Woody Allen

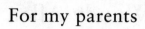

For my parents

Woody Allen

New Yorker

Graham McCann

Polity Press

HOUSTON PUBLIC LIBRARY

Copyright © Graham McCann 1990

First published 1990 by Polity Press in association with Basil Blackwell.
First published in paperback 1991

Reprinted 1991

Editorial office:
Polity Press, 65 Bridge Street, Cambridge CB2 1UR, UK

Marketing and production:
Basil Blackwell Ltd, 108 Cowley Road, Oxford OX4 1JF, UK

Basil Blackwell Inc., 3 Cambridge Center, Cambridge, MA 02142, USA

ISBN 0 7456 0639 3
ISBN 0 7456 0890 6 (pbk)

British Library Cataloguing in Publication Data
A CIP catalogue record for this book is available from the British Library.

Library of Congress Cataloging in Publication Data
A CIP catalogue record for this book is available from the Library of Congress.

Typeset in 10½ on 12pt Sabon
by Ponting–Green Publishing Services, London
Printed in Great Britain by
T J Press Ltd, Padstow

Contents

Acknowledgements

For rather obvious reasons, I am particularly grateful to Woody Allen for sparing the time to answer some of my questions; I will not forget his kindness. Although Mr Allen does not encourage books about himself, he was gracious enough to co-operate with me; I sincerely hope that he finds something worthwhile in what follows. My work was made much easier due to the splendid assistance given me by the staffs of the Library of the Performing Arts (the New York Public Library at the Lincoln Center), the British Film Institute Library, Cambridge University Library, and King's College, Cambridge. I interviewed a number of colleagues and former school friends of Woody Allen, each of whom, for various reasons, asked to remain nameless; I am, nonetheless, indebted to all of them for their help. Several people were kind enough to read certain sections of this book in draft form: Peter Aspden, John Downey, Harry Ferguson, Tony Giddens, Jan Gortler, David Harvey, Marissa Quie, Alex Schuessler, and John B. Thompson.

Intellectual debts, so many of which are oblique, are harder to acknowledge, but some of the more important ones should be mentioned here. Christopher Taylor helped me think through my ideas for this book – and he was generous enough to laugh at my jokes. I am truly indebted to David Reason for the encouragement that allayed my intellectual doubts and anxieties and restored my confidence on the innumerable occasions it failed. John Dunn – a model, for me, of the finest sort of teacher and thinker – has been a most kind and loyal friend. None of these scholars should be held responsible for my arguments, some of which they may find impossible to agree with.

I would also like to thank the following people for their

advice and support: Norma Lee Clark, Quentin Crisp, and Gil and Michele Schaye. Each played a different role, some close to the themes of this book, some in easing the way, others in shaping impressions into ideas, or simply contributing the essential enthusiasm that meant so much to me. Claire Andrews, Rebecca Harkin, Pip Hurd, Alison Kelly, Gill Motley and Mary Robinson worked extremely hard to ensure that the book was ready for publication. Mic Cheetham, my agent, has been an invaluable advisor and supporter. Finally, I am grateful to Silvana Dean for a flawless preparation of the manuscript; for her remarkable industry, tolerance, and thoughtful criticism of content as well as form, she is deserving of a sense of pride equal only to the pride of authorship. Heartfelt thanks to all.

March 1989   *Graham McCann*
Cambridge

Picture Credits

The author and publishers are grateful to the following for permission to use plates: p.8 photograph © Steve McMurry/ Magnum Photos; p.128 photograph: Fritz Schimke/Camera Press; p.220 photograph: Jean-Pierre Couderc/Camera Press.

Introduction

I just met a wonderful new man – he's fictional, but you can't have everything

                                                  The Purple Rose of Cairo

If you want to tell people the truth, you'd better make them laugh – or they'll kill you

                                                  George Bernard Shaw

'Today,' said Woody Allen, 'I'm a star. What am I going to be tomorrow? A black hole?' Although the idea of movie stardom has been a source of fascination for us since the beginnings of the cinema, and despite the innumerable articles, books and documentaries on the subject, the process by which an enduring star personality is created and sustained is one of the least intelligently examined phenomena of popular culture. Many observers have been content to settle on the fairly contemptuous belief that movie stars 'play themselves' – as if playing oneself were easy, given the complex, self-contradictory material at hand and the problem of fixing upon a version of oneself that is both coherent and recognizable. In recent years, no star has illustrated these matters more memorably than Woody Allen. He protests that he plays characters who seem to be very much like him (a New York Jew), with similar careers (comedians, writers, directors), simply because it helps him make his performance believable: 'Because I make the lead character a comic or a writer, I play it myself. I can't play an atomic scientist. I'm not going to make the lead a mechanic. I know the language of certain people.' His fans, however, and many of his critics, remain unconvinced. His biographers have contributed to this view, uncritically accepting the ideas, values and concerns of his fictional characters as 'more or less', autobiographical. Thus we can read that Allen's 'childhood ambition was to be a lavatory attendant' (McNight, 1983), and that 'as a boy he was regularly teased and beaten up' (various sources), neither of which is true. This book is not intended as another account of the 'real' Woody Allen; rather, it is an attempt at understanding how we see him, what we look for in his films, and why we respond to his screen image in the ways in which we do.

Woody Allen does not enjoy his celebrity status. Contemporary photographs more often than not depict a figure whose glare – where the eyes are shielded behind a defensively raised hand or a low-brimmed hat – expresses the weary indignation of someone who has just seen another part of his soul hived off to a public auction. Those people who turn to the movies for enlightenment find what appears equal parts candour and deception, without ever being entirely sure which is which. What seems even more puzzling than this supposed autobiographical coyness is why people should *want* to look at movies for such information. What *is* beyond doubt, however, is that Allen is America's most significant comic movie-maker since the silent era, and, arguably, one of the most important and influential figures in the movie world as a whole. He makes movies, he says, to please himself and a few close friends – in direct contravention of the Hollywood principle of eking out the tried and tested – and exercises a quietly authoritative control over virtually every aspect of the movie-making process. His work offers, amongst other things, a remarkable collection of visions of a modern urban environment – New York City (see chapter 1).

Allen is fortunate, and unusual, in being able to draw upon several different comedy forms (see chapter 2). Where the brilliance of a Perelman or Flann O'Brien is limited to words on paper, and that of a Chaplin or Keaton to the organization of images on film, and that of a Jackie Mason or Henny Youngman to the delivery of one-liners on stage, Woody Allen can slip smoothly from one form to another with an assurance that rivals the specialists in their own field. His prose pieces for the *New Yorker* magazine are models of absurdity – 'How wrong Emily Dickinson was! Hope is not "the thing with feathers". The thing with feathers has turned out to be my nephew. I must take him to a specialist in Zurich' (Allen, 1978: 5); his night-club act was hugely successful and endearingly eccentric: 'I lived in

Manhattan, uptown east, in a brownstone building. But I was constantly getting mugged and sadistically beaten about the face and neck. So I moved into a doorman apartment house on Park Avenue that's rich and secure and expensive and great, and I lived there two weeks ... and my doorman attacked me'; and his movies, at least since *Annie Hall* (1977), have shown a sensitivity for visual vocabulary that is fully the equal of all but a few contemporary directors.

Comparisons have often been made between Allen and his comic predecessors, such as Chaplin, Keaton, Groucho Marx and Bob Hope, but there are many people who first embraced Allen and his image not for his impeccable lineage, but as a representative of a generation that was beginning to speak with increasing volume against the evils of the time, best symbolized by the futile war in Vietnam. Repelled by machismo, disaffected by the acquisitive consumer society, wary of convention, Allen, though he could never be bracketed with 'political' comedians such as Lenny Bruce or Mort Sahl, lampooned everything for which people have been taught respect. This was the work of the anti-hero: Allen's screen persona was ideally qualified for such a role on three counts: as a Jew in a WASP-dominated society; as an awkward weakling in a culture that worships physical strength and idealizes beauty (see chapter 3); and as a private, contemplative person in a world that lionizes the extrovert (see chapter 4).

In the mid-seventies, Allen's movies began to deal more directly with contemporary American life, and his characters became increasingly dissatisfied: they want better sex (or, if not better sex, at least *more* sex), they want to tell funnier jokes, they want to find finer philosophies, and they want to watch grander movies (see chapter 5). Something is missing in the life of the Allen hero, and part of the problem is finding out what that something is. For instance, one of his characters 'often thought there was a great difference between Being and Being-in-the-World, and figured that no matter which group he belonged to the other was definitely having more fun' (Allen, 1981: 15-16). Allen himself has often been described as an 'intellectual' comic, searching for meaning in a meaningless universe. He is painfully aware of the curious spectacle presented by the autodidact fumbling with the great metaphysical questions. Intellectual poseurs are among his favourite targets (they are, he says, 'like the Mafia – they only kill their own'). Yet for all his innate distrust of things cerebral,

Allen, who had been a voracious reader since the late fifties, found himself drawn irresistibly to such areas, with the consequence that, by the mid-seventies, his work began to jar with the more blatantly physical comedy. His characters started to question the worth of their own comic gifts, feeling that life is simply too serious to be funny about anymore.

Recent Allen movies feature individuals determined to believe in something: 'I gotta get some answers!' is a characteristic cry. Such a concern is entirely absent in his early work, in which his characters seek the maximum pleasure and the minimum pain. 'I'm really a timid person,' Allen once said during his night-club act. 'I was beaten up by Quakers.' One is reminded of a remark in the autobiography of the political theorist Thomas Hobbes, in which he tells us that his mother gave birth to twins – himself and fear. Allen's early screen persona seems in many ways the modern counterpart of Hobbes' insecure, self-seeking little man: 'The first Humphrey Bogart movie I saw was *The Maltese Falcon*. I was ten years old and I identified immediately with Peter Lorre. The impulse to be a snivelling, effeminate, greasy little weasel appealed to me enormously.' Indeed, much of Allen's early comic material seems to concern itself with a world in which no one can be trusted – especially one's own family:

> I formed a corporation this year, and I'm the president ... and my mother's vice-president, and my father's secretary, and my grandmother's treasurer, and my uncle is on the board of directors. And we got together the first week ... and they tried to squeeze me out. I formed a power-bloc with my uncle and we sent my grandmother to jail.

Hobbes argued that human beings are always necessarily selfish and inherently untrustworthy, because the good for each of us is simply that thing which happens to be the object of our own desire. Every motive which may at first sight appear to distinguish human beings from other animals is reduced by Hobbes to one or the other of two basic tendencies: fear and self-interest. A sense of humour might, for instance, be taken to be a distinctly human trait and laughter a sign of friendliness and good nature. Not so, according to Hobbes. On the contrary, he claims it is occasioned in people 'either by some sudden act of their own, that pleaseth them; or by the apprehension of some deformed thing in another, by comparison whereof they suddenly applaud themselves'. Moreover, those who laugh most readily 'are conscious of the fewest abilities in themselves; who are forced to keep themselves in their own favour, by observing the imperfections of other men' (Hobbes, 1981: 125). 'Our society places a great value on jokes,' says one of Allen's characters, and Allen himself has come to view his own, prodigious, comic abilities with considerable anxiety. Is comedy only a way of mocking other people's misfortune and suffering? Can there be a humane form of comedy, a comedy that can *help* people, or is Hobbes correct in styling comedy as destructive and self-serving? Allen's attempts at 'serious' movies, such as *Interiors* (1978) or *Another Woman* (1988), are signs of his uneasiness about the role of comedy. His recent comic characters seem haunted by the Hobbesian vision of human beings: time and again the Allen hero is heard to say, 'Listen, will you just trust me?' This need to be trusted, and to trust other people, has become the most important theme in such movies as *Manhattan* (1979) and *Hannah and Her Sisters* (1986). It informs his characters' attitude to their relationships, to their city, and to society in general (see chapter 6).

This book will look at how this concern has developed in Allen's work, from his days as a gag-writer and stand-up comic to his present-day status as an internationally respected writer, actor and director. It is intended as a sympathetic, but not uncritical, account of the cultural significance of the man Groucho Marx once described as 'an absolute comic genius ... the best there is'. It is not so much a discussion of what Allen himself means with his movies; rather it is a consideration of what those movies *may* mean, or come to mean, for us. Ironically, such an emphasis reflects that of Allen's own characters, who are drawn to particular movies and movie stars for very specific and personal reasons – witness the use in *Play It Again, Sam* of Bogart and *Casablanca*, or *Hannah and Her Sisters'* use of *Duck Soup*. Woody Allen's hero is the emigré, the gadfly, the unloved; his hero dreams of home, faith, and love. The outsider yearns to come inside, but not at any cost; the problem remains how to distinguish between genuine belief and blind faith, between a haven and a hovel. In *Stardust Memories* (1980), Allen's character is charged with being an atheist. 'To you, I'm an atheist,' he replies. 'To God, I'm the loyal opposition.' This anxiety about belonging to any institution that would have him for a member is what makes Allen's comic figures so fascinating and, at times, so unsettling.

As George Orwell once wrote: 'You cannot be really funny if your main aim is to flatter the comfortable classes: it means leaving out too much. To be funny, indeed, you have got to be serious' (Orwell, 1970: 329). A Woody Allen comedy is indeed a serious matter.

1

New Yorker

New York was his town. And it always would be.

The opening of *Manhattan* (1979): black-and-white shots of the New York skyline, one image quickly giving way to another, a montage of city sights. The narrator begins: ' "Chapter One. He adored New York City. He idolized it out of all proportion". Uh, no make that: "He romanticized it out of all proportion ...." ' Gershwin's 'Rhapsody in Blue' is heard, as we see further images of Woody Allen's favourite milieu: New York. He takes us on a tour of the city's most famous and impressive landmarks, a stunning array of architectural daring and optimism, finally seen from the Hudson as black shapes against a grey sky lit up by a firework display. The movie's beginning, and its subsequent development, is a remarkable achievement for a writer and director who only a few years earlier was best known for his ability to fill his movies full of hilarious but rather disconnected gags. Woody Allen had made a dramatic progression to conceive *Manhattan*, described by critic Andrew Sarris as 'the only great film of the Seventies'. Furthermore, with this movie Allen, America's most respected contemporary humorist, had made clear what had often been left implicit in his previous work: his identification with New York.

Allen's movies do well in the big cities because in what they describe, dramatize and satirize they are quintessentially urban. Indeed, outside New York, Los Angeles, Boston and San Francisco, Allen's movies are not particularly popular in America; as Allen says,

> There are some towns which have never played [my movies] for years. Honestly. I don't mean much to the Rambo crowd. That's why I am so

grateful for all the support I get from Britain and Europe. It's an
enormous help to me (*Guardian*, 11 August, 1988)

Allen has made a personal province of his native city. New York
is the subject and setting of many of Allen's movies, but he is
also its spokesperson in a way that goes beyond the call of civic
duty. Through his movies, and even outside them, he seems to
carry the city within him; it imbues him and he imbues it, it has
created him yet he constantly recreates it. We now respond to
New York with greater warmth and wonder, so deeply have
Allen's movies worked their way into our consciousness: the
luminous black-and-white image of the 59th Street Bridge, accompanied by the plaintive strains of Gershwin's 'Someone to Watch
over Me'; a scene set in Bloomingdales, moving on to the Stanhope
Cafe; shots of a couple embracing each other, high above the
Central Park fireworks – no movie maker has *engaged* so
thoroughly, movingly and intelligently with a single modern city
than Woody Allen. The publicity for his movies forever emphasizes the inviolability of this bonding: stories of his apartment on
Central Park, his frequent dining at Elaine's, his weekly performances at Michael's Pub. It has become impossible to separate
entirely the New Yorker from his visions of New York: the
perspective projected onto the movie screen is a profoundly
personal perspective, with very selective readings of the city
sights and people, often with our vision trained on Allen's own
surroundings – his balcony in *Manhattan*, Mia Farrow's apartment on Central Park West in *Hannah and Her Sisters*.

   Along with the city's mythology come its cultural assumptions
and presumptions, which Allen's work exemplifies, even as they
surround it and protect it. There is, for example, his attitude
towards movies. Allen is a movie lover with a phobia about
where the movies, for the most part, are made in America. The
movies are made on the West Coast, but their culture is made on
the East Coast: this is the view that is at the centre of Allen's
work. Allen's sensitivity to Hollywood and his big-city aesthete's
dread of California do not mean that he is an opponent of
American movies, but he *has* used his cultural attitude to acquire
a sense of separateness from Hollywood's formulaic traditionalism.
His humour has, in fact, as much to do with the *New Yorker* as
with the movies, drawing on the brilliance of Benchley and
Perelman, as well as Groucho Marx and Chaplin. New York is
one of the most important themes in Allen's night-club routines,

shortstories, plays and movies. New York is a repository of cherished memories from childhood (*Radio Days*), a source of hope amidst a climate of decay and inauthenticity (*Manhattan, Hannah and Her Sisters*), an extension of Allen's own psyche (*Annie Hall*: 'You're like New York. You're an island unto yourself'), and a place of cultural creativity (Allen's New Yorkers are sometimes egotistical and neurotic, but they *always* appear more 'alive' than the 'mellow' inhabitants of California's 'munchkinland'). If Woody Allen is engaged in any particular dialogue, it is surely a dialogue with New York.

New York offers an exhilaration that is also a kind of *terror*. New York needs to be paced, to be left and returned to, like an epic novel. Henry James called his native city, half-lovingly, half-bitterly, 'the terrible town'; he pondered its 'pin-cushion profile', its 'prosaically peopled' shore, its 'impudently new' buildings. He witnessed a new city spread itself into the modernity of the new century. James had lost the New York of his childhood, and he felt 'amputated of half my history'. Yet James cared for the city, cared for it as one born in it; it hurt him that people could create so blindly and so quickly and so crudely the foundations of inevitable 'blight'. Although the changing city caused James to feel concerned (for the increasingly alienated inhabitants and the degradation of their language and literature), he never ceased to *respond* to New York, preserving in his work the memory of 'old' New York, *his* New York. Countless writers after James have returned to experience similar feelings of anxiety and desperate hopefulness. The hopefulness comes with the creativity of the writer: to return to New York is to repossess it, reclaiming it through conscious redescription. 'New York was his town. And it always would be.' Woody Allen is one of New York's foremost creative individuals; he has contested the descriptions of his work as 'Jewish humour' or 'intellectual humour', but he quite openly deals with his identity as a New Yorker. The city figures in his stories and movies as both grail and ghetto, death-mask and birthmark; his values, concerns, ideals and ambitions are seen through the prism *New York*.

The reality of New York is selective, optional, fantastic: there is a New York for each of us. Manhattan is a place for coming and going; for raising up and pulling down; for making money and for spending it. It is a port, a bank, and a fleshpot. It is also a universal image of modern life. Many of the city's most remarkable structures were conceived specifically as symbolic expressions of modernity: Central Park, Brooklyn Bridge, the Statue of Liberty, Coney Island, Manhattan's many skyscrapers, Rockefeller Center, and much else. Many other areas of the city – Wall Street, Broadway, Madison Avenue, Greenwich Village, SoHo and others – have acquired a symbolic weight and force as time went by. The cumulative impact of all this is that the New Yorker finds him or herself in the midst of a Baudelairean forest of symbols. It is a place where new meanings are forever springing up with, and falling down from, the ever-changing environment. Through its very construction, the city corsets-in tremendous excitement and vigour and pace. Intensely clever, cynical, intro-spective, feverishly tireless, Manhattan has all the febrile bright-ness, alternating with despondency, that sometimes attends in-somnia, together with the utter self-absorption of the schizo-phrenic. Manhattan is the part of New York that intimidates the rest of America – nobody is intimidated by Staten Island or Brooklyn or the Bronx. Nowhere in the Western world are there so many (and so explicable) human derelicts alongside so much glaring wealth; Manhattan has the promise of high culture and low life – it is the great challenge. Its inhabitants seem unusually sensitive to the prick of ambition, the fear of failure. They exhibit that explosive mixture of an eager need to please and a determination not to bother that perhaps only the exile, the emigré and the underprivileged can truly understand.

The city has the largest population in the country, yet the country's laws are made elsewhere; it produces the nation's plays, advertises its goods, publishes its books, shapes its opinions and looks after its investments, yet it does not govern the nation. Hence, its curious air of irresponsibility, and its occasional show of hurt. Just as the city constrains the expression of individuality, threatens us with absorption into total anonymity, so it makes self-assertion and projection into overwhelming necessities. As Simmel (1903) observes: 'man is tempted to adopt the most tendentious peculiarities, that is, the specifically metropolitan extravagances of mannerism, caprice and preciousness.' Implicit in Simmel's statement is the suggestion of utter arbitrariness: the city is so large, so amorphous, its ends so remote from us as individual members of it, that any eccentricity might function as a token of our personal uniqueness.

The city is a highly appropriate locale for Allen's solitary, anxious, confused individual – a creature of urbanism, an American who seems to have been forced into the most

'European' part of the country by the threatening spread of hard-headed commercialism, a writer who has been placed in the most intellectually impatient community in the United States. What Allen finds in New York is America at its most oppressive *and* at its most attractive. The city's juxtaposition of people highlights the contrasts of behaviour and heightens the conflict between reactions in the human subconscious towards buildings: both shelter and prison, security and threat. At the same time as the city's organization assists the efficiency of our lives it threatens to dehumanise them. Its monuments are rather ordinary skins of metal and stone that fill up, over time, with dreams. Manhattan is a defiantly artificial megalopolis in which glass and stone and concrete seem on the verge of overwhelming what is now, rather distressingly, called 'the human element'. The art of overcoming these self-created obstacles is urban living at its most extreme and rhapsodic. This is a curious gift of Allen's: the image of one of New York's most nervous, vulnerable inhabitants ceaselessly fighting back and asserting his independence. We are shown, in very vivid ways, how we have assumed certain *perspectives* on the city. New York is more than an agglomeration; it is an assertion, an image, an idea. It is a city of shapes that seem magically to rearrange themselves as one walks along its streets, every few strides brings into view a different concatenation of skyscrapers, and no two views are the same. It is like a book that changes its meaning each time one opens it up. With cannibalistic delight New York consumes itself, tearing down the old and then creating a new structure in its place – forever surprising the observer, constantly tightening the screws of its own intensity, repeatedly assaulting the senses – the ultimate city of the modern world. As though flicking channels on a television set, one can effortlessly view the eclecticism of the neighbourhoods: the astonishing drama of Manhattan, the downtown skyline, the swathe of Broadway; one sees also the genteel charm of Greenwich Village, the peaceful wooded slopes of Morningside Heights, the vaguely sinister silent warehouses of the Hudson shore, and the tenseness of Harlem.

Saul Bellow has remarked how tempting it is to see New York as a microcosm of America, compressing its ethnic, religious, sexual, and political divisions into a single city. Allen arrived at a similar conclusion in *Manhattan*, describing New York as 'a metaphor' for decaying values, a lost innocence, and a breathtaking arena for a nation's conflicting hopes and dreams.

As Allen identifies so strongly with the city, these hopes and dreams are, in part, his own; his reading of New York is inescapably connected to his understanding of himself. His Manhattan is inhabited mainly by Jews and WASPS – there are few blacks, or Hispanics, Italians, Chinese, Irish or Haitians (compare this with the New York of *Moonstruck* or *Mean Streets, They All Laughed* or *Wall Street*). Significantly, when *Manhattan* was sold to cable-TV in the US, Allen insisted that the movie could not be 'reduced' to standard screen size, but would have to be shown with the full Cinemascope image shown with the top and bottom of the screen blanked out with borders. Any tampering of the movie's screen size would have meant that the memorable scenes showing the characters interacting with the city's sights would have been reduced to close-ups of the characters' faces, thus vitiating the real meaning of the movie. We are watching individuals dealing with life in a modern city, and this city could be nowhere but New York. The character Allen plays is clearly, indisputably, a New Yorker. He has been rewriting, revising his image of the city and his character since the start of his career.

Woody Allen was born on 1 December, 1935 in Brooklyn. He was named Allen Stewart Konigsberg, adopting the pen-name 'Woody' when he first began writing gags. He attended Midwood High School in the Flatbush district of Brooklyn. His parents, Nettea Cherrie and Marty Konigsberg, had married during the Great Depression following the First World War. Marty Konigsberg was an engraver of jewellery, but he was forced to take various short-term jobs, such as a waiter (at the Sammy Bowery Follies in Manhattan) and a cab driver. Nettea worked as a book-keeper in a Manhattan florist shop. Both parents were of European Jewish descent, and a great number of emigrants from Hitler's Europe had recently arrived to make the neighbourhood an interesting mixture of cultures. The Marx Brothers were products of the Jewish ghetto which was not yet integrated into the so-called melting pot of American society. However, Flatbush was a comfortable 'silk-stocking' area, populated by quiet, peaceable families from the middle class. Allen appears to have ignored his parents' emphasis on the need for a good education, and he spent most of his time teaching himself magic, reading comic books, and listening to jazz. In 1963 Allen told Helen Dudar of the *New York Post* of these early years in Flatbush: 'It was hectic. Partly because of economic circumstances, partly because of war-time apartment shortage. My family was always getting

billeted with relations. There were always uncles and cousins
running in and out of rooms, and we were always moving.' His
single popular quality, as far as he was concerned, was his use of
words:

> I've always had an extremely easy talent for writing. I was always the
> one who wrote essays at school and read them out loud in front of the
> class. (Benayoun, 1986: 21)

At school, Allen was neither a leader nor a rebel, and his presence
passed largely unnoticed. Most of Allen's contemporaries and
teachers at Midwood remember him as always smartly dressed
and extremely quiet and reserved. It is generally agreed that as a
student Allen was able yet unwilling to do more than pass his
exams with the minimum of effort. Few students now feel able
to recall Allen in detail; his extra-curricular interests kept him
away from all but a few of his schoolfriends. Years later, when
he had achieved fame as a stand-up comic, Allen was asked
about Midwood by an old school-friend; he placed his hands
over his ears and said, 'Don't talk to me about that place. I
hated everything about that period' (private correspondence with
author). Although he has always played down the early tensions
between his parents and himself, at times they must have been
severe. In a rare moment of candour he told Dudar of his
parents: 'Even now [1963], they'd feel much better if I had lived
up to their dream and been a pharmacist. There's tremendous
pressure where I come from – a middle-class Jewish neighbourhood – to be an optometrist or a dentist or a lawyer, and that's
what my friends have become.' (One is reminded of the old
Jewish joke about the woman whose son becomes President of
the United States: 'You must be so proud,' says her friend.
'That's nothing,' replies the mother, 'my other son's a doctor!')
   'I lacked for none of the creature comforts,' said Allen. 'But I
was shy and everything dissatisfied me although I don't know
why'. Later, in *Annie Hall*, Allen has Alvy Singer tell an audience
of when, after he was thrown out of college, his mother locked
herself in the bathroom and took an overdose of mah-jong tiles.
Indeed, there are so many references in Allen's work to his
character's struggle with his parents that it is hard to resist
seeing them as playfully autobiographical. Allen's first marriage
collapsed after a short time, and in a night-club monologue
Allen says that his mother, upon hearing this news, opened the

door of the furnace and got inside ('Took it rather badly I felt'). *Zelig* features a character who is locked in a closet by his parents when he misbehaves; and, when he is *particularly* unruly, they punish him by locking themselves in the closet with him. In another comic monologue, Allen recalls a time when 'he' was kidnapped: his parents 'snapped into action ... they rented out my room.' His father, 'who has bad reading habits,' takes the ransom note to bed, reads a few lines, gets drowsy, and dozes off; later he lends the note to friends. In *Hannah and Her Sisters* Mickey Sachs tells his parents of his plans to become a Catholic: again, his mother shuts herself in the bathroom. During Allen's *own* adolescence, it seems that his parents were anxious and concerned about his increasingly stubborn refusal to 'apply himself' at school. When he began to devote most of his energies to writing jokes and studying comic techniques, his parents almost certainly felt that he was becoming self-destructive.

Allen regularly attended the movies (the Marx Brothers, Ernst Lubitsch, Bob Hope, Preston Sturges were all great favourites). He visited the Flatbush Theater five times a week, seeing 'every comic, every tap dancer, every magician, every kind of singer ... I could do everybody's act. I used to tear up the Raisinets boxes and write jokes down.' In time, he started sending off gags to the newspapers and (when aged seventeen) saw his first words in print in the Earl Wilson and Walter Winchell columns. A year later, under a $25-a-week contract for the David O. Albert public relations firm, Allen was creating up to fifty jokes a day for such clients as Bob Hope, Guy Lombardo and Danny Kaye. After graduating without distinction from Midwood High School, Allen spent a single semester at New York University, majoring in film; he usually preferred to miss lectures and spend his time in movie theatres. After leaving University, he just as briefly attended the tuition-free City College night courses ('in an effort to keep my mother from opening her wrists'), and in the late fifties, while he was working on television shows, hired a tutor to coach him at home. During the 1950s, Allen contributed to several highly successful shows, writing material for Herb Shriner, Sid Caesar, Art Carney, Jack Paar and Carol Channing. His comedy ideas became progressively more personal, eventually causing his employers to feel that they only really made sense when performed by Allen himself. He was reflecting on himself through his work, and his strong identification with his native city made his work most attractive to his fellow New Yorkers.

Allen, despite being such a distinctive celebrity, continues to live a relatively normal life in Manhattan. He dines out almost every evening, plays jazz at Michael's Pub every Monday evening, and visits the city's best revival movie house, the Regency. On the streets he has friends address him as 'Max' to avoid recognition: 'I still get away with it.' He generally wears a rain hat pulled low over his forehead, avoiding eye contact more than he once did, yet he remains comfortable in the city that prides itself on its refusal to acknowledge the famous in its streets. It seems that Allen has enjoyed something of a charmed life: on the only occasion when his apartment was broken into, not only did the intruders depart empty-handed, they also left behind a video-recorder they had stolen from another building. Most of his friends are old friends; he remains in touch with school-friends such as Mickey Rose (who co-wrote some early scripts with him), and several can be seen in cameo roles in his movies. For a movie-maker who craves complete control over the shooting of his screenplay, the familiarity of the actors and the location is invaluable. Allen has remarked:

> My producer is always saying, 'can't we go someplace else to work?', because everything is so expensive and there are no concessions and it's very hard to work here, you know, but what can you do? I mean, so many of my stories take place in New York and, besides, I'm *comfortable* here. You know, I live here and I'm not a big voyager. (BBC, *Film 88*)

Allen knows his city, he writes with it in mind.

Walter Benjamin remarked that the knowledge one acquires strolling the city streets, moving in and out of the crowd, turning corners into unexpected pathways, is akin to the knowledge one acquires intuitively rather than through conscious study:

> Not to find one's way in a city may well be uninteresting and banal. It requires ignorance – nothing more. But to lose oneself in a city – as one loses oneself in a forest – that calls for quite a different schooling. Then, signboards and streetnames, passers-by, roofs, kiosks or bars must speak to the wanderer like a cracking twig under his feet in the stillness of a clearing with a lily standing erect at its centre. (Benjamin, 1979: 298)

Through wandering through its streets, aimlessly, the city shows itself to us again, with sudden glimpses of long-forgotten sights and unexpected scenes. For Benjamin, strolling through the city

is like rereading a favourite novel, getting reaquainted with its
themes and characters, recovering a sense of things past. Allen
would seem to agree:

> In every crisis of my life, the way I have responded is by immediately
> putting on my coat and walking the streets endlessly. There are places
> that are meaningful to me because they were a part of one of these
> crises – a park bench, maybe, or a coffee shop where I stopped for a
> piece of pie and coffee.

In this sense Allen reminds one of Baudelaire's *flaneur*:

> For the perfect *flaneur*, for the passionate spectator, it is an immense
> joy to set up house in the heart of the multitude, amid the ebb and
> flow of movement, in the midst of the fugitive and the infinite. To be
> away from home and yet to feel oneself everywhere at home; to see the
> world, to be at the centre of the world, and yet to remain hidden from
> the world ... The spectator is a *prince* who everywhere rejoices in his
> incognito. (Baudelaire, 1964: 9)

New York, as the quintessential modern city, satiates his needs:
'If I go to London or Paris or Rome I do the same things that I
do here. I walk around the streets and maybe drop in on a
movie. There's nothing that interests me in a vacationing way.'
In *Manhattan*, the characters (whenever they are depressed or
anxious or cannot concentrate) go out onto the streets, seeking
stimulation and diversion. This city may threaten, it may intimi-
date, but it also offers to save you – it has theatres, libraries,
galleries, restaurants, museums, bookstores and shops, size and
energy and architectural splendour. One is encouraged in one's
voyeurism: public transport and long busy streets make observers
of us all, part-time spies, overhearing private conversations and
secretly surveying other people's expressions. One can rest neatly
beneath one's anonymity. Through wandering the streets one
may lose oneself, and one may even find oneself. The buildings
are a constantly changing constellation of styles and functions,
constructing and deconstructing themselves according to people's
needs and roles. Such an architectural form corresponds with the
conditions of a movie soundstage, the hangar-like building in
which the majority of a movie is shot. The determining factor on
a soundstage is the need of 'now'. All technical abilities, all
lights, all recording equipment, all the energy of actors and
crew, are concentrated in a discrete corner of the building and a

discrete area of passion and action within the larger context of
the movie's script. The localization of the intensity will be transferred as soon as one shot has been completed. The set is then
dismantled, and particular parts of it are employed in constructing
the next set. Like the soundstage, the city encourages a restless,
remorseless theatricality. The metropolis is a splendid stimulus
for the actor in each of us. The city, judged in terms of our
social behaviour inside it, is not a 'natural' circumstance; and its
public arenas – restaurants, department stores, museums, tube
trains, certain streets and squares and parks – are licensed for a
degree of theatrical abnormality. New York is at all times a
spectacle and a drama, always self-consciously on stage; there is
a staccato briskness to the New Yorker's stride, and a punchy
rhythm to the speech. Many Hollywood stars, including Brando,
Monroe, Garbo and de Niro, expressed feelings of liberation
during their stay in New York – exploiting its sheer size in order
to drift unnoticed through its streets, 'becoming' a succession of
unknown selves. Indeed, in cities people are given to all kinds of
acting, putting on a show of themselves. For someone as shy as
Woody Allen, there could surely have been no better environment for him to test himself and develop his personality.

Chaplin was an obvious early influence upon Allen: 'As soon
as Chaplin comes down the street I start to laugh – his really
primitive unmotivated hostility.' Chaplin's tramp is an immigrant
in a silent, anonymous urban America: he waddles down grey
streets, one like any other, dodges into alleyways or empty
buildings – he is like a visible poltergeist, causing havoc in a
country still struggling to settle its identity. Allen, on the contrary,
is the 'little man' in advanced industrialized America, an individual in an oppressively 'settled' milieu. Allen is aware of the
changes that New York is undergoing, and the sense in which
those changes impinge on himself and his past. He has spoken of
the old movie theatres of his youth, now demolished and all but
forgotten:

> One day I stood there and the buildings were gone. The lot was
> completely empty and the sun shining down on it made it seem even
> more desolate. And I kept thinking how I used to sit there in the dark,
> with an entire exotic world engulfing me. Life up there on the screen
> was so vivid and so real. You couldn't believe that one day it wouldn't
> exist... It's occurred to me that I'm in on the tail end of something.
> That some day they're going to invent a wonderful high-resolution
> television screen and kids are going to grow up without having the

experience of going to a well-appointed theater, that they won't know what it's like to go to a *movie*. (*New York Times Magazine*, 19 January 1986)

Woody Allen is clearly fascinated by both the complexity of Manhattan and the magical splendour of the movies. His subject matter has become the two lost cultures, those of the gracefully glorious city and the gracefully glamorous cinema. *Manhattan* reflects this concern for what is absent, missing, what has come to exist only in memory: Gordon Willis' black-and-white cinematography recalls the imagery of thirties Hollywood and the glamour the old movies imputed to New York as a setting for sophisticated romance. Allen said, 'that's how I remember it from when I was small. Maybe it's a reminiscence from old photographs, films, books and all that. But that's how I remember New York. I always heard the Gershwin music with it, too.' Allen is trying to break out of habitual ways of seeing the city. Gone is one's familiarity with streets and houses, although they may still surround one; one sees them with a doubly alien view: with the view of the child one no longer is, and with the view of the child to whom the city was not yet familiar. The adult's glance does not yearn to merge with the child's glance; it is directed toward those moments when the future first announced itself to the child. Everywhere in the city, in the streets and parks, in the movie houses and the monuments, *Manhattan* is on the trail of such moments, the memories of which are preserved by the child until the adult can decipher them. *Manhattan* captivated European audiences, suddenly showing a sense of history that had often been lacking in American movies. New York had never seemed so attractive, so memorable, as in this movie. Americans had commonly regarded the idea of a desirable urban culture as a European invention, for there is a fashionable contempt for the city in branches of American culture popularized by Thomas Jefferson, and a tendency to focus nostalgia on the innocence lost when the old agrarian ways were abandoned. Woody Allen, mid-way through his career, seemed almost single-handedly to be shifting the emphasis on America's past, revealing both a new sense of pride and a new form of regret for the things that have been lost.

Manhattan's use of the music of George Gershwin is particularly poignant: Gershwin, like Allen, was a New York Jewish popular entertainer who wanted to be accepted as a 'serious' artist. His music illustrates the depth of nostalgia in Isaac Davis, a man who is unknowingly but manifestly in search of an identity, even a simply historical one. Manhattan is no melting-pot; many of its fragments refuse to melt, so stern is their loyalty to racial or national identity. New York has a strong claim to be the 'most Jewish city' in the world. It has been estimated that the City's Jewish population is around 1,118,800 – almost 16 per cent of the total (see Auletta, 1979: 215). Yet New York's intensely Jewish status is much more than a merely statistical one: it is to do with flavour, with outlook, with culture, with commitments, with influence, with the deep impression that generations of Jews have left on the community as a whole at almost every level. As the *Encyclopaedia Judaica* (vol. 12: 1124) puts it:

> If the Jews gave to New York unstintingly of their experience, energies and talents, they received in return an education in urbanity and a degree of cosmopolitan sophistication unknown to any other Jewish community of similar size in the past. It is little wonder that many Jews developed an attachment to New York that bordered on the devotional. Above all, when the 20th century New York Jews thought of the city they lived in, they did not simply consider it a great capital of civilization that had generously taken them in; rather, they thought of themselves – and with every justification – as joint builders of this greatness and one of its main continuing supports.

Many studies divide the New York Jewish community into two distinct groups: one is of those who have become assimilated into the community at large, liberal in their political and social attitudes, sometimes treating their own Jewishness casually; the other consists of those to whom Jewishness is the overriding factor in life, who see everything in strictly Jewish terms, and who see it as a sacred duty to keep the faith as in olden times. It has been said that the East River defines the limits of Jewish liberalism in New York. This is not quite what Norman Podhoretz meant when he wrote, 'One of the longest journeys in the world is the journey from Brooklyn to Manhattan', to convey the sense of gradual estrangement of the Jewish boy from his deepest cultural traditions as he ambitiously pursued his individual star (quoted in Bloom, 1986: 25). It would be misleading to imply that the assimilated Jewish community dwells exclusively in Manhattan, while the 'ethnics' reside in Brooklyn. Nothing is more ethnic than the old Jewish part of the Lower East Side, contracted though it has become in recent decades. What is left, however, would be recognizable to the people who came off the ferries from Ellis Island a century ago, with knish bakeries on every block, and other stores selling everything Jewish from kosher wines to bar-mitzvah sets. Certainly, Woody Allen's move from Flatbush to Central Park has represented a remarkable cultural transition which has not been lost on the Jewish community. In this sense, Allen is the perfect movie comedian for an age in which the movies have ceased to be mass entertainment.

Allen, as a Jewish comic, followed in a fine and formidable tradition. The streets of immigrant America spawned an extraordinary number of Jewish performers who became well known in the entertainment worlds of vaudeville and movies: Al Jolson, George Gershwin, the Marx Brothers, Eddie Cantor, Irving Berlin, Jack Benny, George Burns, Milton Berle, Sid Caesar, Phil Silvers, Bert Lahr, Jackie Mason, Henny Youngman, and innumerable others. The crowded ghetto streets of New York nurtured the comic and imitative talents of these performers, while the growing number of summer resorts in the Catskill Mountains, a circuit known as the *Borscht Belt*, provided an excellent training ground for aspiring entertainers. The 1950s witnessed the emergence of Elaine May and Mike Nichols, Mort Sahl and Lenny Bruce: all Jewish, all capable of sophisticated material attractive to a young, college-educated and politically-aware audience. In clubs all over urban America, the traditional comic patter was being challenged by individuals who had been brought up in a more educationally-oriented system. The 'college-kids' slowly began to make an impact on the American comic circuit formerly shaped by the international success of Bob Hope and his contemporaries.

Broadway Danny Rose (1984) is one of Allen's poems to New York that invokes moments from Manhattan's past. It draws on Allen's own memories of his night-club years, focusing on a small-time booking agent for parties, small clubs and the *Borscht Belt* who falls for a mob moll. The movie is a consciously romantic vision of the real Manhattan. Like so many children who grew up in modest surroundings in the outer boroughs, Allen viewed Manhattan as a mysterious and exotic place, full of promise and potential:

My father first brought me to the city in 1941. I remember getting out of the subway at 42nd Street and seeing for the first time 30 theatres standing in a row. To this day I always have a Runyonesque feeling when I'm in the streets. Cole Porter's New York I'm always trying to find. (*New York Times Magazine*, 19 January 1986)

Danny Rose is one of Allen's most poignant characterizations, for he seems to exude a certain kind of New Yorker – a man who has struggled for years to survive in the city, a man who was never given the time nor the opportunity to learn his trade, a man who thus was forced to settle for outcasts as clients (skating penguins dressed as rabbis, one-legged tap dancers) and a hopelessly meaningless 'patter' ('May I just interject one concept at this juncture?'; 'It's the classic pattern of a definitive situation', 'It's an entire mental syndrome'). His endearingly bland instruction to his clients is: 'Look in the mirror and say, "Star", "Smile", "Strong".' His solitary, precious, pampered 'star' is an over-weight Italian singer who includes in his act an ode to indigestion, 'Agita', and the ridiculously raucous 'My Bambina'. He drinks, he flirts, he fails; to Danny he is Sinatra. Such indomitable faith has kept Danny going, and also kept him vulnerable. 'You can't ride two horses with one behind,' he says as he struggles, incomprehensibly, to explain his career. His only tangible legacy is found in the Carnegie Delicatessen, where there is a sandwich named after him – the 'Danny Rose Special Sandwich'. The overall effect is one of desperation amidst a ceaselessly changing world: Danny Rose exists in a fast-moving city that moves him on whenever he tries to pause and reflect or learn. He can only grab at overheard clichés and partially understood schemes as the great and powerful threaten to trample over his dreams of 'making it'. City life heightens one's sensitivity to multiple stimuli, but erodes one's patience to reflect on any one of them. Danny Rose struggles on, clinging to the wreckage of his past as the city pushes him into the future. Allen himself began when the Danny Roses were already fading from Broadway, and he was far more aware of the problems of 'showbusiness'.

When Allen, having dropped out of university, was given a post in the Writers' Development Program of America's leading television network, NBC (Working on *The Colgate Comedy Hour*), he was obliged to work in Hollywood. It seems that the change of locale was intolerable: Allen could not take to the West Coast, with its tremendous parochialism and its subservience to the values of the market-place. 'I was always very careful not to get seduced into TV writing,' Allen recalls. 'I was making a lot of money and knew it was a dead end; you get seduced into a lifestyle, move to California, and in six months you become a producer.' Allen has frequently commented that he feels at home in the city: he does not enjoy travelling, or spending long periods in the countryside: 'I'm used to urban life. I'm used to the pace of New York, and it has everything that I need.' Finding himself writing sketches for people who panicked at the first sign of declining viewing figures made Allen feel thoroughly alienated. From the beginning of his career he has been obsessively hard-working, yet he has never been driven by anything other than a *personal* interest in his craft. To make Allen conscious of some external, 'commercial' standard of quality was thus to undermine his sense of pride and purpose in his work. Having married Harlene Rosen, a student at Hunter College, Allen seized the opportunity to return to the east. He acquired a rented Manhattan apartment, and his wife helped him to develop his knowledge of art and philosophy.

Mort Sahl's 'jazz-like' style was an inspiration to Allen at this time. 'My interest in nightclub performing was nil until I saw him,' Allen told Lax (1975). 'Then it occurred to me that, "Hey, you could be a comedian because you have the equipment; that is a very valid way to express yourself" '. Allen supplemented his income by working at Tamiment summer camp in the Pocono Mountains in Pennsylvania. Tamiment was on the *Borscht* circuit, providing its comics with a particularly intimidating environment in which to learn their craft. As Adams (1966: 57) recalls:

> The roughest thing in the whole world is to lay an egg at a show in the Catskills. There is no place to hide. If you die at a night club or in a theater, you can always run home ... But when you bomb in the mountains, it's like a concentration camp with sour cream. You just want to walk into that pool and never come out. There's no sunshine strong enough to dry up the flop sweat ... The only intelligent thing to do is to crawl into the ground, but the musicians are there ahead of you.

It was here that Allen first performed his own material in public – after having been literally pushed on stage. He was noticeably tense in front of the audience. He stammered and could not pace his delivery. He had periods when his self-control seemed to crumble and he would start fiddling with the microphone or muttering at the audience. The early experiences were intense, challenging, and very painful. The considerable numbers of autobiographical themes in Allen's stage act perhaps slowly caused some tension between his wife and himself. They separated and, according to one of his routines, they chose divorce over a vacation in Bermuda because 'the vacation is over in two weeks, but a divorce is something you have forever.' In 1960, with encouragement from his new managers Jack Rollins and Charles H. Joffe, Allen began performing his own material at small Manhattan clubs like the Village Vanguard and The Blue Angel. Whereas Lenny Bruce satirized middle-class tastes, and Mort Sahl satirized middle-class politics, Woody Allen satirized himself. 'I don't get an enormous input from the rest of the world', he said. 'I wish I could, but I can't.' Perhaps he was just being rather more honest than others, but his public self-analysis was certainly original. It was some time, however, before Allen found the right audience for his stand-up routines. Max Gordon, who ran the Village Vanguard, remembers that only 'the sophisticated few' responded to Allen's act. According to Gordon, Jack Rollins immediately sensed Allen's anxiety.

> To me he said: "Max, *please* tell him he's doing okay." The kid wouldn't listen to him. He was sitting there with his hands over his ears. "Max, tell him," Jack begged me. "Tell Woody he's not terrible. He thinks he's terrible." Then he swung round and patted Woody's shoulder. "You're doing terrific. You hear? Terrific!" Then he said to me, in a whisper, "Tell him, Max. Tell him how terrific he's doing!".
> (in McNight, 1983: 93)

After the first two years as a stand-up comic, Allen's instinctive timing and distinctive delivery became increasingly evident as he grew in confidence and relaxed: 'I was scared, and I worked at feeling more at ease and getting to enjoy my time on stage.'

When Allen began to establish himself as a performer, it was with a routine that drew upon aspects of New York Jewish culture and the more general interests of modern intellectual life. Described by some at the time as sounding 'like a nice Jewish boy gasping for air', Allen's natural nervousness became a kind of style, with each story being guided around circuitous alleyways and backstreets before the punchline comes into view. The verbal arabesques are deceptively clumsy – stammers, pauses, repetitions, hesitations, backtrackings – the apparently aimless wanderings suddenly being ambushed by a carefully positioned punchline. Allen, according to Arthur Gelb, 'approached the microphone as though he were afraid it would bite him'. 'I'll tell you about my private life,' he often began his sets, 'and then we'll have a question-and-answer session.' He goes on to recall a traumatic childhood: 'breast-fed from falsies', parents whose sole values were 'God and carpeting', a summer at an interfaith camp where he was 'sadistically beaten about the head and neck by children of all races and creeds'. Things improved when he became captain of a latent paranoid softball team, allowing him to visit Europe via a 'neurotic exchange program'. Allen once described himself as 'a product of TV and psychoanalysis': Keaton and Chaplin, said Allen, 'came at the end of the industrial revolution and they expressed the physicality in everybody's life... But now everything has become electronic and Freudian and the interest has shifted. The conflict is no longer about: Can I find work? Can I cope with nuts and bolts in a factory? It is: Can I stand the stress and pressure of working in an affluent society? The conflict is more subtle' (in Benayoun, 1986: 158).

Allen thus began to develop his stage persona: an alienated, anxious Jewish analysand at odds with an often cold, mechanized urban world. His comic sketches slowly add flesh and colour to this world: a Brooklyn where kids steal hub caps from moving cars, and where a suicidal man in a basement apartment jumps out of the window *up* onto street level; the rabbi who becomes a TV star and confuses the Ten Commandments with the Seven Dwarfs; the man who, threatened by a thug, 'very quickly lapsed into the old Navajo Indian trick, of screaming and begging'; a Madison Avenue advertising agency that hires a 'show Jew' who has to 'look Jewish' and read memos from right to left (he is eventually fired for taking off too many Jewish holidays); and, perhaps most memorably, the unfortunate Mr Berkowitz who, leaving a fancy dress party dressed as a moose, is 'shot, stuffed, and mounted at the New York Athletic Club'. Allen's monologues humorously investigate the *quality* of modern life, the problems which arise from an abundance of commodities and services but a dearth of values and principles. This New York has a tremendous diversity of racial and economic groups, a breathtaking variety of cultural pastimes, yet few people seem either content or settled. Movie producers ask Allen to take the music and lyrics out of *My Fair Lady* and turn it back into *Pygmalion*; they hire him to write a non-fiction version of the Warren Report, and to make a comic musical based on the Dewey decimal system. No one can be trusted anymore: Allen's rabbi cheats him out of a lucrative job; his grandfather, just before passing away, sells him a watch. Getting into an elevator with a built-in voice which asks for your floor number, Allen hears it make an anti-semitic remark. His father is made redundant, replaced by a computer that does everything he could 'only better'; Allen's mother rushes out and buys one.

As Allen has said, his comedy became sensitive to the reflectiveness of modern life, focusing upon inner tensions and anxieties exacerbated by the pressures of urban living. Allen started having analysis in the 1960s, and his night-club act was a veritable casebook of psychoanalytic theories. Unlike Chaplin or Keaton, who used their bodies to express so much, Allen tends to concentrate his acting in his facial expressions and his manner of speaking: his eyebrows arch upwards at the slightest sign of trouble, the glasses are constantly being readjusted and touched, the mouth conveys meaning with the slightest of twitches, and the voice (surely one of the *classic* comic voices) is an extraordinary collection of intonations and curiously comprehensible stutters: 'tch', 'um', 'uh-huh'. Allen has spoken of the period at the start of his career when he 'read voraciously', catching up with every important thinker he could find: Freud, Kafka, Schopenhauer, Kierkegaard, Ibsen, Shaw – the result is rather like a cross between George Steiner and Bob Hope. At the same time that Allen began examining human behaviour by 'looking within', he also started examining his city as a kind of self, charting the various levels of meaning and its unconscious impulses. He probes the city by exploring its layout, its active and passive areas, its hardened public exterior and its nervous private interior. His stories of New York are thus, in part, *questions*: his characters and situations react to these questions, not always answering them in expected or satisfactory ways. In *Annie Hall*, one sees the New Yorker ask, 'How can romantic love survive the pressures of modern life?' In *Manhattan*, the question becomes even more problematic: 'How can one individual be successful and personally fulfilled without living in bad faith?' The increasingly sophisticated questions lead to increasingly 'open', ambiguous responses: maybe, Allen suggests, there are only more questions.

In one of his *New Yorker* pieces, Allen depicts the Brooklyn of his childhood as a hopelessly illogical place where it is impossible *not* to grow up with the suspicion that nature is fundamentally devious and immune to rational analysis:

Tree-lined streets. The Bridge. Churches and cemetaries everywhere. And candy stores. A small boy helps a bearded old man across the street and says, 'Good Sabbath'. The old man smiles and empties his pipe on the boy's head. The child runs crying into his house ... stifling heat and humidity descend on the borough. Residents bring folding chairs out onto the street after dinner to sit and talk. Suddenly it begins to snow. Confusion sets in. A vender wends his way down the street selling hot pretzels. He is set upon by dogs and chased up a tree. Unfortunately for him, there are more dogs at the top of the tree. (Allen, 1981: 83)

This is the kind of New York that shows itself to the *schlemiel* – the 'little guy' who is both victim and outsider, who is confronted by failure and responds with ironic complaint. 'The *schlemiel*', according to a Jewish proverb, 'falls on his back and breaks his nose'. He is the butt of jests both local and cosmic. Like Lear's fool (whom Allen 'plays', fleetingly, in Godard's *Lear*), the *schlemiel* knows more than anyone else, but that sometimes only underlines for him the cruelties in life. Only the *schlemiel* knows that the dogs are waiting at the top of the tree – but that knowledge is no help when there are also dogs pursuing one at the base of the tree. Nature seems to keep its most absurd tricks for the *schlemiel*: in *Sleeper*, Miles Monroe wakes up after centuries of sleep only to slip on a banana skin 'as big as a canoe'; he is told that scientists have found that the *really* healthy food is the junk food of *his* time. In this environment, where *nothing* can be taken for granted, Woody Allen begins his artful struggle to survive.

'You don't *have* to be Jewish to be traumatized,' said Allen, 'but it helps'. Most of Allen's important male characters have been New York Jews. *Annie Hall* (1977), in particular, demonstrates Allen's urban, Jewish consciousness in a series of extended Jewish jokes that become the daily life of his screen persona, Alvy Singer. The movie underlines the fact that the Jewish–American experience has become an intrinsic part of the modern American experience. Alvy Singer is probably the most Jewish of all Allen's screen characterizations, a man obsessed with paranoia, guilt, sexual hang-ups and childhood fantasies. He claims, for example, that the federal government's refusal in the early 1970s to support fiscally the ailing New York, the city of 'left-wing, Communist, Jewish, homosexual pornographers', is clearly an anti-semitic act; he explains that such a refusal is 'a matter of foreskin, not economics'. Such anxiety insinuates itself into his personal relationships: his colleagues, instead of asking, 'Did you eat?' say (according to Alvy) 'D'jew eat?'. An innocent visit to a record store is cut short after a tall, blonde-haired salesman tries to sell him cut-price Wagner. Marcel Ophuls' four-and-a-half hour documentary on the Nazi Occupation of France, *The Sorrow and the Pity*, is the harrowing fate awaiting Annie Hall when she becomes Alvy's lover. Alvy's affair with Annie, a *shikseh* from Chippewa Falls, is doomed to failure because of their cultural and emotional differences. Alvy is the aggressively cynical New York Jew, the morbid intellect who reads only books with death in the title, who divides humanity into the 'horrible' ('blind people, cripples' and so on) and the 'miserable' ('everyone else'), who refuses to lose his integrity by accepting a reassuring but unfounded faith. Like many other fictional Jewish characters (such as Bellow's Moses Herzog or Roth's Alexander Portnoy), Alvy Singer displays an obsession with his past. The whole movie is about a love affair that is now over, and as the story develops (as fragment is added to fragment) we see Alvy delving ever deeper into his own personal background, trying to 'figure out, where did the screw-up come?'. We see Alvy's mother, distressed by her son's passivity. We see Alvy's father, sitting polishing a pith helmet as he engages in pointless arguments with his wife ('Leo, I married a fool!'). In a series of flashbacks we see how Alvy's Jewish childhood influenced his life: the anxious mother–son relationship, the reactions to his 'deviant' sexual behaviour ('I never had a latency period'), and the suffocating crowd of relatives who queue up to advise the young boy. Thanksgiving Day at Annie's parents' home is the movie's ethnic highlight: in beautiful heartland America, amid baked ham and Granny Hall's stare (she regards Alvy as a *real Jew*), Alvy magically turns into an Hasidic Jew – a visual representation of Alvy's sense of strangeness. Healthy and prosperous, Mr and Mrs Hall engage in oppressively insular conversations about local matters, ignoring Alvy's desperate efforts to involve himself: even the conversation is restricted. We see the differences between the Halls and the Singers ('oil and water') through the use of the split-screen: the refined Halls at their ham dinner and the raucous, noisy Singers arguing over a brisket. The scene becomes even more striking when Mrs Hall suddenly discusses the issue of guilt with Mr Singer:

Mrs Hall: How do you plan to spend the holidays, Mrs Singer?
Mr Hall: Fast?

> *Mr Singer*: Yeah, no food. You know, we have to atone for our sins.
> *Mrs Hall*: What sins? I don't understand.
> *Mr Singer*: Tell you the truth, neither do we.

Beginning with *Annie Hall*, Allen abruptly shifted the tone of his movies, dropped the earlier improbable formats, drew on autobiographical themes and details, and began using humour as a counterpart to stories he intended as poignant studies of New York life. *Sleeper* (1973) had found Allen in a future world, *Love and Death* (1975) placed him in Napoleonic times, but *Annie Hall* was a movie about and for America in the mid-1970s. The old worries still persist in the movies that follow – the philistines still hedge him in, eliciting more worried looks and wounded stares and painful, self-annihilating jokes – but new, more profound worries appear: a gnawing, almost panic-stricken doubt about the value of his own celebrity, and attached to that doubt, as if by handcuffs, the harrowing question of women and their power to save or destroy him. In *Annie Hall*, Allen's insecurity takes the form of Pygmalion – playing Alvy Singer, New York comedian, who meets Midwestern WASP Annie, decides he is in love, and immediately starts trying to turn her into somebody she is not – somebody as bright, guilt-ridden and insecure as he is – so he does not have to risk something 'permanent'. Eventually, it works: Annie discovers that life with Alvy is no longer fun, leaves him, and goes out to Hollywood – the ultimate betrayal. Alvy can thus safely retreat back into the lonely land of the misunderstood. He stays in New York and rewrites the relationship as a play – this time with a happy ending. Wish-fulfilment also forms a key theme in *Manhattan*, whilst perceptions of the real and the imaginary provide the structure of *Stardust Memories* (1980), which depends even more than did *Annie Hall* on the interrelationship between the movie's protagonist and Woody Allen himself. Besides pointing the way forward into the director's subsequent work, *Annie Hall* demonstrates, through the exact craftsmanship that underpins its ostensibly casual service, that Woody Allen is a good deal better than Alvy Singer at transmuting untidy life into something that is rather close to being art. As Maureen Stapleton was heard to say after attending the New York premiere of *Manhattan*: 'It almost makes you forget all the dog poop on the streets.'

Allen's treatment of New York is clearly an *overtly* subjective one. He adopts a perspective, and invites us to share it with him. Such openness is significant, for it guides us towards the distinctive relationship between the author and his environment. In *Annie Hall*, Allen begins by looking straight at the camera and thereby establishes himself as the master of ceremonies, the person who will summon the characters and arrange the order and duration of the scenes. *Manhattan* opens with another variant of the controlling monologue as Allen's voice-over recites different versions of the first paragraph of his character's work-in-progress about the city. The manner of the opening alerts us to the fact that what we are about to witness is Woody Allen's Manhattan, and no other.

> 'Chapter One. He adored New York City ... He romanticized it all out of proportion. Now ... to him, no matter what the season was, this was still a town that existed in black and white and pulsated to the great tunes of George Gershwin.' Ahhh, now let me start this over. 'Chapter One. He was too romantic about Manhattan as he was about everything else. He thrived on the hustle ... bustle of the crowds and the traffic.'

We see further visions of New York: construction men drilling a street; schoolchildren running home; Delancey Street overflowing at noon, Park Avenue in rare repose at dawn; joggers in Central Park; slim glass boxes and squat Belle Epoque curiosities; the Plaza Hotel; the 59th Street Bridge. Each image accompanies one of Isaac's word-pictures:

> 'To him, New York meant beautiful women and street-smart guys who seemed to know all the angles.' Nah, no ... too corny for my taste.

He tries again:

> 'Chapter One. He adored New York City. To him, it was a metaphor for the decay of contemporary culture. The same lack of individual integrity to cause so many people to take the easy way out was rapidly turning the town of his dreams in – ' No, it's gonna be too preachy. I mean, you know ... let's face it, I wanna sell some books here.

Isaac pauses, sighs, and makes yet another attempt at starting his story:

> 'Chapter One. He adored New York City, although to him, it was a

metaphor for the decay of contemporary culture. How hard it was to exist in a society desensitized by drugs, loud music, television, crime, garbage.' Too angry. I don't wanna be angry.

As the discrete scenes from New York life pass before us, some attractive and others rough and routine, one begins to wonder whether the narrator will ever succeed in finding the 'correct' introduction. He gathers his thoughts together, sighs once more, then says:

> 'Chapter One. He was as ... tough and romantic as the city he loved. Behind his black-rimmed glasses was the coiled sexual power of a jungle cat.' I love this. 'New York was his town. And it always would be.'

Although it seems that Isaac has 'found' his beginning, the actual effect is the exact opposite. The final 'draft' ("He was as ... tough and romantic as the city he loved") is the only one that does *not* sum up one of *Manhattan*'s several themes. The movie does deal with a man who 'was too romantic about Manhattan as he was about everything else'; it also features a man who, at first, has a weakness for 'beautiful women and street-smart guys' until he sees how 'corny' it all is; the movie also shows the city as a 'metaphor for the decay of contemporary culture' and focuses upon the 'lack of individual integrity'; we can also see in the movie a serious criticism of 'a society desensitized by drugs, loud music, television, crime, garbage'. The multiple introductions alert us to the multiple meanings in the movie; as with a good novel, one can find several levels (streets and alleyways), several themes in the narrative. Allen's opening to the movie is literally that: an opening, an explicit recognition of the artificiality of 'structuring' a story, devising a beginning, middle and end (in that order). We note the allusions to the subsequent 'ordering' of New York, and the multiple stories, sights and sounds of such a fast-moving, fast-changing city.

The movie is by no means an entirely approving portrait of New York. On the voice-over, we hear Isaac (Allen) continually repeat that he sees 'New York as a metaphor for the decay of contemporary culture', rather as other critics have described the city as 'the nation's thyroid gland'. A few days after the movie was released, Allen explained that he saw, as the backdrop for this story, a society that had been 'desensitized by television, drugs, fast-food chains, loud music and feelingless, mechanical sex'. Towards the end of the movie, Isaac complains into his tape recorder that 'people in Manhattan are constantly creating these unnecessary neurotic problems for themselves because it keeps them from dealing with the terrible, unsolvable problems of the universe'; Allen himself insisted that 'until we find a resolution for our terrors, we're going to have an expedient culture'. In order to demonstrate this fear, the movie shows that under their shimmering surface, his characters are shallow and scared.

To some extent, New York's development over the past century can be seen as symbolic action and communication: it has been conceived and constructed, not merely to serve immediate economic and political needs, but also to demonstrate to the rest of the world what modern human beings can build and how modern life can be imagined and lived. *Manhattan* explores this theme, exploiting its ambivalent results. The silken elegance of the black-and-white imagery evokes a sense of bygone Manhattan, but the characters and concerns of the movie are very much in the present: the old New York thus seems to haunt their actions. *Manhattan*'s New Yorkers congregate at Elaine's and Museum of Modern Art parties, publish books about their failed marriages, and mourn the loss of romantic innocence. Isaac Davis is an accomplished writer of TV comedy shows who aspires to more 'serious' literary work; his best friend Yale (Michael Murphy) is slaving away at a biography of Eugene O'Neill. In both cases the chaos of their emotional lives makes it unlikely that they will fulfil their professional ambitions. Tracy (Mariel Hemingway) becomes Isaac's lover, but she is so much younger than he and their relationship seems destined to be short-lived. Yale begins an affair with Mary Wilke (Diane Keaton), an egregiously competitive intellectual who declares Ingmar Bergman and Gustav Mahler 'overrated' while she churns out 'novelizations' of screenplays. No one is happy; everyone seeks 'authentic' love.

Allen's Manhattan, where the reality of the aesthetically and morally diverse modern city must contend with Isaac's selective romantic impressions, is complimented by Gershwin tunes, seductive visual romanticism, and narratively in characters whose attraction for Isaac is difficult to defend in terms of real qualities. Isaac is the moralist who finds himself in Schnitzler's *La Ronde*, the romantic surrounded by pragmatists. He married his first wife Jill (Meryl Streep) knowing that she was bisexual, thinking that he could 'change' her; when she leaves him for another woman, he is stunned. When she publishes a book disclosing the 'disgusting little moments' of their married life, including the time when he tried to run over her female lover, he is outraged. Isaac is, in his own words, 'winner of the August Strindberg Award' when 'it comes to relationships with women'. He is obviously stimulated by 'trouble', and moves from his affair with seventeen-year-old Tracy to one with Yale's ex-lover Mary, who is 'both attracted and repelled by the male organ'. Isaac informs her that he is working on a novel about his mother, entitled *The Castrating Zionist*. When he feels successful with his work (TV comedy) and his relationship (with Tracy), he panics and leaves. Isaac is similarly emotionally confused over his relationship with modern Manhattan. He cannot abide its 'fake values', the pretentiousness and narcissism of its intellectual elite, its banal television shows and its crude materialism. Yet at other times he makes it clear that he cannot live anywhere else. 'He can't function anywhere other than New York', says a friend. The most moving and beautiful moments in the movie occur when Allen's first love for the woman and the city are seemingly at one with each other. Taking an old-fashioned carriage ride through Central Park one evening, Isaac looks tenderly at Tracy and remarks, 'You're God's answer to Job ... You would've ended all argument between them ... He would've pointed to you and said, you know, "I do a lot of terrible things, but I can also make one of these." And then, Job would've said, "Yes, okay – well, you win." ' Looking out at the 59th Street Bridge, with dawn about to break, the sound of 'Someone to Watch Over Me' gently growing louder, Isaac and Mary are seen from a distance as two grey silhouettes; Isaac says, 'it's really – really so pretty when the light starts to come up...' he sighs, '... this is really a great city. I don't care what anybody says. It's just so-really a knockout, you know?'

We are reminded of Isaac's Jewishness when, at a party, he responds to a discussion of a satirical article on anti-semitism by advising everyone to put down their pens and pick up baseball bats. As Yacowar (1979) has noted, Isaac's Jewishness shapes the often contradictory aspects of his personality: wise-cracking onlooker, persecuted victim, anxiety-ridden weakling, eternal outsider, guilty paranoid, gifted comedian, hopeless but unbowed lover, figure of moral rectitude. Isaac's put-upon Jew thus finds himself locked into conflict with the alien world surrounding him: 'Jewish' New York versus WASP America, the Left intelligentsia versus the Right establishment, and the wandering Jew versus international prejudice. 'Life,' said Allen, 'is like a concentration camp. You're stuck here and there's no way out. You can only rage impotently against your persecutors.' For Allen, that rage is expressed through a series of tragi-comic jokes that address our fears and uncertainties while they gently mock our inadequacies. When Isaac rages against authoritarianism and prejudice, we may laugh, yet we do not doubt his sincerity.

Eventually everyone in *Manhattan* reveals just how terribly vulnerable and isolated they are. Mary's analyst, Donny, telephones *her* in the middle of the night for comfort and later takes an overdose. Mary, who seemed so self-assured and independent, allows herself to be duped by Yale's empty promises. Yale, for all of his lofty talk about his important book project, is unable to write and unable to defend his extra-marital affair. Isaac, who was lured away from Tracy by Mary and then abandoned by Mary, finishes by begging Tracy to go back to him. Ironically, Tracy, so young and apparently so vulnerable, seems to emerge as the most well-balanced of all the characters when the movie ends. She is about to leave for six months of study (on, rather ironically, how to act) in London. Isaac approaches her as the soundtrack plays 'They're Playing Songs of Love, But Not for Me.' He pleads with her to unpack her bags and stay. 'What's six months, if we still love each other?' she asks. 'Not everybody gets corrupted ... have a little faith in people.' Isaac, exasperated, is aware that he cannot control the other, he cannot halt the process whereby everything changes, and yet he cannot bear to see that quality he loves disappear. The movie thus ends with Isaac, half-smiling, mixing unfounded hope and lingering scepticism in an uncommonly charming, vulnerable expression. He is on the verge of faith, of hope. He had been seduced, temporarily, by the facile and flashy charms of Yale and Mary, but now (rather like Fitzgerald's Nick Carraway in *The Great Gatsby*) he is waking up to the authentic, vulnerable beauty of a relationship with Tracy.

Manhattan was in one sense Allen's most courageous study of New York, for, unlike *Annie Hall* (where Alvy Singer seems to haunt the city, stopping passers by and observing them like some fascinated anthropologist), in this movie Allen's character is very much a part of the analysis, very much a member of the community he is criticizing. His world is Manhattan's East Side, extending from the forties to the nineties. Isaac dines at Elaine's (like Allen himself), and he takes his son for lunch at the Russian Tea Room. Before he quits his job he lives in an impressive duplex. Isaac, clearly, is a successful New Yorker, a man who has 'made it' on terms that the slick Manhattan society would instantly recognize and acknowledge.

With *Manhattan*, Allen said that he wished to communicate his 'subjective, romantic view of contemporary life in Manhattan. I like to think that, 100 years from now, if people see the picture, they will learn something about what life in the city was like in the 1970s.' Indeed, *Manhattan* carries the authentic aura of an artist who knows this language and lifestyle as only a participant can do, allowing Allen to achieve that delicately ironic tone which is located between celebration and critique. He commented at the time:

> What I feel about New York is hard to say in a few words. It's really the rhythm of the city. You feel it the moment you walk down the street. There's hundreds of good restaurants, thousands of brilliant paintings, you see all the old movies, all the new ones ... It has to do with nerves, with the blood that runs through the city. It's dangerous, noisy. It's not peaceful or easy and because of it you feel more alive. It's more in keeping with what human beings are meant to feel about the world ... There's more conflict than anywhere else. The struggle to survive here is much more exciting than Los Angeles, say, where everything is pleasant. I mean, all those people sitting in their tubs, can you imagine it? (quoted in Palmer, 1980: 16–17)

In Allen's writing this attraction to New York both as a place and as an idea is accentuated by the *negative* idea of Los Angeles. Allen has been rewriting the East and the West coasts throughout his career, using them as positive and negative poles for his thinking and his narratives. New York symbolizes creativity, Los Angeles symbolizes ennui; New York contains individuals of integrity, Los Angeles embraces individuals of shameless narcissism; New York is organized and centralized, Los Angeles is disorganized and yawningly open-ended; New York is intellectually active, Los Angeles is spiritually bankrupt. In short, what is hopeful resides in the East, what is hopeless lies in the West. Allen once said to Groucho Marx: 'I don't know how you live in California. For a man of your piercing intellect to be able to live on the West Coast is incredible to me' (in Chandler, 1980: 468). He is repelled by the bone-white pleasure palaces of California because life there is too shamelessly easy. With 'the Frontier' now only a myth, to leave the city for the 'freedom' of the West is, for Allen, tantamount to social and political isolationism.

Allen's movies contain constant references to this dialectic. In *Sleeper* one finds Allen's character waking up in the future after being asleep for 200 years; he compares this lengthy inactivity to spending a weekend in Beverly Hills. In *Bananas*, Allen is a products tester: his verdict on a coffin that contains a built-in music centre – 'It'll go down well in California.' The threat of a visit to Los Angeles never fails to strike fear into Allen's characters. In *Annie Hall*, Alvy Singer is forced to attend an awards show in Hollywood, but he becomes nauseous just watching TV directors using canned laughter ('Do you have boos on that machine?'). Told that the weather is always bright and warm, Alvy complains that his skin is not suited to the sun: 'I don't tan, I stroke.' The more his old friend praises the place, the more acerbic Alvy becomes: 'I don't want to live in a city where the only cultural advantage is that you can make a right turn on a red light.' A party at Tony Lacey's represents the beginning of the break-up of Alvy and Annie – once away from New York, and love surely fades. While Annie enjoys LA's balmy, relaxed climate, Alvy adheres to his view that, 'When I get mellow, I ripen and rot.' In *Hannah and Her Sisters* Micky Sachs laments that his former partner has settled into a comfortable but amoral lifestyle in California. The spiritual and cultural sterility of LA thus serves to underline the warmly redeeming qualities of New York *and* keeps Allen firmly within the city's limits.

Allen's New York is not, however, free from 'Californian' elements: witness, for example, the succession of 'partners' Allen's movie character breaks away from – Rob in *Annie Hall*, and the Tony Roberts character in *Hannah and Her Sisters*, both of whom horrify Allen by leaving Manhattan for lucrative jobs making comedy shows in LA. Anyone can get into bad habits: New York, and New Yorkers, live in constant danger of losing touch with what is valuable and worthwhile in the past, so keen are they to modify, move on and change. Allen strives to preserve the sense of wonder and mystery associated with traditional society while he engages with the challenges of modern urban life. For Allen, to sever the tension between tradition and modernity is to leave oneself either trapped in nostalgia or else anonymously adrift in the ever-new. The question is, how to

accept New York's dynamism without dismissing its history. For
Henry James, the future is tolerable only if it is a hesitant
growth from the past; for H. G. Wells, the future is an obliteration
of that past. One can recognize the Jamesian element in Allen's
treatment of New York, his sometimes melancholic remarks about
an earlier version of the city, a time being erased from memory
by the sweeping changes of the present. James had the intention
of retrieving America's brief but fast vanishing past, which
coincided with a search for his own youth; his quest had been
for 'the America of my old knowledge'. Allen, one feels, *wishes*
to believe in the Jamesian New York, yet he cannot ignore the
realistic coldness of the Wellsian metropolis. What one sees in
Manhattan and other movies is Allen's anxious critique of the
Wellsian New York, the 'metropolis that works', but which
needs more than simple mechanical efficiency to survive as a
place where one *lives*, and Allen's Jamesian exploration of an
earlier New York and, by implication, his own early life. He told
me: 'I must say it's getting harder and harder to romanticize
current-day New York, and so I *am* becoming increasingly
nostalgic.'

His play *The Floating Lightbulb* (1981), set in Brooklyn in
1945, features a Jewish couple, beset by poverty, and their elder
son, who escapes his stammering awkwardness through magic
tricks. *Annie Hall* shows us a young Alvy Singer, desperately
trying to control his nerves as a big-dipper rattles by over the
roof of his parents' house – they live underneath a funfair. The
young Alvy finally loses his optimism when he discovers that the
universe is expanding and thus all things will eventually be
destroyed: like Isaac in *Manhattan*, the fear that the thing he
cares about will be lost or damaged is terribly unsettling. In
Zelig (1983), a New Yorker becomes so receptive to modernity,
to change, to shutting out all knowledge of an ordered, familiar
past, he is the ultimate child of modernity – he marries several
women and fathers several children ('because it seemed the
right thing to do at the time'), he passes through a series of jobs,
trades and identities, travels through most countries, adopts
innumerable guises, accents, affectations and intellectual positions, and finds everything except himself. He is the shocking
confirmation of the structuralists' suspicion: that history has no
subject, that all individuals are the passive victims of their environ-
ments. When Leonard Zelig eventually comes to recover his
sense of selfhood, it is like the end of a nightmare, but the

nagging thought remains that perhaps only another dream has begun. Mickey Sachs, in *Hannah and Her Sisters*, tries every religion and philosophy he can find in order to retrieve some feeling of meaning for his life, yet nothing convinces him. Each movie sifts through the past, as though a *raison d'être* was hidden behind some half-forgotten memory, waiting to be discovered.

'Forgive me if I tend to romanticize the past,' Allen tells us at the beginning of *Radio Days* (1986). Yet such a confession is never entirely without irony: this particular confession is heard as we are shown a rain-soaked, gloomy grey Rockaway, the 'seaside' district of Brooklyn. Once again, Allen draws on his Brooklyn childhood, using autobiographical figures and events as starting-points for novel digressions: little red-haired, bespectacled Joe looks on as his parents heatedly debate which is 'the greater ocean' – the Atlantic or the Pacific; Joe's father ('a big butter-and-egg man') who, like Allen's own father, is forced for a time to earn a wage as a cab driver; Joe's mother, who is plagued by her son's reckless 'experiments' with a chemistry set; and the family's shared interest in radio and movies. Little Joe is immediately fascinated by radio's magical reconstruction in sound alone of Manhattan as a place full of glamour, life and laughter, cigarette smoke and champagne, tuxedos and tap-dancers, all moving to the music of Tommy Dorsey, Artie Shaw, Louis Armstrong, and Glenn Miller. In the mundane world of Rockaway, the wireless inexplicably forms the link with the foreign and the fantastic, giving people a sense of ritzy Manhattan that, for some, remained more 'real' than the place itself. The movie theatre is another, even more exhilarating dream screen for young Joe, projecting an astonishing invocation of 'America'. His first trip, to see *The Philadelphia Story*, is truly enchanting: we hear Sinatra singing 'If You Are But A Dream' as we follow the boy into the building (half temple, half theatre) exuding a rich lustre of golds, yellows, pinks, and reds. 'It was like entering heaven,' says Allen's narration, with no sound of irony. Suddenly the colours peel away and we have a black-and-white screen and awesome sightings of stars, promissory notes from the next 'dream place'. Allen compares the movie theatre to 'heaven' and the comparison is not a careless one; he knows the illusory, wistful, *promissory* quality of the movie images. It is something about that sense of wishing and wanting and hoping and having that attracts him to the medium. *Radio Days* is inspired by Allen's perennial nostalgia for the days when New York was seemingly a kinder, gentler place. As with *The Purple Rose of Cairo* (1985), *Radio Days'* movie theatre offers sanctuary from reality, momentary yet memorable, the ever-changing images seeming somehow to move to a logic more reliable than the logic of everyday life. When the screen turns to black-and-white, and the stars come out of hiding, it is not far from the beauty of *Manhattan*, with all of its gracious hope and flickering fragility.

Allen has in recent years become a willing prisoner of New York. He works almost exclusively within the City, because

> I live here, and I don't like to travel that much, and I certainly don't like to travel and to have to commit myself to the place and stay in a hotel for six months' time or four months' time. You know, it's too big a commitment. So life is much easier for me if I live in New York; I can sleep at home, I can go to my restaurant, see my friends... (*Film 88*, BBC TV)

'I still walk around, you know,' he told me, 'but people *do* interfere'. After suffering the delays and unpredictable incidents that came with location shooting for *Love and Death* in the mid seventies, Allen vowed never again to stray outside New York City. He now says that he would rather spend time making New York seem like Vermont or even Europe rather than travel to the places themselves. Whenever possible he will use real buildings as locations because, as he says, they match his imagined scenes better than any studio could do. He edits his movies in New York's Manhattan Film Center, a converted bridge parlour on the first floor of an old Park Avenue hotel. Despite his movie character's jokes ('I believe there's an intelligence to the universe, except for certain parts of New Jersey'), New York is somewhere that he can learn increasingly more about through years of inhabiting it, a place where he can discern difference in the apparently identical and similarity in the diverse, a city where he can understand the way people act, think and express them-selves:

> I don't think I'm *excessively* isolated. I live in New York City, and I'm politically aware to a reasonable degree. I think one would be more isolated in California – a cliché, I know, but I think it's true. Here, in the course of a week, I see a lot of different people in different professions, whereas in California, I think you tend to be isolated. The

community tends to revolve around film making and television. (*Esquire*, April 1987)

The natural world – the country – is an alien land, disturbing and in some ways belittling his creative appetite. 'I've always been at two with nature,' goes one of Allen's oldest gags. The countryside is one of the few subjects on which Allen, when being interviewed, is prepared to agree with the views of his movie persona: 'I'd rather die than live in the country,' he told *Time* magazine in 1979. He pointed out that he disliked the insects, the quiet, the 'alienation' – 'there are the woodchucks too...' One can almost hear Alvy Singer's famous frenzied critique of country life:

> The country makes me nervous. There's ... you got crickets and it – it's quiet... there's no place to walk after dinner, and ... uh, there's the screens with the dead moths behind them, and ... oh, you got the – the Manson family possibly, you got Dick and Terry...

A Midsummer Night's Sex Comedy (1982), Allen's only movie to take place out in the countryside, is thus, rather predictably, the least convincing of Allen's 'mature' works; we watch in disbelief as Allen's character extols the 'enchanting' qualities of nature and frolics in the forest. Unsurprisingly, it seems that Allen found a location only one half-hour north of Manhattan in order that he could drive back to his beloved New York every night. Allen's unsympathetic view of country life is in stark contrast with the classic Hollywood comedies of the 1930s and 1940s. Cavell (1981) has found in these movies a 'green world', a place where the perspective of cultured people can be regained, and psychic renewal obtained. This was often identified in Hollywood movies as Connecticut. Thus, Cary Grant's hapless scientist in *Bringing Up Baby* finds his sense of adventure when he is dragged off to the country. The divorced couple in *The Philadelphia Story* fall back in love with each other when away from the city. Yet, in stark contrast, Allen's *September* (1987) has everyone experiencing psychic disintegration and decay in the country: wild thunderstorms never stop, electricity cuts out, visitors fail to arrive, and the atmosphere is stifling. Love falls apart, old wounds resurface, and the only prospect of renewal and happiness is a move to New York and a new career. The skyscrapers of the city isolate New Yorkers from their natural environment and create an artificial climate with synthetic wind tunnels and geysers of steam. For the New Yorker the countryside is the Other, the non-urban – in Tony Hancock's phrase, it is 'a large town with no buildings in it'. It is the city, Allen's own city of New York, that holds him. Here, far more than in Paris or Rome or London, certainly more so than elsewhere in America, Woody Allen is at home, in tune with the rhythms of the city, the interests of the inhabitants.

New Yorkers are Allen's most critical audience. They share so many of his memories, his concerns, his tastes. When he interprets the city he also interprets his fellow New Yorkers. 'What are future generations going to say about us?', he asks a character in *Manhattan*. The question is at the centre of all of Allen's inter-rogations of New York, touching a nerve under the nostalgia. His stories have done for New York what Updike has done for New England and Chandler for Bay City. 'He idolized it out of all proportion,' 'Forgive me if I tend to romanticize the past': the admissions and apologies keep recurring in Allen's movies, yet the images often contradict the alleged 'romanticism' – such as when Isaac sits in a boat on Central Park lake, dips his arm in the water, and finds it is now covered with mud and dirt. 'I'm really a typical Jewish intellectual with all that implies,' he once said. Allen certainly appears to embody the essence of the neurotic, inquisitive, intelligent New York Jew, resembling thousands of others who roam the city's streets. New Yorkers have no trouble in recognizing Allen's skewed assemblage of features, expressions and gestures as those of a particular, familiar type. However, Woody Allen is triumphantly himself, a unique individual – a wonderful comic archetype, a New Yorker who is an outstanding interpreter of New York. This is *his* city and, one way or another, 'it always will be.'

2

The Bluebird of Anxiety

It's not that I'm afraid to die, I just don't want to be there when it happens.

Do I like happy endings? Only when they are possible.

'Early in life,' says Woody Allen in one of his night-club routines, 'I was visited by the bluebird of anxiety.' Richard Schickel (1973) once described Woody Allen as 'a walking compendium of a generation's concerns, comically stated'. Allen is a loser who still manages to get his moment of glory. He is the only short, bespectacled figure included in a *Playgirl* list of the 'ten sexiest men'. In 1966, *Current Biography* recognized his universal appeal: 'He demonstrated a singular ability to distill humor from the small frustrations of daily life.' Allen began his career as a stand-up comedian by confiding in his audience, inviting them to share in his anxieties: 'A lot of significant things have occurred in my private life that I thought we could go over tonight...'. The humour, it seemed, was drawn *from* everyday life rather than posing as an alternative to it. By constructing an image of a failure, a nobody ('People forget me ... even while they're shaking hands with me'), Allen made contact with many people's most intimate feelings of alienation and self-doubt. 'His one regret in life,' says Allen's biographical blurb, 'is that he is not someone else'. This well-known self-loathing first revealed itself when Woody Allen made his first, nervous and unpredictable appearances as a night-club comedian in New York. When he made that nervousness into a *strength*, a habit to be cultivated, his audience expanded.

'I have, by nature, an enormously sad face,' Allen has said.

'I'm not a smiler. If you didn't know I was a comic, I would be a study in sadness.' Allen's face is beguiling in its ordinariness: the red hair is ruffled and lifeless; his eyebrows seem to be floating just above his black-rimmed spectacles; the poached-egg eyes peer out through the lenses, timid and vulnerable; the large nose and thin lips are defiantly 'imperfect' and ill-matched. His walk manages to seem both ungainly and rhythmic, a mass of moving arms and legs. His whole body, when in motion, seems to fragment into a cluster of exclamation marks, reacting in amazement to the shocks in city life. He is dressed informally, to the point of seeming unkempt. One feels that one would not notice such a person ... if only he were not so memorable. There is a nimbus of oddity that everyone carries around with them, as ineffably subtle as the twitch of an eyebrow or the flick of a finger. With Allen this oddity is writ large, an uncaged selfhood that attracts us with its emphatic normality. In his short stories, plays and movies, Allen developed this illusion of intimacy, this appearance of an autobiography in the offing, this context of confession. Over the years he has made his public persona so 'real', so fascinating, that we shake our heads in disbelief when he insists that this 'Woody' is not him. Allen has successfully *worried* his way into our consciousness. This success was something Allen worked for during years of careful experiment.

Woody Allen today stands somewhat alone in the movie-making community. Unlike many of America's other well-known directors currently working – such as Steven Spielberg, Francis Ford Coppola, George Lucas and Martin Scorsese – Allen did not seriously study movies as an academic subject at university. Although he is a man who clearly loves the medium of movies, Allen is unusually versatile – being internationally respected for his work as a stand-up comic, a playwright, an actor, an author, a screenwriter, and a director. Such a remarkable set of abilities is one of the reasons that Allen has so much control over his movies, but they have not always developed at the same pace or indeed in the same direction. The 1960s saw Allen move from being an unknown writer of other comedians' material to being the star and director of his own movie. It was a decade in which Allen had the opportunity to experiment with his comic ability using several different media: written essays for the *New Yorker* magazine, scripts for popular movies, and stage plays. Few humorists have stretched their talents so far in so short a period of time. By the 1970s the man who regretted not being someone else was admired for his openness about himself. 'Woody Allen, *c'est moi*,' said Schickel, and many people agreed with the verdict.

The dearth of information concerning Woody Allen's first two decades makes his eventual breakthrough into television and movies seem quite meteoric. He really started to make a reputation for himself in the fifties, writing for Sid Caesar's *Your Show of Shows*, along with such young comics as Mel Brooks, Carl Reiner, Larry Gelbart, and Neil Simon. Working as a member of a team, attending prolonged sessions during which everyone would listen to and comment upon each other's jokes, Allen gained experience without enjoyment. A veteran of the show's staff, Al Goldman, recalls:

> Every morning they all arrived, straight from their shrinks. They lit up their cigars and got into a circle around Sid, who recited, alone, the outlines of a sketch which had previously been prepared. As soon as he finished, everybody jumped up like a bunch of madmen. They screamed at each other, and hurled jokes at each other, improvising bits of dialogue, until they were tired out from laughing and sat down again.

Allen himself recalls a similarly chaotic atmosphere:

> I mostly remember an infernal noise, everybody shouting like we were in a madhouse, fighting for our lines. Nobody had a lack of confidence. We worked like a kind of steamroller. There were loud screams in the alley, then two of us would isolate in another room and write a page or two. (in Benayoun, 1986: 161)

For an exuberant man such as Mel Brooks (who seems to perform as much *off* screen as on), these sessions were opportunities to perform his own material. In contrast, for a man as introverted and shy as Woody Allen, these sessions were not occasions he savoured. He was being well paid, he was learning much from his fellow-writers, but he was not the kind of person who is comfortable in a group. His humour, even at this early stage, often sounded too obscure or odd until he demonstrated how he thought it should be delivered. His new managers, Jack Rollins and Charles Joffe, began to consider how Allen could begin to develop this distinctive kind of humour. Suddenly, on their advice, he quit and tried to perform. There followed a period of tremendous anxiety that has often been referred to in Allen's movies; as a stand-up comedian he sometimes needed to be pushed onto the stage, and he only gradually allowed a semblance of self to slip through the tangle of nervous mannerisms and the tense, erratic delivery. The mercilessly self-critical performer was also the writer revelling in the freedom to use his own material. *Annie Hall* (1977), *Manhattan* (1979) and *Hannah and Her Sisters* (1986) all feature a successful television writer quitting his job and then almost immediately declaring, 'I made a terrible mistake.' His night-club act exhibited a tremendously inventive use of language at the same time that he implied it would not save him: one story has him buy a pen from *Esquire* that can emit tear gas if he is attacked: a 'Neanderthal man' confronts him in the lobby, and *ink* squirts from the pen. Allen tries writing all over the assailant, and makes a 'mental note to complain to *Esquire*'. The character that was being created in these routines was Woody Allen the *schlemiel* – the hapless, helpless little man who is engaged in a ceaseless struggle against every conceivable natural and human obstacle.

According to Woody Allen's stand-up routine, his childhood was a traumatic time in his life. His parents (both of whom resembled Groucho Marx) bronzed his baby shoes while his feet were still inside them ('they were sentimental but impatient'). His father was a caddie at a miniature golf course. His mother would often sit at home, knitting a chicken. His inferiority complex was, it seems, hereditary: 'My grandfather was a very insignificant man. At his funeral his hearse *followed* the other cars.' The young Allen was bullied by neighbourhood kids such as Guy de Maupassant Rabinowitz and Sheldon Finkelstein. Too poor to buy their son a real pet, Allen's parents bought him a dog with a stutter from a Damaged Pets store. Allen's one childhood success, at age five, was his acclaimed performance as Stanley Kowalski in his school play. He fared no better at New York University – expelled for cheating in his metaphysics exam by looking into the soul of the boy sitting next to him. Even when he began working on *What's New Pussycat?*, he told his audiences that he was still the same old *schlemiel*: when the movie star Peter O'Toole arranged to go on a date with a beautiful woman, Allen begged her to bring along a sister for him. She did: Sister Maria Terese. 'It was a very slow night.' They discussed the New Testament into the early hours, and they finally agreed that Christ was very well adjusted for an only child. Allen's first marriage was the cause of yet more torture: his wife would involve him in long philosophical arguments to prove that he did not exist. She was, he claims, a very immature person: 'Once, while I was taking a bath, she came in, and sank my boats.' They divorced. Alfred Hitchcock expressed an interest in the movie rights to the marriage. Even mechanical objects conspired against Allen: his sunlamp rained on him, his television set avoided him, and his 'deluxe' dictaphone replied 'I know, I know...'

Unlike some of his contemporaries on the club circuit, Allen paid little attention to politics. 'Current affairs' material, he said, had a short shelf-life and was always full of awkward contradictions concerning its function. Allen focused on himself, his experiences of life in New York City and the everyday fears and hopes that figure in modern society (and, implicitly, this carried political themes). The comedy was deliberately small-scale, personal, made up of common problems exaggerated and multiplied for comic effect. There are certainly surreal moments and characters: a man who is half-Mexican, half non-fat milk; a disco run by 'topless rabbis' (without yarmulkes); a Village club called the Integration Bagel and Yoga where an Eskimo sang 'Night and Day' for six months at a time. Allen worked hard to make his stage persona comical yet likeable, a *schlemiel* whom everyone knows as part of themselves. Each routine is constructed so as to draw the audience in, making it identify with Allen. For example, he tells of once being offered a fortune to make some vodka commercials (his name had been come across on a list in Eichmann's pocket) and not knowing whether to accept. 'I needed the money,' he laments, 'but I feel that drinking intoxicating beverages is immoral.' Wracked by indecision, he seeks trustworthy advice – from his psychiatrist, his bank manager, and finally his rabbi. 'Don't do it!' cries the rabbi. 'Vodka is evil! Refuse the money!' He does, and immediately feels a better person for having done so. Later he sees one of the advertisements he has righteously turned down. It shows Senta Berger in a skimpy bikini reclining on a sun-drenched beach holding a cool vodka and tonic. Her lips are provocatively parted, her eyes smoulder with desire for the man sitting beside her. That man is Allen's rabbi.

As Allen's appeal with the public expanded, he elaborated his act to the point where its highly personal nature made it uniquely his own. His most successful and original routines could be endlessly improved with exotic flights of fancy. One of these routines has Allen kidnapped. The police surround the house where the kidnappers are hiding out; they have run out of tear gas, so they capture their quarry by enacting the death scene from *Camille*. Tear-stricken, the culprits are sentenced to fifteen years on a chain gang, but they escape past the guards, posing as 'an immense charm bracelet'. Allen's small but loyal group of fans would keep attending his shows, listening out for every new detail in each routine. 'The Moose' is a classic routine that epitomizes everything that was new and distinctive about Allen's work at this time, and it deserves to be quoted at length:

> I was hunting up-state New York and I shot a moose. I strap him on to the fender of my car and I'm driving home along the West Side highway. What I didn't realize was that the bullet did not penetrate the moose. It just creased his scalp, knocking him unconscious. So I'm driving through the Holland Tunnel, and the moose woke up. Now I'm driving with a live moose on my fender ... and the moose is signalling a turn. And there's a law in New York State against driving with a conscious moose on your fender Tuesdays, Thursdays and Saturdays. I'm very panicky ... and then it hits me. Some friends of mine are having a costume party. I'll go, I'll take the moose. I'll ditch him at the party. It won't be my responsibility. So I drive up to the party. I knock on the door. The moose is next to me. My host comes to the door. I say, "Hello ... you know the Solomons?" We enter. The moose mingles ... did very well ... scored. Some guy was trying to sell him insurance for an hour and a half. Twelve o'clock comes, they give out prizes for the best costume of the night. First prize goes ... to the Berkowitzes, a married couple dressed as a moose. The moose comes in second. The moose is furious! He and the Berkowitzes lock antlers in the living room. They knock each other unconscious. Now I figure here's my chance. I grab the moose, strap him to my fender and shoot back to the woods. *But* I got the Berkowitzes. I'm driving along with two Jewish people on my fender ... and there's a law in New York State ... Tuesdays, Thursdays and *especially* Saturdays. The following morning, the Berkowitzes wake up in the woods in a moose-suit. Mr Berkowitz is shot, stuffed, and mounted at the New York Athletic Club – and the joke is on them, 'cause it's restricted.

The routine is deceptively simple; to listen to Allen tell it one could easily imagine that he is making much of it up as he goes along. He gives the impression of hesitating, of making random comments and extraneous allusions. Once the moose begins to make signals to the traffic, we are distracted from the initial absurdity of how it got to be on Allen's fender in the first place. The structure of the story is, in fact, carefully worked out. When Allen first mentions the New York State law for moose drivers, it seems a throw-away remark. When Allen first mentions that the couple in the moose-suit are Jewish, we think little of it (this is mentioned as we imagine a moose humiliated by a more realistic moose-suit). Suddenly Allen's punchline arrives to illuminate an elaborate network of comic links: the New York Athletic Club's laws ban Jews, but the moose that its members proudly display is in fact a Jew-in-moose's clothing. The routine is made particularly successful by Allen's intelligent use of short sentences which instantly conjure up images that allow us to follow the story ('So I drive up to the party. I knock on the door. The moose is next to me'.) Such sentences slow down the pace at regular intervals, playing on our curiosity as to what the next extraordinary occurrence will be. There is even a gentle note of social comment in the routine: the roar of celebration and laughter comes after Allen shows how the anti-semitic law is overcome.

Although the most gifted of stand-up comedians give us the impression that they are being 'naturally' funny on stage, in fact they are doing something far removed from instinctive humour. The problem with the commonplace laughter of everyday life is that the ludicrous context which is generated spontaneously very much depends upon a shared understanding of relatively intimate facts, nuances, and gestures; this context is highly transitory and difficult, if not generally impossible, to reassemble. Thus, the amateur joke does not travel well, and when one repeats an amusing comment that made one's companions laugh the day before yesterday, one is usually forced to excuse oneself with the phrase, 'You really should have been there!' Lovers can exclude everyone except each other with a private joke or catchphrase. The professional comedian cannot count on any special relationship with an audience; a joke must be general (or ambiguous) enough to make people laugh in New York, Chicago, London, and Liverpool. The comedian's jokes are an *adaptation* of commonplace humour towards generalization and reliability. Jokes are obliged to compete in the market-place of pleasures associated with laughter, and for that reason their materials must be less privileged, less personally limited, and their ludicrous context must be wider than obtains in daily extemporaneous provocations to laughter. Jokes create the comic experience in an extremely radical and economical form. In a very short scene, they must engender a ludicrous context, engage the audience's participation, and establish in the briefest way those peculiar incongruities of plot, character, or concept that continue to support the ludicrous context and that elicit the laughter which signals a successful conclusion. This is what Allen learned to achieve: the effective comic line, delivered in a recognizably humorous manner, with a sufficiently wide-appeal to register with audiences of varied backgrounds and tastes. As Richard Shickel (1973) wrote: 'Listening to his public monologues has always given me and mine the peculiar sensation that our own interior monologues have been tapped and are being broadcast.' Allen's night-club act, in the years just before and during his entry into movie-making, was extremely professional and remarkably distinctive. He used his relatively short stature (five feet, six inches) to emphasize his inadequacy. He began slowly, hesitantly, quietly, feeling his way. He appeared as a performer in search of a theme ('What else should I tell you about myself?'), wondering aloud about what might interest the audience. Gradually, this apparent absence of direction is revealed as a shrewd act, a subtle flow of comic invention. His aura of chaotic desperation made his sharpness all the more striking. 'I'm basically ... a stud,' he announces. A woman in the audience shrieks with mocking laughter. 'She wants me,' Allen improvises. Seemingly casual, unstructured affairs, his sets were actually scrupulously timed, with cunning pauses and hesitations at precisely the same point every night. An early fan recalls: 'Some of us would go each night and repeat some of his lines along with him. We'd wait for the favourite stories' (correspondence with the author, 9 May 1988). The small, intimate night-clubs allowed Allen to develop the low-key, conversational style that became his trademark. His voice is deeply Brooklynese (the Dutch traces contributing to the accent) – not as aggressive as Mel Brooks, friendlier than W. C. Fields. He did not need to pitch his delivery to the balcony, but he could understate, confide, subtly convey his comments. In this sense his night-club beginnings were conducive to his entry into movies: unlike theatres, the clubs demanded a style that was closer to the understatement of the screen actor than the physical and vocal exuberance of the stage actor. This environment also discouraged the kind of physical routines performed so brilliantly by earlier comedians such as W. C. Fields and Charlie Chaplin before they started making movies. The intimate club atmosphere brought the audience close to Allen, and the microphone made him relatively stationary. His image was based on his face and its expressions, his voice and its inflections.

Allen was fortunate to begin his performing career during a period in which the stand-up comic was very much in vogue; as he has said,

there was that whole rush of comedians in the Sixties. Mike Nichols and Elaine May, Shelley Berman, Mort Sahl. Bill Cosby and I were on the tail end of it. Just like a lot of folk musicians, we got our start in small clubs that just don't exist anymore, which is perhaps why there aren't that many young comedians anymore either. (in *Rolling Stone*, 30 September 1971)

These comics attracted a new, well-educated audience. By the early 1950s, the university population was on the increase, and by 1968 it reached a total of six million – four times the number of 1940. Allen's most important models at this time were probably Mort Sahl, his fellow stand-up comic, and Bob Hope, whom he first saw in 1942 in *The Road to Morocco*. Allen said that Mort Sahl 'made it different for all of us who came after him. He changed comedy for all of us.' Sahl would amble onto the stage, wearing an open-necked shirt and an old pullover, daily paper tucked under his arm, and he would sit down and respond to the current news items: 'I see here in the paper....' Looking back on his early years from the vantage point of 1977, Allen reiterated his admiration: 'It's not the political commentary that's important, but the way Sahl lays his jokes down. He does it with such guile, such energy. He's my favourite performer.' Both Sahl and Allen were big-city Jews, but whereas Sahl exempted himself from his satire and built his act around a left-of-centre political viewpoint, Allen criticized general values and manners through a merciless self-analysis. Ironically, by the late 1980s Sahl had drifted so far to the Right that his 'ideological' act was made somewhat specious because of his support for Republican politicians; Allen, who has never tried to 'politicize' his comedy, has nonetheless remained quietly but consistently liberal in his political activities. This independent, anti-authoritarian aspect of Allen makes Bob Hope a rather ironic influence. Hope has come to be seen as the Great American Comic, the scrupulously WASPish man who is forever seen with friends such as Nixon, Ford, Reagan, and Bush. However, Allen has always been a shrewd observer of comic technique, and he immediately recognized Hope's superb timing and disciplined performance. For Allen, Hope was an inspiration: 'The jokes become a vehicle for the person to display a personality or an attitude, just like Bob Hope ... You're laughing at character all the time.' Hope was the non-ethnic version of the *schlemiel*: an inveterate womanizer, a *naif*, a coward, a fall guy, yet also a winner. 'Hope was the guy next door,' said Allen. 'You really believed in him ... He was much more real than Groucho.' In 1979, when the Film Society of the Lincoln Center honoured Hope with a compilation movie of his best moments, Woody Allen helped compile and narrate it. Allen's narrative contained the comment:

> Hope's bantering style – the fantastic ad-lib style, the verbal interplay – reached a point of graceful spontaneity rarely equalled in films ... The lightness is everything. The puns, the asides, the fast one-liners, the great quips that appear throughout his work are quick, bright, and delivered very lightly.

Allen cited a scene in his own *Love and Death* (1975), where his sword gooses a Russian aristocrat and he goes on to flirt with a countess from across a theatre: (first by peeping at her around a fan and wiggling his eyebrows, then melodramatically brushing his hair, then panting with his tongue hanging out, finally by wiggling his sword). It was not imitation, Allen explained, but the scene showed how well he had learned the light comic touch and the endearingly gauche expression from Hope. Allen has also drawn on a certain kind of English humour: 'When I was young on certain wavelengths I could get the *Goon Show*. Sellers and Milligan were terrific.' He added, 'I'm a big, big English comic fan. Alistair Sim, the *Beyond the Fringe* players. They always make me laugh, to this day. Whenever I see Cook in New York, I always find him hilarious. I always watch Monty Python when I have a chance to' (BBC *Film 78 Special*). Groucho Marx undoubtedly made a great impact on Woody Allen, with his quickfire comic quips and his playful use of language:

> From the moment I picked up your book until I laid it down, I was convulsed with laughter. Someday I intend reading it.

> I could dance with you 'til the cows come home. On second thoughts, I'll dance with the cows and you come home.

> Why, I'd horsewhip you if I had a horse.

Like Groucho, Allen is eminently *quotable*: the two comics

speak and write in crafted, concise aphorisms which defy paraphrase or imitation. However, Groucho did not use his own
anxieties and inadequacies as the source of his comedy; Groucho's
strategy was to talk so much, so rapidly, and so belligerently
that talk becomes a kind of weapon. Groucho Marx, one under-
stands, is invulnerable: he wanders through a scene, pointing out
the absurdities of others, and we laugh with him but never at
him. Allen may recall Groucho in his manipulation of language
in order to mock the conventions of others, but he is nearer to
Hope in his *vulnerability* (women answer back to Hope and
Allen, and when they insult authority figures they may well end
up behind bars). Allen employs a *gentle* irony, whereas someone
such as Swift is habitually savage. Both Socrates and Swift are
self-consciously articulate moralist–critics, while Allen's screen
power is partly dependent upon his nervous inarticulacy – good-
ness wells up as it were.

Allen was, from the beginning, more of a story-teller than a
joke-teller. He usually exploited the *schlemiel* by placing him in
amusing contexts – driving around New York trying to lose a
moose; a holiday in Europe with Hemingway and Gertrude
Stein; or running down a street dressed only in his red flannel
underwear after being accidently hypnotized into thinking he is a
fire engine. Many of these stories cannot be paraphrased without
the loss of much of their humour: Allen's delivery is so distinctive,
and the comic detail so precise, that it is understandable why he
has become so heavily quoted. As Allen's story-telling developed,
the closer he came to the themes and styles of other American
Jewish writers. These Jewish comic figures are erudite unfor-
tunates; their jokes are no mere laughing matter, but profound
reflections on the foibles and fixations of our time. This comic
must be a *khukhem*, the wise figure of old. Allen's *schlemiel*
began to share certain characteristics with Isaac Bashevis Singer's
Gimpel the Fool, Saul Bellow's Herzog, Malamud's Fidelman,
Joseph Heller's Yossarian and Philip Roth's Portnoy. These
famous fictional characters have been mangled by their families,
unlucky in love, and haunted by guilt and anxiety, yet they are
also brilliant talkers, articulate and inventive. Moses Herzog
begins: 'This is the story of my life: how I rose from humble
origins to complete disaster.' Herzog is a modern, big-city *schlemiel*, a well-educated man who has made a mess of his life; he has
suffered two failed marriages, his academic promise is
unfulfilled, and he is at the mercy of lawyers, psychiatrists, and

his own uncontrollable sexual appetite. Portnoy is the *schlemiel* as a nice Jewish boy who has grown into the supreme modern sexual neurotic. All of these characters are fine story-tellers, cataloguing their *tsuris* (the history of injustice that trails them) with irony and bitterness. Compulsively analytical, self-absorbed, and acutely self-conscious, they are intellectuals with fine ideals whose bodies ache for sexual adventure. They have been through the 'civilizing process', and they *still*, on occasion, find themselves moved by primitive lust; they understand Plato, Kant, Hegel and Heidegger, they have a strong sense of moral urgency, yet they still tumble and fail and fall in love and hurt themselves and their hopes and their lovers. Intellect and lust fight each other to the death inside these characters, and they convey to us their terrible sense of helplessness as they experience the battle.

The 'Woody Allen' character that took shape during the 'night club years' has similar concerns: he combines the cleverness of Groucho Marx with the helplessness of Stan Laurel; he talks of philosophy, literature, politics and morality, but he still manages to allow himself to be humiliated in his endless search for love. One of his pseudonyms, 'Fears of Hoffnung', encapsulates the key tension: fear may be the acquired trait, but Hope is the family name. Although Jews have sometimes been accused of being 'rootless' rationalists, a character like Woody Allen knows very well that habit, custom, tendency, temperament, inheritance, and the power to recognize real and human facts have equal weight with ideas. His ambivalent attitude toward the Jewish community comes out in a great deal of his night-club and prose material. Allen once wrote in *Esquire* magazine: 'I landed at Orly airport and discovered my luggage wasn't on the same plane. My bags were finally traced to Israel where they were opened and all my trousers were altered.' His warmer portraits of Jewish people often combine a gentle irreverence with a general sense of empathy. In a short piece featuring Rabbi Zwi Chaim Yisroel, the most assimilated of rabbis, Allen mocks the authority figures at the same time as he sympathizes with the human being; when asked why Jews are not supposed to eat pork, Rabbi Yisroel replies: 'We're *not*? Uh-oh.' Allen himself is anxious about his fragile position *vis-à-vis* his Jewish background and the WASP-dominated world. He is dwarfed by the monsters of industry, science, business, and government. Like such characters as Portnoy, he goes out into a hostile world armed with a fine education, and then, when it is time to take aim and fire, instead of the desired shot of knowledge comes a pathetic little flag saying '*Bang*'. If intelligence is no protection against impotence, what is the fate of the modern intellectual? This is the question that lurks beneath Allen's comic stories.

Allen was not content with his night-club act. He was fascinated with writing. Writing offered even more control over his ideas than stand-up monologues; he could develop sophisticated parodies, puns and word-pictures without the need to make them immediately comprehensible to a wide audience. In 1965, he began publishing his short stories and comic essays in the most admired of American humorous journals, the *New Yorker*. Roger Angell, the senior editor who handled Allen's copy, said: 'There was no doubt in anybody's mind here but that we'd discovered a very funny writer.' Allen entered into a tradition in American letters distinguished by the brilliant comic styles of writers such as Robert Benchley, James Thurber, and S. J. Perelman. Together these individuals epitomized the urbane, incisive style of the *New Yorker*. Benchley's style is cooler, outwardly more conventional than Allen's. Impeccably precise and cultivated in his prose, the well-bred Benchley delighted in depicting himself as a man puzzled by the small, nagging discomforts and inconveniences of modern life. Perelman, whom Allen resembles most in style, presented himself as more outgoing and less cautious than Benchley; he would try anything once, whether it involved writing a Hollywood movie or a classic Russian novel. He told Kenneth Tynan that the main reason for the remarkable number of Jewish comics in America was 'because the Jews were immigrants. They were wrestling with English as a foreign language. They'd take an Anglo-Saxon cliché – like "I disbursed a goodly sum" and make it funny by pronouncing it in the wrong accent' (quoted in Tynan, 1967: 328). Perelman was fascinated by language and its uses, the strange and exotic meanings that might come from placing a word in an unfamiliar context, the absurd effect of clichés and jargon. He could make any form of discourse seem ridiculous:

> As recently as 1918, it was possible for a housewife in Providence, where I grew up, to march into a store with a five-cent piece, purchase a firkin of cocoa butter, a good second-hand copy of Bowditch, a hundredweight of quahogs, a shagreen spectacle case and sufficient nainsook for a corset cover and emerge with enough left over to buy a

balcony admission to *The Masquerader* with Guy Bates Post, and a box of maxixe cherries. (Perelman, 1949)

Perelman was parodying the common nostalgia for some pre-inflation edenic past, but it is hard to read 'cocoa butter', 'quahogs', 'shagreen' and the rest without a sense of wry amusement. He worked for a kind of insane exactitude in his prose and it was rare for him ever to settle for 'sad' if he could risk getting away with 'chopfallen'. Perelman's punning, parodistic style certainly influenced Allen's early writings. Angell has said:

> Woody, I know, admired Perelman extravagantly. And Sid Perelman's language is recognizable in almost everything he wrote for us in the early years. I had to point that out to him.... I told him, "Look, we already have one Perelman!". And he took it rather well. Just the same, it's a very hard thing for any writer to change his style. It took Woody quite a long while to get Sid's mannerisms out of his system. (McNight, 1983: 111)

Perelman's work was often darkened by his own melancholic, perhaps rather misanthropic, view of others. Allen was not yet ready to invest his prose with his full personality.

Allen's *New Yorker* pieces, most of which he has collected into several volumes, are full of striking comic absurdities such as, 'Dostoyevsky, if he could sing, would sound like Ray Charles.' Allen's comedy comes from the recognition of a discrepancy between what is said and what is meant (consider *Annie Hall's* use of subtitles to show the lustful thoughts beneath the intellectual conversation), between who one is and what one does (the sexual misfit who thinks he resembles Cary Grant), between what the character sees and what we see (the pratfalls ahead that we see coming). Humour encourages us to free-associate, interpreting odd combinations of ideas in the most idiosyncratic of ways. When a writer such as Philip Larkin presents us with an incongruity, we attempt to decode it to find the meaning he intended. However, in comedy there is no such 'solid' truth. No form of culture is more unfriendly to rational analysis than the incongruity that causes laughter. Allen's incongruities are ludicrous – that is why we laugh at them (unlike, for example, *poetic* incongruities, which do not strike us as funny). Almost all comedic experiences require some form of *cueing*. Virtually all examples of ludicrous incongruity succeed precisely because the nature of the work is known in advance (Allen's hapless lover would seem unfunny in, say, a melodrama). The context puts us on alert for the kind of response that is expected of us, encouraging us to prepare the humorous frame of mind and mood necessary to receive ludicrous incongruities, and condones the wider range and depth of association and the more idiosyncratic significances that characterize our mental process in dealing with a ludicrous as opposed to a serious incongruity.

Allen's early contributions, collected together in *Getting Even* (1975), were often parodies of other writers and genres, such as Hemingway, hard-boiled detective stories, political memoirs, academic course descriptions and Hasidic tales. In 'Death Knocks', Death arrives at Nat Ackerman's house. Death is something of a *schlemiel*: 'I climbed up the drainpipe. I was trying to make a dramatic entrance. I see the big windows and you're awake reading. I figure it's worth a shot. I'll climb up and enter with a little – you know ... (*snaps fingers*). Meanwhile, I get my heel caught on some vines, the drainpipe breaks, and I'm hanging by a thread. Then my cape begins to tear. Look, let's just go. It's been a rough night!' Things get even worse: Nat persuades Death to play a game of gin rummy - if Nat wins, he gets an extra day alive. He wins. Death is humiliated, has to go to a hotel for the night, but falls down the stairs. The story ends with Nat on the 'phone to a friend: 'But Moe, he's such a *schlep*!' In the next collection, *Without Feathers* (1978), the humour is less derivative and increasingly surreal: 'Dr. Joshua Fleagle, of Harvard, attended a seance in which a table not only rose but excused itself and went upstairs to sleep.' 'If only God would give me some clear sign! Like making a large deposit in my name at a Swiss bank!' Allen plays with the *physicality* of words, finding humour even in the look of language: Lovborg was originally called 'Lövborg, until, in later years, he removed the two dots from above the *o* and placed them over his eyebrows'; 'Shall I marry W.? Not if she won't tell me the other letters in her name'; 'He differentiated between existence and Existence, and knew one was preferable, but could never remember which.' The third collection, *Side Effects* (1981), is more caustic in its approach and more subtle in style: one article parodies those academic memoirs that seek to 're-evaluate' notorious colleagues:

Needleman was not an easily understood man. His reticence was mistaken for coldness, but he was capable of great compassion, and after witnessing a particularly horrible mine disaster once, he could not finish a second helping of waffles. His silence, too, put people off, but he felt speech was a flawed method of communication and he preferred to hold even his most intimate conversations with signal flags.

'Confessions of a Burglar' features a thief with a defiantly bourgeois sensibility: 'On the way home from a heist, I'd steal some pajamas to sleep in. Or if it was a hot night, I'd steal underwear'; 'Jenny married money. Not an actual human being – it was a pile of singles.' There are several techniques that are evident in Allen's *New Yorker* work. Verbal surprise, placing isolated words or phrases into inappropriate contexts, is one way in which he deflates pretentiousness: for example, a respected writer named Metterling is known as 'the Prague weirdo'; in an academic metaphysics course description, we read, 'students achieving oneness will move ahead to twoness.' The real hero of Russian history is, it seems, one Sidney Applebaum. Through inversion, Allen has a trivial thought or phrase come at the end of a profoundly serious disquisition: 'Eternal nothingness is OK if you're dressed for it'; 'How is it possible to find meaning in a finite world given my waist and shirt size?'; 'The reality I speak of here is the same one Hobbes described, only smaller'; 'Is there anything out there? And why? And must they be so noisy?'; 'Not only is there no God, but try getting a plumber on weekends.' This technique is probably Allen's most well known and widely-imitated. The passages seem to be at their most innocuous, and then comes the absurd ending: 'Illicit activities engaged in by Cosa Nostra members included gambling, narcotics, prostitution, hijacking, loan-sharking, and the transportation of a large white-fish across the state line for immoral purposes.' Another strategy is to take a common metaphor or phrase and treat it at its most literal – a technique Allen later uses brilliantly in *Stardust Memories* (1980):

> Sydney Finkelstein's hostility has escaped. Finkelstein, a short man with glasses, told police that he had been fighting to hold his anger in for years. And he's very embarrassed that it broke loose while he napped. Police are combing the countryside and warn all citizens to stay indoors.

'Juan Gris began to break [Alice Toklas'] face and body down into its basic geometrical forms until the police came and pulled him off.' As with Perelman, Allen's parodies of pretentious styles are often devastating. His target is often academic language, its pomposity and pseudo-democracy:

> Film is a young art and as such is not truly an art but an art within an art employing the devices of mass communication in a linear, nonmodal, anti- or nondiversified, creative otherness which we will call density. If a picture is dense, it has density.

Movie clichés are also common targets: 'I'm a psychoanalyst. This is my pipe!'

Allen's short story 'The Kugelmass Episode' is one of his most brilliant, winning him an O. Henry Award. Sidney Kugelmass, an unhappily married humanities professor at City College, weighed down with worries about alimony and child support, is suffering from *ennui*. 'Kugelmass was bald and as hairy as a bear, but he had soul.' His wife has become uninteresting to him: 'I'm a man who needs romance,' he whines to his long-suffering analyst, who replies that he is not a magician. Kugelmass takes this as a hint, and contacts a magician, the Great Persky. Persky has a magic cabinet: enter it with the novel of your choice, and you can enter into its pages, have sex in the text with the fictional lover of your choice; one yell, and Persky will bring you back into reality. Kugelmass chooses *Madame Bovary*, and starts an affair with Emma Bovary. Everything is perfect – 'she speaks in the same fine English translation as the paperback.' Kugelmass is ecstatic, although students up and down the country cannot understand who the bald-headed Jew is who keeps kissing Mme Bovary and then suddenly disappears before Rudolph appears around about page 120. Kugelmass is smitten. He begins to address Emma with the question, 'How you doing, cupcake?' He persuades Persky to summon her to present-day New York for a wild weekend at the Plaza Hotel, after which a hitch occurs – Persky cannot get her back in the book, and Emma Bovary is running up an enormous bill and demanding that Kugelmass marry her. She keeps demanding new activities: 'I want to see *Chorus Line* and the Guggenheim and this Jack Nicholson character you always talk about.' Students, now finding no trace of Emma Bovary in their books, conclude: 'Well, I guess the mark of a classic is that you reread it a thousand times and always find something new.' Finally, Persky restores the woman to her fictional world. Kugelmass thinks he has learned his lesson, but after three weeks he begs Persky to let him return for just one more session of sexual adventure: 'Listen, you've read *Portnoy's Complaint*? Remember The Monkey?' Philip Roth's book is placed in the box with Kugelmass, but this time the box pops and fizzes and finally explodes. Kugelmass, unaware of Persky's disaster, is preoccupied with more pressing matters. Inexplicably, instead of *Portnoy's Complaint*, Kugelmass is trapped in a textbook, *Remedial Spanish*, being chased by the word *tener* ('to have') – 'a large and hairy irregular verb'. This story, one of Allen's later, more 'mature' pieces, shows how much he has developed over the years. The Perelman-styled, somewhat self-conscious use of language has given way to an assured, quietly ironic touch that is never intrusive. Characterization is stronger: Kugelmass is a believable character, who knows something of what we know about this story – 'I'm going to regret this' he ruefully remarks at one point. As with Alvy Singer in *Annie Hall*, Kugelmass keeps doing what he knows he will regret because he *needs* the irrational, painful, wonderful love of another. As with *The Purple Rose of Cairo*, the 'drop into the magical' that we feel when we allow ourselves to be engrossed in fictional worlds is an experience that can become an addiction. Thus, Allen's written essays exhibit some continuity of themes both with his night-club act and with his later movies, and he increasingly used them to experiment with ideas that sometimes led to screenplays.

The same year in which Allen began contributing pieces to the *New Yorker*, he staged his first play: *Don't Drink the Water* (1966). It was intended as a straightforward, commercial Broadway comedy. Walter Hollander is a New Jersey caterer; during a vacation with his wife and daughter, he innocently takes a photograph in what turns out to be a communist missile zone, and the secret police chase the Hollanders into the arms of the American Embassy. The rest of the play deals with the attempts to get the Hollanders home again. The play, although rather too slight to merit close attention, was a decent beginning. Tony Roberts, who acted in *Don't Drink the Water*, recalls that Allen said 'that his sole ambition at that time was to reduce an entire theaterful of people to such an intense level of hysterical laughter that they would beg for the play to stop in order to catch their breaths. He was even sorry that there had to be straight lines, because that meant people would have to stop laughing for a moment in order to hear the next setup' (Roberts, 1988: 520). Allen said that his model had been George S. Kaufman, and one can certainly recognize some Kaufmanite wisecracks and carefully-timed repartee. 'I hope I can write as well as Kaufman did and be as entertaining to people who buy tickets,' said Allen at the time. 'I want to write show shows... No messages, no undercurrents, no blasphemies, no dirty language, no people in ashcans.'

Although Allen began to acquire less conventional aspirations when he started writing and directing his own movies, he has continued to make his plays appear very conservative in form. *Play It Again, Sam* (1969), although it was later made into a movie, did little to suggest that Allen's approach was getting in any way more ambitious in his dramaturgy. However, his two one-act plays, *Death* and *God*, were not staged by Allen during the sixties, but they are remarkable early examples of Allen's more adventurous style of writing, reminding one of the tone and concerns found in his later movies. *Death* features Kleinman ('little man') who is disturbed, at night, by the knock of destiny. A maniac has murdered several people and he is on the loose in the neighbourhood; a vigilante group has decided to take the law into its own hands and capture him. Kleinman, another *schlemiel*, is pressured into joining the group. What follows is one of Allen's earliest attempts at exploring the dramatic, unsettling side of comedy. There is, Kleinman is told, a 'plan': everyone has a role to play in the killer's capture, but no single person must know the others' role (in case they are found out). No one stays long enough to convince Kleinman that there really is a plan, but they do enough to make him feel guilty about such doubts:

> I'm going home and that's it. Except then tomorrow they'll come around and ask where I was. They'll say, the plan went wrong, Kleinman, and it's your fault. How is it my fault? What's the difference. They'll find a way. They'll need a scapegoat. That's probably my part of the plan. I'm always being blamed when nothing works. I – What? Who's that!?

As Kleinman feared, the evening ends in disaster when he is accused by the others of being the maniac; when the real maniac is heard, the bloodthirsty mob leave Kleinman alone, to meet his fate. *Death* is sketching in the wings of theatre of the absurd: it is very contradictory in aim, seeming to oscillate between a serious study of paranoia and a fairly black comedy about a hapless man caught up in a bureaucratic world.

Allen really allowed himself to experiment with *God*, which is a quite vertiginous play-within-a-play, subverting conventional formal expectations as it explores the actual and manufactured distances between fiction and real life. The play is set in ancient Greece. Hepatitis, a dramatist, complains to his leading actor, Diabetes, that his new play lacks a satisfactory ending. Trichinosis arrives, saying that he has just the thing for the ending, a new machine, with God in it, which descends from the rafters to resolve the action. 'I'm going to make a fortune with this invention. Sophocles put a deposit on one - Euripides wants two.' Although no one is convinced by Trichinosis, they agree to go ahead with the play. An announcer in modern dress introduces the show. In the play within the play, the Fates (Bob and Wendy Fate) dispatch the slave Diabetes to take an urgent message to the king. The message is: *Yes*. The question was: *Is there a God?* The King is distressed upon hearing this news, for he reasons that 'if there is a god, then man is not responsible and I will surely be judged for my sins.' As Diabetes is about to be killed for bringing the King such bad news, Zeus appears, strangled by the wires of his machine. God is dead. Thus, Diabetes and Hepatitus are back at the beginning again, in search of an ending again. 'The trick is to start at the ending when you write a play. Get a good, strong ending, then write backwards,' says Diabetes. 'I've tried that,' Hepatitis replies. 'I got a play with no beginning.' 'That's absurd,' says Diabetes. 'Absurd? What's absurd?', asks Hepatitis, and then the lights go down and the play is over. *God* is one of Allen's most significant (and lasting) early works. It draws on several different traditions: the comic action of the Marx Brothers, the Perelman-styled wordplay, the Living Theatre, and perhaps even the self-questioning anxiety of Samuel Beckett (with or without the ashcans). It is a chaotic play, but intentionally so: characters arrive from different time periods, there are wild anachronisms in language ('Shmuck, you're the King'), and constant reference to things beyond the fictional frame. Woody Allen is at one point 'phoned up by a character in order to ask what should be done about Doris Levine, who has left the audience and wandered onto the stage:

Actor: This is Diabetes.
Woody: Who?
Actor: Diabetes. I'm a character you created.

Woody: Oh, yes ... I remember, you're a badly drawn character
... very one-dimensional.
Actor: Thanks.

Life is pictured as a layering of roles within roles, of fictions
within fictions, with no fixed, clear and single reality to be
determined. The play toys with all fixed positions, opening trap-
doors whenever one settles on a clear distinction between fiction
and reality, determinism and free-will:

Lorenzo: I created your son; he's fictional. Not only is he
fictional; he's homosexual.
Man: I'll show you how fictional I am. I'm leaving this theater
and getting my money back. This is a stupid play. In fact, it's
no play. I go to the theater, I want to see something with a
story – with a beginning, middle, and end – instead of this
bullshit. Good night. [*Exits up the aisle in a huff*]
Lorenzo: Isn't he a great character. I wrote him very angry.
Later he feels guilty and commits suicide. [*Sound: gunshot*]
Later!]
Man: [*Reenters with a smoking pistol*] I'm sorry, did I do it too
soon?
Lorenzo: Get out of here!
Man: I'll be at Sardi's.

God addresses, in *Hellzapoppin* fashion, the power of the
author over the reality of the fictional world. It is a theme that
recurs in Allen's work (*Annie Hall* and *Purple Rose of Cairo*
being two of the most notable examples), and it surely reveals
his own desires to control his work and his environment. In this
play that control is in a constant state of change, apparently
slipping from each author's grasp, but always, in the last instance,
in the possession of Woody Allen. Each important move in
Allen's career – from writing gags to performing his own material
to appearing in his own movies to directing them – was motivated
by Allen's tremendously powerful desire for a feeling of complete control over every aspect of his work, from its conception
to its exhibition. He told an interviewer, when questioned about
whether one needs a degree of 'creative tension' on a movie set:

Tolstoy sat home, and Flaubert, and they wrote their thing. I don't
think there has to be friction at all. I think it's a debilitating factor. I
think we'd have better films if directors controlled them completely.
(*Esquire*, April 1987)

Allen's popularity in the United States was already impressive by the mid-sixties, especially with critics and intellectuals familiar with his club routine and his *New Yorker* pieces. He had made several appearances on television chat shows, and his night-club act had acquired an enthusiastic audience. One of the people who came and admired his humour was a Hollywood producer named Charles K. Feldman. He believed that Allen's unusual ability to deal with sexual yearnings and inadequacies with such charm and wit would make him a suitable screenwriter for a new movie he was planning. Feldman hired Allen to write *What's New Pussycat?* (1965), a light comedy featuring an eligible bachelor who struggles to control his impulse for seducing every woman he meets. Allen had wanted Groucho Marx for the role of the analyst in *Pussycat* and a major part for himself. The producers decided to cast Peter O'Toole in the leading role of the sex-obsessed magazine editor and Peter Sellers as his consulting psychiatrist, the emotionally-disturbed Fritz Fassbender. Allen was given a supporting role which gave him little scope to develop a strong character. Despite the fact that Allen's screenplay underwent considerable 'revisions', it is still possible to discern several themes and traits which reappear in Allen's later work: the difficulty of romantic love, the interest in psychoanalysis, and the varied cultural allusions that range from Voltaire's *Candide* to Fellini's *8½*. Charles Feldman went on to cast Allen as James Bond's cousin, the cowardly Jimmy Bond, in the ill-conceived spoof, *Casino Royale* (1967). By this time *What's New Pussycat?* had defied the critics and become one of the most popular comedies for many years. Allen hated the theme song, regretted the pseudo-'permissiveness' of the story, and he could not bear to watch the movie, remarking ruefully that, 'If they had let me make it, I could have made it twice as funny and half as successful.' He continued with his night-club performances, but *Pussycat* had made him a 'bankable' writer. This period was not a time when Allen could assert his own ideas on movie-making, and it seems unlikely that he really possessed any substantial, well worked-out views on the subject at this early stage.

What he was doing involved seizing every opportunity offered him, tolerating the interference from the producer and director as he observed them, studying their techniques and occasionally scoring isolated triumphs in what were generally dispiriting movies. *What's Up, Tiger Lily?* (1966), for example, had Allen working on a Japanese James Bond adventure (*Kagi no Kagi*, 1964). He redubbed and re-edited the movie, making it into a surreal story concerning the search for a missing egg salad recipe. The movie does succeed in being occasionally amusing, and it exhibits Allen's early interest in experimentation with film form – juxtaposing Japanese visuals with Brooklyn accents, 'breaking' the celluloid as the story unwinds, and superimposing one set of images over another. The tone of Allen's narration wavers somewhere between contempt and fondness for the clichés of the original material: he has the Japanese Bond-figure intro- duce himself as 'Phil Moscowitz, lovable rogue', and at one point Moscowitz will say of a passer-by, 'this is the obligatory scene – the director always has to walk through with his wife.' For much of the time Allen is simply going through the motions, but occasionally he will exploit a scene in order to make a splendid joke about *American* movie clichés: in one scene we see Moscowitz in a room with a woman clad only in a bath towel; she smiles at him, winks, slowly and seductively walks toward him and says, 'Name three presidents.' One character, who has been acting as a true Oriental throughout, is shot and he groans: 'I'm dying – call my rabbi.' The yiddish Allen inserts is particularly effective at undermining the original drama: the egg salad recipe is so good 'it could make you *plotz.*' Allen's narrative emphasizes the ways in which movies work on us in order to achieve their effect, thus reminding us that no movie exists in a vacuum, but rather is part of our ongoing love affair with the very *idea* of movies.

Allen's initial experiences of movie-making made him wary of *any* outside factors that hindered the realization of the original ideas contained in his written scenario. More so than many recent movie-makers, and certainly more so than most movie comedians, Allen has always had a strong commitment to some conception of authenticity. Each actual movie is, for Allen, a failure, a necessarily flawed approximation of what he had originally envisaged. After *Pussycat*, the ambition was to acquire sufficient power to keep the 'distortions' (unexpected interpreta- tions and inflexions of his words by actors, directorial revisions of his story, screenwriters' doctorings of his script, and so on) to a minimum: 'the only way to make a film is to control it completely.' He explained to Douglas Brode: 'I hate everything about the movie-making process but the writing. I hate the acting, the editing, the hours, the camera – everything. Sets are not fun. No one is amusing. It's a thoroughly unpleasant experience' (Brode, 1986: 27). Allen sought autonomy from the Front Office and as total a control on the set as is humanly possible – writing the screenplay, choosing his cast and crew, acting in and directing the movie, supervising the editing, having approval over advertising the finished work. 'It's so much easier that way,' he said. 'Sometimes it's a physical strain, but it makes things so much simpler' (*Guardian Weekly*, 28 June 1987).

Television had long been available to Allen, but after only two comedy specials he had outgrown the medium. In 1969 he said: 'Television is a medium run by cretins to pander to the lowest taste of the American public.' He did agree to make one more special for public television in 1970 (entitled *The Politics of Woody Allen*) – a very uneven spoof on Nixon and Kissinger – but the show was cancelled after legal advice, and Allen turned away from television. His fascination with movies had been evident before and during his early stand-up years, as his stories increasingly took on the form of screenplays – short, elliptical sentences which still managed to make one visualize rooms, faces, gestures, and poses. Indeed, some of Allen's short stories for the *New Yorker* were so vivid and rich in comic potential that he later reworked them into movies (compare 'The Kugelmass Episode' with *The Purple Rose of Cairo*). Although a strong-willed, independent person, Allen has always been aware of his own short-comings, and it is probable that he endured the shrill silliness of *What's New Pussycat?* and *Casino Royale* in the hope that it would lead him to an opportunity to make his *own* movie in his own way. Allen was able to begin his directorial career on the basis of his work on the extremely commercially-successful *Pussycat*, and, especially, with the invaluable support of Jack Rollins and Charles Joffe, his producers and managers. *Take the Money and Run* was Allen's first movie as leading actor and director, and he co-wrote the script with his old friend from Midwood, Mickey Rose.

Using a pseudo-documentary style of narrative, the movie follows the career of Virgil Starkwell, social misfit and born failure. The narrator is Jackson Beck, whose deep, authoritative voice is also known from the 'March of Time' newsreels. Starkwell is pathetically ill-equipped for life: 'He takes to crime at an early age, and is an immediate failure.' He struggles as the cello player in a marching band; committing petty crimes in order to pay for more lessons. 'His cello playing was just plain terrible,' his teacher recalls. 'He had no conception of the instrument. He was *blowing* into it!' He is repeatedly bullied by friends and strangers alike (all of whom stamp on his spectacles). He turns to crime and his poor handwriting foils his first attempt at holding up a bank. The teller reads the note and Virgil tries to speed up the process: 'I am pointing a gun ... at you...'. 'That looks like "gub", that doesn't look like "gun".' 'No that's "*gun*".' The argument continues, and a second teller reads the note: ' "Please put fifty thousand dollars into this bag and abt natural" – what's "abt?" ' By this time a queue has assembled and is growing impatient. Virgil produces a gun. 'Oh, I see – this is a hold up.' The teller calmly informs Virgil that he will have to get his note initialled by one of the vice-presidents before he can get any money. Virgil mutters that he is 'in a rush', but finally resigns himself to another session of handwriting analysis. The scene is a superb parody of both a movie crime cliché and the tiresome nature of modern bureaucracy. Following the style of Allen's *New Yorker* writing, the narrative has some amusing word-plays and absurd concluding lines: 'For a while, Virgil Starkwell earns a meagre living selling meagres.' One of Virgil's colleagues is arrested for assault, armed robbery, and dancing with a mailman. Another is booked for marrying a horse; a third for dancing naked in front of his in-laws. Like the later *Zelig* (1983), *Take the Money and Run* consistently offers an ironic comment on the documentary genre. We see Virgil's parents being interviewed, both of them hiding their embarrassment behind Groucho Marx masks. There are 'on the spot' interviews, including one with the amateur cameraman who seems incapable of ever getting to the point: 'I was having breakfast ... two fried eggs, toast, I can't remember what kind of juice ... don't know whether it was, er, orange juice or grapefruit ... but, I, I remember I *had* a juice ... oh yeah, it was orange juice...'. 'He never made the most wanted list,' complains Virgil's wife, adding: 'it's unfair voting ... it's who you know.' A former neighbour of Virgil's says at the end: 'You'd never believe it. It was the best cover up job you're ever seen ... that there was a *mind* in there that could rob banks! He was the biggest *schlemiel* and nothing you ever saw.' 'I think crime pays,' he tells an interviewer in his prison cell. 'The hours are good, you travel a lot.' Where is his old gang? 'A great many have become homosexuals ... others have entered into politics and sports.' *Take the Money and Run* is the movie of a young and very gifted stand-up comedian: it draws on some of Allen's old routines (most memorable, the prisoners disguising themselves as a charm bracelet), and it is as impatient and as frenzied as one might have expected from someone so accustomed to switching from one self-contained story to another.

Allen has described his first five movies as 'comedy that was strictly for laughs'. Although they become progressively more skilful, they have a certain style in common. Their composition is purely functional, the gags are more important than the narrative, the camera is tied down, and the movie is made with cuts. Allen calls them 'light conceits', 'Tom and Jerry cartoons'. Although *Take the Money and Run* received several reviews which evaluated the movie's structure as 'endearingly arbitrary', its release was in serious jeopardy when preview showings left audiences silent or even hostile. The editor of several other 'problem' movies, Ralph Rosenblum, was called in by the producers in order to salvage the material. He found Woody Allen in a 'despondent' mood, and the production manager, Jack Grossberg, was against releasing the movie unless it was radically revised. Viewing the movie in its current form, Rosenblum found it 'was put together in a strange, inept way, with little rhythm and a very bad sense of continuity...'. Worst of all, the story 'was capped with a grotesque and offensive ending': Virgil is caught leaving a bank and is gunned down by the police. 'The last shot in the movie has the camera pulling away from Starkwell's blood-drenched, bullet-ridden body. It was very chilling' (Rosenblum and Karen, 1979: 245). In effect, the movie was saved by Allen's consenting to Rosenblum's suggestions: cutting the 'tragic' denouement, rearranging the scenes to give some sense of lineal development, and shooting new scenes to link the old sections together. Rosenblum was impressed by Allen's lack of vanity and by his ability to learn at great speed. What held Allen back, said Rosenblum, was an acute lack of patience with his own performances; whenever a scene was not quite working, Allen lost confidence and tried to start again ('I'm an imperfectionist,' he joked). There was no audience and no immediate laughter; this was a different form of comedy.

The most important effect of the movie was to establish 'Woody' as a popular character, retaining his old night-club following and attracting a new audience of movie-goers. What is clearly lacking at this early stage is Woody Allen's specifically *movie* skills and techniques: he is still evidently a stand-up comedian who has wandered into the frame, anxiously forcing his material to fit the new medium. The problem is that Allen's comedy is still designed for *reading* or *hearing* rather than watching, and his visualization of very funny *ideas* is often simply superfluous: to punish a prisoner by locking him in a sweat box for several days with an insurance salesman is an amusing thought which does not require us then to *see* it; to hear that a side-effect of an experimental vaccine causes Virgil to turn into a rabbi for several hours is funny until we are then *shown* Virgil dressed as a rabbi. Such scenes are heavy-handed and ponderous, serving as visual echoes of lines that are self-sufficient. For instance, in his night-club act he told a story about his newly-found fame, when he rents an expensive Fifth Avenue apartment and hired a Swedish maid three days per week. His mother was horrified: 'What are you doing with this Swedish person? I could clean just as well for you – and cheaper!' For a while, the arrangement works well. However, he eventually has to let her go. She stole. In his act, Allen made this story sound extremely amusing; to film it, however, would be to transform it into a leaden and somewhat crude little scene.

Although with each new movie Allen's sense of narrative pacing improved, his grasp of the medium's potential seemed to lag behind. Rosenblum recalled that if Allen 'thought he needed 150 jokes in an hour and a half, he wrote and photographed 300. And he made them tighter, a joke at every turn, so that the pace would never slacken' (Rosenblum and Karen 1979: 259). Allen, looking back on his work after this period, remarks: 'When I first started making films, I was concentrating on getting laughs exclusively and trying to make laugh-machine films' (*Esquire*, April 1987). Allen in these early movies is much more effective as a comic *writer* rather than a comic performer. These movies communicate their ideas through the creator's brain, not the actor's body. Rather than putting a central comic figure through a series of physical adventures, these movies combine conceptual parodies (some fine, some forced) – of social attitudes and psychological stereotypes, of television and movie genres, styles and conventions, even of specific media sequences and programmes – with surrealistic gags, wild juxtapositions, strange situations, unlikely characters, and anything else that seems to occur to Allen at the time. The adventures of Allen's character in these movies are irrelevant; the real material is the comic style that Allen conceives for depicting and commenting on each event in the 'plot'. The written humour is *transferred* to the screen, it has yet to be *transformed*.

Allen also took some time to carve out a distinctive character for himself. This movie persona was not immediately convincing: Virgil Starkwell could have been played by another actor. The unique way of speaking and gesturing that we now recognize as Woody Allen's only developed over time. The early movies show him moving backwards into the future, making references to the great movie comics of the past. Chaplin was an obvious influence on Allen. He admired him for his willingness to take risks, attempting a fine blend of comedy and pathos. For Allen, this reached its climax in *City Lights*. *Take the Money and Run* begins the slow process whereby Allen's 'little guy' identifies with, and then distinguishes himself from, Chaplin's 'little man'. The scene where Virgil Starkwell tries to kill the woman who is blackmailing him reminds one of the black comedy *Monsieur Verdoux*; in *Bananas* Allen's character tests a product that starts to misbehave violently in a way that recalls *Modern Times*. Although Allen's screen persona lacks the balletic grace and physical agility of Chaplin's tramp, he makes every effort in his early movies to overcome this apparent limitation: in *Take the Money and Run*, *Bananas* and *Sleeper*, Allen performs more sight gags than in any of his later movies. In 1970 he said: 'I could probably deliver lines better than Chaplin can, because I don't think he talks very well. But I would like to develop into a better physical comedian. I think I have the instincts, but not the grace to do it.' In fact, Allen *did* develop into a very subtle physical comedian (watch the way he walks in *Annie Hall*, or his delightful robot shuffle in *Sleeper*), but only after a period in which he tried too hard and acted too frantically. Allen's humour, as he has noted, reflects a less physically-oriented society than Chaplin's; the physical aspect is still there, but it is more subtle and understated.

Allen's character also drew upon the example of the Marx Brothers. The early 'Woody' persona is nearer to Chico and Harpo than to Groucho, for he has a hapless quality that the super-self-assured Groucho never showed. As Allen progresses, adding depth and intelligence to his characterization, the 'Groucho' comparison perhaps becomes more appropriate. Yet the Marx Brothers differ from Allen in that they create chaos out of order, they *seek out* trouble, whereas Allen is ambushed by chaos as he claws his way toward orderliness. The Marx

Brothers are nihilists, Allen is a sceptic who longs to be an optimist. Groucho is the quintessential outsider; Allen does not enjoy being outside. Groucho will never give himself to any single person; Allen is in constant pursuit of intimacy. Allen's early movies reflect the Marx Brothers in their *structure*: the storyline is treated with irreverence, forever being invaded and distracted by visual and verbal gags. Allen plays games with movie plots and realism, there are some wry asides to the camera, and the hero plays the role of the cowardly braggart and great lover as a private joke between himself and the audience. Sex is a prominent theme in all of these movies, either as the knowing aside (such as when, in *Bananas*, Allen's character slips a porn magazine inbetween *Newsweek* and *Encounter* only to have the shop assistant shout out: 'Hey Ralph, how much is a copy of *Orgasm*?'), or as pithy aphorism, such as his remark in *Annie Hall*: 'That's the most fun I've had without laughing.' Another of Allen's enduring concerns began during this early stage: the relationship of movies with other movies, the effect of familiar forms on individual subject-matter. *Bananas* (1971), *Play It Again, Sam* (1972), *Sleeper* (1973) and *Love and Death* (1975) derive much of their humour from their ironic use of the conventions and clichés from well-known movie genres – the revolutionary epic, the science-fiction fantasy, the 'Bogart' figure, the Hope–Crosby 'road' picture. Allen is influenced by the very *idea* of movies, as well as by their makers. *Play It Again, Sam* opens with Allen's face in close-up, the movie *Casablanca* reflecting on his glasses as he sits in silence, enthralled by the experience of watching a movie. This tremendous reverence for the movies is something that Allen returns to again and again as one of his most optimistic themes. What his early work specializes in is the healthy irreverence towards certain genres and directors that only a genuine movie lover could successfully bring off.

Bananas (1971) features Allen as Fielding Mellish, a character reminiscent of Bob Hope with his nervous, wise-cracking dialogue: 'Blood! That should be on the inside!' He is an idiot: 'Eastern philosophy is metaphysical, redundant, abortively pedantic'; 'Mmmm, that's wise, that's, that's very pithy ... it had ... great pith.' The movie is a superficial satire of dictatorships and the genuinely unpleasant aspects of political revolution. More pointedly, the movie is an often sharp critique of *kitsch* culture: the invasion of private life and thought by the clichés of television, the emptiness of popularized high culture ('I'm into Kierkegaard.' 'Well, of course, he's Danish.' 'Yeah! He'd be the first to admit that'), the arrogance of American 'lifestyles'. The modern obsession with 'experts' is hilariously parodied by an 'interpretor' who, instead of translating, repeats everything Fielding says: 'I am very pleased to be here', 'Ay em vurry plessed to be ere.' Fielding Mellish (Allen) is an apolitical products-tester who becomes entangled in a South American revolution, in the course of trying to impress his activist girlfriend. Fielding is a typical *schlemiel*: his girlfriend Nancy says he 'lacks' something. 'Is it personality or looks?' he whines. 'No,' she replies, 'it has nothing to do with the fact that you're short, or your teeth are in bad shape'; 'Don't you have fun when you're with me?' he asks. 'No ... And it's not because I don't love you ... I'm interested in so many vital political things. I want to go and work with pygmies in Africa, with lepers in a leper colony.' Fielding's whine is now shrill: 'I *love* leprosy. I like cholera, I like all the major diseases...'. It is no good. When Nancy sleeps with her Castro-like hero (who is actually Fielding with a beard), he takes off his disguise and smiles. 'Oh my God,' says Nancy. 'I *knew* something was missing.' The story begins with live TV 'Wide World of Sports' coverage of a presidential assassination ('we've seen a series of colourful riots beginning with the traditional bombing of the American Embassy'), complete with an exclusive Howard Cosell interview ('Let me through. This is American television!') with the expiring victim ('Well ... Good luck to you, sir!'). Fielding's exploits with the rebel army serve as opportunities to make unlikely jokes about fast food and imperialism. The guerrillas stop by a cafe and Fielding orders a thousand grilled cheese sandwiches, three hundred tuna fish and two hundred lettuce and tomato sandwiches. The CIA flies over troops to fight for *both* sides – 'this time,' it is said, 'no chances are being taken.' Fielding tries to attract foreign aid: 'We ... we lead the world in hernias'. Fielding, on trial back in the US, is allowed to interrogate the witnesses: 'Does the code name "Sapphire" mean anything to you?' A black woman testifies under the name of J. Edgar Hoover ('I have many enemies'). Howard Cosell (who is either a very good sport or else *very* naive) reappears at the end to commentate on the honeymoon night of Fielding and his new wife, Nancy. 'The action is swift, rhythmic, coordinated.' The sexual act is nearly halted after a cut is found above Fielding's right eye, but he is allowed to resume and the 'bout' is concluded. Cosell moves in the cameras and interviews the couple. Nancy: 'I just had no idea that it would be so quick, you know, I was expecting a longer bout. He needs a little seasoning, but he's not the worst I've had.' Fielding: 'I was in great shape. I thought I had her in *real* trouble...'. One finds several aspects of Allen's work developing before one's eyes: the movie (unusual for a comedy) *looks* attractive, and in his next few efforts this visual sophistication will improve until a kind of beauty has been achieved. The comic touch is more delicate and apposite (Fielding's anxious moments with his hidden *Orgasm* magazine are superbly acted by Allen), although this is still the work of a *gag*-writer – if one fails to elicit a laugh, another one follows almost instantly. The almost obsessive gathering together of clever lines, coupled with the often intrusive movie references (*Potemkin, Tom Jones*), indicate a certain insecurity, a lack of confidence in his ability to hold an entire movie-length narrative together. However, unlike Mel Brooks, Allen appears to take some notice of the *critical* reception of his work. *Bananas* shows him still trying too hard to please all audiences simultaneously. 'My first two pictures were full of areas ruined by my inexperience,' said Allen. However, 'You can say they weren't factory-made films ... they're not machine made. I do have a certain kind of style, and it's my own.'

Everything You Always Wanted to Know About Sex (But Were Afraid to Ask) (1972) is a frustrating revue which seems to drift along without ever becoming a 'real' Allen movie. Once the 'sketch' format is accepted, the feeling remains that there should have been more of them: when Gene Wilder becomes the lover of a sheep, a potentially *very* funny sketch is allowed to overstay its welcome. In one sketch Allen plays a sex-starved court jester as a kind of homage to Bob Hope ('It's great to be back at the palace!'). He has never sounded so much like the classic Hope comic: 'I would give my life for a bare bodkin, to see a queen's bare bodkin, or *anyone's* bare bodkin, or even one with a little clothes on it.' The two most amusing sketches featuring Allen are full of his most inventive humour. 'What Happens During Ejaculation?' has Allen as a spermatazoon about to be shot out of an erect penis. 'Do you know what it's like out there?' he cries. 'What if he's masturbating? I'm liable to end up on the ceiling! I'm due at my parents for dinner.' He is warned: 'You took an oath when you entered sperm training school: to fertilize an ovum, or die trying.' If this sketch is made into a spoof on the science-fiction genre, another episode parodies the horror genre. Allen here is the author of 'Advanced Sexual Positions: How to Achieve Them Without Laughing'. A mad scientist ('Clitoral orgasm should not just be for women. There is a connection between excessive masturbation and entering politics') loses control of his experiments, and a gigantic breast ('about 4000 with an X cup') is let loose on the countryside ('They usually travel in pairs!'). Allen's character, Victor Shakapopolis, has to coax the giant breast into an enormous brassiere. The sketches all have their moments (in the 'medieval' scene Allen struggles to remove the Queen's chastity belt: 'I must think of something quickly, because before you know it the Renaissance will be here and we'll all be painting...'), yet generally the revue format seems uninspired and Allen seems to be pausing before stretching his talents once again.

Also in 1972 came *Play It Again, Sam*, adapted from Allen's successful stage play. Allen claims it was never his intention to make any of his plays into movies; he sees them as quite distinct. The movie looked like a more 'conventional' comedy, and this was due perhaps in part to the direction from Herbert Ross. The movie placed the Allen persona in its most realistic setting yet, and the narrative developed in a pleasantly predictable manner which encouraged a greater empathy with the character than in Allen's previous work. He plays Alan Felix, a divorced movie critic, who, though wretchedly ineffective with women, inconveniently finds the romantic entanglement he craves with his best friend's wife (played by Diane Keaton). Coached throughout in the art of seduction by his tough guy role model – a phantom Humphrey Bogart – Felix ultimately finds a kind of satisfaction simply by 'being himself'. The movie is a curious version of the 'buddy' genre – one man resists taking his lover away from his best friend – and offers a 'neater' conclusion to the problem of romantic love than Allen will tolerate in the future. The notable tendency, looking at the movie today, is the increasing emphasis on relationships and analysis, relying rather on plot than on the lack of it for comic possibilities.

Alan Felix is the first recognizable Woody Allen 'type', although a certain quality has yet to emerge: the character could still conceivably be played by another actor (indeed, Dudley Moore took the role in the London production) . All of the characters speak in a style of self-conscious witticism that is a legacy of the night-club years. Most of the movie's best moments occur during

Allen's monologues (in effect, his stand-up comic routine once again):

> I hate to be there on a blind date when the girl sets eyes on me. What if she looks at me and laughs or screams? Has a girl ever once reacted by laughing or screaming? ... Once. That little co-ed from Brooklyn College came to the door, saw me, and passed out ... but she was weak from dieting.

> If only I knew where my damn analyst was vacationing. Where do they go every August? They leave the city. Every summer New York is full of people who are crazy till Labor Day.

As a writer, Allen is only slowly acquiring his own vocabulary and his descriptive technique is still tied to a number of old movie quotations – Felix is shown to fear the discovery of his affair through the use of several 'dream' scenes which refer to Italian dramas and Hollywood romantic epics. One feels that Allen must take command of this tactic before it completely overpowers him: *Play It Again, Sam* has a movie critic living out a *Casablanca* fantasy, advised by a Bogart apparition, constantly referring to other movies, even *dreaming* other movies – the cleverness is at times a kind of clutter, a claustrophobic context for a performer who has yet to achieve a fully-rounded personality.

Allen's next movie was yet another movie satire, this time on the science-fiction genre. However, *Sleeper* (1973) escapes the constrictions of the previous few movies, providing a relatively elaborate story-line and, significantly, concentrating on the interaction between the comic talents of Allen and Diane Keaton. Miles Monroe (Allen), is owner of the Happy Carrot Health Food Restaurant on Bleecker Street, Greenwich Village, and a clarinet player with the Ragtime Rascals. He entered St. Vincent's Hospital for a dyspeptic ulcer one day in 1973, and the next thing he knows is that he has just been defrosted two hundred years later: 'I knew it was too good to be true. I parked right near the hospital.' The 'cosmic screw-up' that has left Miles stranded in a police state forces him to become an outlaw. Along with former hedonist, Luna (Keaton), he attempts to sabotage the government by kidnapping the leader's nose (the only part of him remaining after an assassination attempt). The backward glances are still very evident: *Metropolis* (1927) and *2001: A Space Odyssey* (1968) are gently parodied, and Allen also produces a kind of homage to the acrobatic slapstick tradition (with some delightful twists, such as reviving the banana skin gag but making the banana larger than the person slipping on it). At the same time as these familiar references occur, we witness the impressive growth of Allen as a movie-maker: visual punchlines often replace the expected spoken remark, and Allen's battle with an endlessly expanding soufflé and his sudden erotic fascination with 'the Orb' are brilliantly funny scenes which contain hardly any dialogue at all. The Miles–Luna relationship offers a gentle sparring match between equals, reminiscent of the Spencer Tracey–Katherine Hepburn classics. Allen's character has outgrown the 'incompetent' image of previous incarnations: he woos Luna away from Erno, a man who goes to 'handsome lessons'. The great themes of Allen's later movies – sex, the evanescence of love, and the awareness of one's mortality – are now firmly established and are explored here with confidence and style. 'Sex is different here in the future,' says Luna, 'We don't have any problems, everyone's frigid, except for the ones whose ancestors are Italian.' Miles, threatened with the reprogramming of his brain, gasps: 'My second favorite organ!' At the end of the story, Luna warns Miles: 'Meaningful relationships between men and women don't last.... There's a chemical in our bodies that makes it so we get on each other's nerves sooner or later.' 'I'm always joking, you know that,' confesses Miles in a rare moment of openness. 'It's a defense mechanism.' Allen is now sufficiently relaxed to close the movie with a simple dialogue interchange. When Luna accuses him of nihilism, he corrects her: 'Sex and death: two things that occur once in a lifetime ... only after death you're not nauseous.'

  Love and Death (1975) can be seen as a transitionary work in the Allen series, providing a bridge between the earlier genre parodies and the later 'autobiographical' works. Two styles mingle with each other in this movie: the crowd-pleasing sight-gags typical of his early approach and the subtle treatment of serious social issues which will remain in his later philosophic movies. Allen himself rated this effort as his favourite for many years, and was actually disappointed at the audience's joyful reaction to the story: 'People don't connect with the seriousness of that picture because of the [comic] tone'. On the surface, *Love and Death* is an affectionate parody of Eisenstein's films and the masterpieces of Russian literature: Boris (Allen) is in love with his cousin Sonia (Keaton); he is forced to go off to war against the French, and by accident he escapes injury and even achieves a certain notoriety, returning to marry Sonia. Together they become involved in a plot to kill Napoleon - a chance to redesign history – but they bungle it. Boris is captured and sentenced to death. Eventually Allen steps outside of Tolstoy and Dostoevsky and writes a very uncompromising dénouement. Boris is visited in his death cell by an Angel who promises a last-minute pardon (which Dostoevsky actually receives before *his* execution); Sonia next sees a disconsolate Boris, accompanied by the Grim Reaper, shouting out, 'I got screwed....' In the Bergmanesque final shot, Boris accompanies Death, dancing down a line of trees. One may remember that Allen originally wanted *Take the Money and Run* to end with his death. With *Love and Death*, Allen has found a way to *begin* his examination of his major tragic themes without alienating his audience or ignoring the inbuilt expectations of the comedy form.

Love and death: two persistent problems that lead all of the future Allen movies in far-reaching directions, two veins that carry the creative pulse of his subsequent narratives. Boris concludes: 'Man consists of two parts, his mind and his body, only the body has more fun.' This thought genuinely troubles Allen: he questions the relationship between desire and reason, truth and rhetoric, fact and fantasy. He is suspicious of 'disinterested' intellect, and he is fearful of unchecked passion: in *Annie Hall* he puts sexually-loaded subtitles beneath his and Diane Keaton's sophisticated conversation, and in *Love and Death* he works in a similar exchange:

Sonia: Immorality is subjective.
Boris: Yes, but subjectivity is objective.
Sonia: Not in any rational scheme of perception.
Boris: Perception is irrational, it implies immanence.
Sonia: But the judgment of any system or *a priori* relation for phenomena exists in any rational or metaphysical or at least epistemological contradiction to an abstract and empirical concept such as being or to occur in the thing itself or of the thing itself.

He struggles to continue, until Sonia says: 'Do we *have* to talk about sex all the time?' Language as a means either to articulate or to obscure sexual desire is one of the strands woven into *Love and Death*: two others deserve mention – the relation between sex and death, and the connection between eating and sexual intercourse. Even as a boy, young Boris bumps into Death and asks him: 'What happens after we die?... Are there girls?' When the adult Boris seduces a beautiful countess, her husband demands that they fight a duel. Allen, again, is reminiscent of Bob Hope in his flippant line of patter: 'We could run a check on your erogenous zones, but what about the dybbuck?' It is Boris' love for Sonia that makes him try and kill Napoleon. He hears that one man died in the arms of his wife as he tried to satisfy her – 'Died smiling, no doubt.' The equation of sexual appetite with the desire for food is another important theme: when Sonia confides that she may be 'half angel, half whore', Boris replies with the enigmatic comment, 'Let's hope I get the half that *eats*!' When Sonia finally invites Boris to meet her in her bedroom, he says: 'I'll bring the soy sauce!' In a series of cross-references, food, sex and death are wrapped around each other. Sonia asks the recently-deceased Boris what death is like: 'You know the chicken at Treskie's Restaurant? It's *worse*!'

Love and Death was Allen's most balanced and mature work to date. The familiar broad humour and one-liners were given depth by some superbly restrained observations that derived their humour from their context. In one of the most brilliant of these scenes, the newly-married Sonia and Boris go to bed: Sonia lies with her back to Boris, he gazes lovingly at her, slowly moves toward her and touches her shoulder. 'Not here,' says Sonia. The movie, in retrospect, seems at the crossroads between a tradition and a new kind of vision, the seriousness and *anxiety* of Allen the person forcing him to redefine the boundaries of comedy that Allen the performer has hitherto rigidly respected. The relationship of love and death is, from this point on, what the cinema of Woody Allen is primarily about: the manner whereby the seemingly diametrically opposed forces are revealed as actually the positive and negative aspects of the same condition. The comedian does not search for the meaning of life, but on the contrary reveals the hopelessness of such a search. How then does one come to terms with the evanesence of love, or life, or movies? The tragedian focuses upon the one who hopes, not the one who observes these hopes. Allen insists upon doing both: he has often admitted to interviewers that he is fascinated by the 'great philosophers', yet he says that he also finds them funny. Allen sees the humour in human incompetence, yet at the same time he acknowledges that, for each individual, that incompetence can be intolerably distressing. The potential is thus present for Allen's humour to be unusually *inclusive*. The typical, crude kind of humour is only superficially 'democratic': we are, in fact, merely invited to join together and laugh at another's misfortune (the person slips on the banana skin, the foreigners look/speak/act in the odd way).

Throughout the 1960s, Allen developed his humour to such an extent that, by the end of the decade, he was a master of comic technique in several media. He had demonstrated his ability to make people laugh with his night-club routines, *New Yorker* pieces, television shows, plays, and movies. He had also constructed a public persona that a remarkable number of people could identify with. Observing Allen, in his 'mature' work, we are invited to share in the recognition of curious or absurd behaviour that *we* might well do ourselves. As Allen has recently commented:

> What interests me is not the hero. It's the coward. It's not the success, but the failure. I think there are so many more of them in life. That's what I try and reflect in my movies. (*Hot Press*, 6 May 1988)

When an Allen character becomes almost paralysed by the sudden realization that at some point he is going to die, we can laugh at him while appreciating that he *ought* to be so anxious. For pragmatic reasons (the fact that we need to be efficient, honour our obligations, interact with other people), we do not puzzle over the horror of Auschwitz, or the mass deaths in Cambodia, we do not remain in mourning for our loved ones or allow ourselves to consider the implications and ramifications of every catastrophe reported in the daily news, or reflect at length on why we came to fill a certain space at a certain time for what sometimes feels like a cruelly brief duration. However, when we hear and see someone (Allen) doing all of these things, thus making himself radically incapable of contributing to the order of things (he seems to quit his job in nearly every movie he appears in), we can laugh *at* him whilst also finding ourselves agreeing with much of what he says. Allen makes a similar point when he tells Diane Jacobs (1982: 85) 'When Keaton's husband dies, and she says, "Life is really terrible – so where do you want to eat?" To me that said more about death and how we deal with it than I could have if I were being genuinely serious.' In the movie which contains so many ironic references to his 'early, *funny* films' – *Stardust Memories* - Allen says: 'I don't want to make funny movies anymore... They can't force me to. I ... you know, I don't *feel* funny. I – I look around the world, and all I see is human suffering.' By this stage it is almost impossible for anyone except the most insensitive viewer to find this either simply comic or tragic – the remark is emotionally iridescent, it has a shallow *and* a serious tone, the one waiting to ambush you if you dare to choose the other. What finally emerges during *Love and Death* is Woody Allen's awareness of his own imperfections and failures, and his ultimate refusal to choose the lesser of two evils – pragmatism or moralism. He is aware of the disjunction between existence as it is and as it ought to be: this self-consciousness is the starting-point of comedy. It is *the* overarching anxiety of his later movies.

3

Love and Death

Sex is like death, only after death you don't feel like a pizza.

Is sex dirty? Only if it's done right.

At the beginning of *Annie Hall* (1977), Woody Allen looks directly at us and informs us of two facts: 'I turned forty' and 'Annie and I broke up.' These remarks capture the quintessential Allen themes: human mortality, and modern romance. During his career he has looked at these issues with exceptional wit and an ever-increasing maturity. As Allen has said: 'I'm not "fey" and I'm not "Chaplinesque". And above all, I'm not "cerebral". Why does a pair of glasses automatically make you "cerebral"?' Sex and death are two fairly elementary subjects, and they are my two biggest themes – because they interest me the most.' No comedian before Woody Allen had spoken candidly and cleverly of masturbation, oral sex, orgasm, menstruation, sexual vibrators or contraception; none had discussed the tensions between love and lust, the breakdown of sexual relationships, or the selfishness that impinges on one's regard for the other. With great wit and imagination, Allen has concerned himself with the diverse ways in which modern society has come to terms with sex or, as Alvy Singer calls it, 'playing hide the salami'. Yet for all the beauty and excitement of sex, Allen asks: 'Is that all there is?' The thought that he will one day die is profoundly unsettling. *Love and Death* (1975) was a comedy about intellect, the distance between bodies which intellect, conversation, sometimes obscures ('But morality is subjective!'; 'Do we have to talk about sex all the time?'). Since *Love and Death*, Allen has left behind the fantasy future and the mythical past, preferring instead to base

his stories in contemporary, familiar settings. The central concerns, however, remain the same: the longing for love and the
awareness of the inevitability of death. His work can be read as
a response to several related questions: why cannot the body
perform what the mind conceives – such as immortality? Why
cannot experience imitate the perfection of art? Why is the ideal
always so much more enchanting than the practice?

*Everything You Always Wanted to Know about Sex (But Were
Afraid to Ask)* (1972) was Allen's spoof on Dr David Reuben's
self-help sex manual (which had been enjoying considerable
popularity in the social battlegrounds of the late 1960s). Allen's
playful satire on Kinsey-type sex researchers, media 'sexperts'
and popular erotic imagery was self-consciously destructive in
design. What Reuben's approach tells us, says Allen, is precisely
what we do *not* need or wish to 'know' about sex. Allen's own
movies deal with love in a manner quite novel in American
commercial cinema. Commonly, movies had shown sexual relations as merely physical: in order to make them visible, they
tended to be treated as a *violent* form of expression, a clash of
bodies. Lovers were seldom allowed to talk together and overcome problems or change one another. With the gradual liberal-
ization of the censorship restrictions during the 1960s, the cinema
became more concerned with the show of sex rather than the
analysis of love. American screen comedy was one of the most
shameless genres in this sense, with the majority of its 'sex
satires' being crude, plotless movies pandering to the American
male's supposed fascination with the female breast. The object
of desire was always the woman, with the man's body shyly
sheltered from the voyeuristic gaze – in *The Graduate* (1967)
Dustin Hoffman, during his torrid affair with Mrs Robinson,
never once had cause to remove his underpants. Woody Allen
began directing movies with the memory of *What's New Pussycat*
(1965) still fresh in his mind: 'They butchered my script,' he
recalled. 'It ended up as a "sex-sex" movie.' His own approach
was to switch the emphasis away from the woman toward the
man as the object of analysis: his gift is the ability to identify
with the sexual failure, the loner, even a spermatozoon. He
shows men in the post-Freudian, industrialized modern society,
finding the very *nature* of love newly problematic in the light of
feminism and higher education. As Shickel (1973) noted:

We were the first generation to accept the psychoanalytic metaphor easily, naturally and, above all, youthfully. A lot of us, like Allen, acquired our first shrinks at the time we acquired our first jobs. And, one suspects, for much the same reason, which is that reality failed to match expectations.

'I'm not afraid to die. I just don't want to be there when it happens.' Death is not so much a separate concern for Allen as the concern for love seen from another angle. For instance, in *Stardust Memories* Sandy Bates is told that *The Bicycle Thief* concerns the basic struggle to avoid starvation. He replies,

> But what happens if you're living in a more affluent society. And you're lucky enough to not have to worry about that... So, then your problems become, how can I fall in love, or why can't I fall in love, more accurately, and, um, why do I age and die, and what meaning can my life possibly have? You know, the issues become very complex...

The *idea* of annihilation preoccupies him more than its outward appearance; it is the wrinkle in his humour, the worry he can never entirely manoeuvre around: 'I'm always asking myself if there's an after-life and if rents are controlled there. Can one get change for twenty dollars there?' In *Love and Death*, the condemned man improvises: 'Yea, though I walk through the Valley of the Shadow of Death – or on second thoughts, even better, though I *run* through the Valley of the Shadow of Death – that way I'll get out of it quicker.' Allen once managed to joke about sex *and* death: he claimed that he longed to die and be reincarnated as Warren Beatty's fingertips.

In the *New Yorker* magazine in 1977 Allen was quoted as saying:

> As soon as you start to want to say something meaningful in comedy, you have to give up some of the comedy in some way. You have got to be willing to go more in the direction of writers like, say, Mark Twain or Salinger or Philip Roth or Saul Bellow – people like that who can be quite funny and unfunny, but what gives the substance to their work is willingness to be unfunny a certain amount of the time.

Stardust Memories has Allen's character in pursuit of authentic love at the same time as he is visited by a sense of his own transient existence: he reflects on other people, 'how unhappy most of them are, and those terrible things they do to each other and, you know. How everything is ... over so quickly and you don't have any idea ... was it worth it or not.' Allen's individual finds himself in an America newly exposed to history, affected by the desperations of existentialism and absurdism, war-pained, urban, materialist, *Angst*-ridden, troubled with global responsibility, struggling to distil meaning and morality from the chaos of utopian and progressive thought.

Allen's early movies lack any real awareness of mortality, and thus he has compared them to 'Tom and Jerry cartoons. A guy runs out and you smash him on the head with something and he doesn't die and he doesn't bleed and it's past and you clear the decks for the next joke right away.' Humour itself, for Allen, seems to distance us from pain: 'Laughter usually occurs when something funny has happened; that is why the death of a friend seldom evokes a chuckle, but a funny hat does.' Indeed, jokes are surely the classic way of jamming intimacy, shielding one's sincerity. All of this changes with *Annie Hall*, in which Alvy Singer is haunted by a sense of his own mortality that is anything but illusory. From this movie on, Allen's characters are painfully aware of their transience, and this awareness makes itself felt in every area of existence, casting a cool shadow over every meaning. In humour, the use of 'death' metaphors starts to unnerve one: 'This joke will *kill* you,' 'They *died* laughing,' Allen's early movies seem to abhor a single minute free from gags, as though a moment of seriousness would spell the end: 'I died in front of that audience.' Allen uses every opportunity to compare an experience with death: marriage (keeping separate apartments is like having 'a life raft'), orgasm ('sex and death – two things that come once in a lifetime'), and the love affair ('She really killed me ...', 'What we have on our hands is a dead shark'). 'Love fades': this is the most disturbing thought for the lover; when the other leaves and leads a separate existence once again, then the lover has died, the lover's identity has lost its affirmation. When Allen's character in *Hannah and Her Sisters* is reminded that death is inevitable, he replies:

> Yes, but doesn't that ruin everything for you? That makes everything ... you know, it just takes the pleasure out of everything. I mean, you're gonna die, I'm gonna die, the audience is gonna die ... Everything!

Upon hearing that he is *not* suffering from any of the horrible things he feared he was, he leaps for joy – but, almost immediately after, the *Weltschmerz* returns, and he remembers that he is just as fragile and finite as he ever was. Love seems so frivolous, so insignificant in this frame of mind, but deceptively so; its existence is our only diversion from death. Allen's movies show human beings ambushed by intimations of mortality: the child in *Annie Hall*, stopped in his tracks by the 'news' that the universe is gradually breaking apart. The adult in *Stardust Memories* reacts in a similar manner:

> Hey, did anybody read on the front page of the *Times* that matter is decaying? Am I the only one that saw that? The universe is gradually breaking down. There's not gonna be anything left.

Allen's heroes are ontological orphans searching for a sense of commitment amidst a chaotic, eclectic culture. The flashbacks take them back to parents, school, childhood friends, as though the meaning of their transience sleeps there, waiting to be decoded. One of the novels Allen repeatedly refers to, *Moby Dick*, contains a passage which seems to anticipate this sense of anxious auto-biography:

> Our souls are like those orphans whose unwedded mothers die in bearing them: the secret of our paternity lies in their grave, and we must there to learn it. (Melville, 1988: 501)

Allen has said:

> I guess you have to explain me, or I have to explain myself, from the fact that I grew up with women. There was my mother and seven sisters. That was bound to have an impact. A Jewish mother and seven sisters. You better believe it! ... Those formative years made their mark. I still prefer the company of women. My secretary is a woman. My film editor is a woman. Most of the people who work for me are women. When I write all the women parts, there is a lot of me in each of them. (*Hot Press*, 6 May 1988)

Allen's empathy for his women characters is one reason why his work does not often include the kind of bitter images of Jewish motherhood that one finds in the writings of Roth. What Allen *does* draw on from his background is the fierce Jewish respect for learning – a respect that conflicts to some extent with his fascination with comedy and unpremeditated pleasure. In *Love and Death*, his character says: 'I have learned that human beings are split in two: mind and body. The mind embraces the most noble aspirations, like poetry or philosophy. But it is the body which enjoys itself.' Like other modern Jewish writers, such as Bellow and Roth, Allen is fascinated by the ways in which knowledge and sexual desire interact with each other. In the myth of Cupid and Psyche, the lovers' thirst for knowledge of each other gradually replaces their trust of each other. Allen is concerned with the possible insensitivity of the intellect and with the dream of uniting intellectual and sexual satisfaction. Sex and philosophy are combined (and, sometimes, contrasted) as the search for sensuous gratification shares the stage with the quest for the meaning of life.

In *Manhattan* we see Isaac Davis surrounded by educated people who use their intellect as a weapon (to hurt others) and as a shield (to obscure their own inadequacies and insecurities). 'Facts', says one character, in a rather tired tone, 'I've got a million facts on my fingertips.' Isaac replies:

> That's right. And they don't mean a thing, right? Because nothing worth knowing can be understood with the mind ... you know. Everything *really* valuable has to enter you through a different opening ... if you'll forgive the disgusting imagery.

Isaac's comment is almost immediately contradicted by his own ineluctable need for knowledge: he makes his excuse and retires to his study, explaining that he has his 'serious' book to write – the book that is so important it caused Isaac to give up his very successful (and lucrative) job writing television comedy. Sex, for Allen's characters, is wonderful, joyous, intoxicating, but it is not enough. The life of the mind, although vital and exciting, is also insufficient. The intellect seems permanently alert to the suffering in the world, whilst the body seems permanently oblivious to everything except its own pleasures and pain. Allen gives us an image of a disoriented individual, the parvenu in the culture, the stranger in the city, the wanderer displaced between origins and the present, offering to substantiate the culture if only that culture will show its humane substance. Making love, Allen suggests, offers a momentary opportunity for empathy, a chance to combine egotism and altruism, personal need and concern for the other. Yet *contemplating* love, for Allen, makes one painfully conscious of the space between oneself and one's lover, between one's least attractive fantasies and one's most important obligations: 'Sex alleviates tension and love causes it.' As Saul Bellow once put it, the ideal is 'two human beings bound together in love and kindness', but the reality is often 'two psychopaths under one quilt.' Allen's manner of expressing this dialectic is reminiscent of the intimate, confessional character of Bellow's letters and Roth's analysis: Allen lays bare his problems, addressing his audience directly on stage (as a comic) and sometimes in movies (*Annie Hall*).

Allen's mind is constantly interfering with his body's concerns. He tells us of how he 'prolongs the moment of ecstasy' during love-making by thinking of a baseball game. An example, one might think, of the imaginative sexual athlete putting his intellect to practical use. However, the fantasy proves too much of a diversion: he is still engrossed in the 'game', occasionally shouting 'Slide!', while his wife is in the shower. The 'happy medium' between mind and body forever escapes one's grasp. Predictably, Allen's characters frequently withdraw into themselves for a more 'ordered' existence: 'You can't control life. It doesn't wind up perfectly. Only art you can control. Art and masturbation. Two areas in which I am an absolute expert.' In this Age of Anxiety, we worry about our sexuality, our identity. As Foucault (1982) argues: Antiquity was the age of pleasure; then there was the age of love; now we live in the age of sex. The point is the antithesis of the third not only with the second but also with the first. To cease to believe in an overblown and overdemanding conception of sex, to return to a rational pursuit of pleasure: that may yet be the way for humanity in the aftermath of AIDS. Modern life, with its febrile activity and its impatient search for 'the new', has changed the nature of sexual experience; sex has become *mannered*, self-conscious, and thus the idea of 'authentic' intimacy (passionate and uninhibited) has been undermined. Our tastes and convictions in love have become externalized, publicized – allowing society to tell us how and what to love and needing it to tell us whether we do. The great fear is that, beneath the language of love and the amorous gestures, nothing is left: when lovers leave, all the recriminations and irritations come out – 'so they were thinking *that* about me all along!'. Sexual activity is something one can simulate: we can study it, *learn* it from books and movies, and these 'performances' may leave us finer actors but less committed lovers. In Allen's movies the lover is also both analyst and analysand: each caress is frozen for scrutiny, each feeling is suspended for examination.

The pure rose of his romanticism seems to flower in the base soil of his body. Love, which is a process (like a movie), is reduced to an isolated moment (like a photograph). Sex without love is an empty experience; however, as Allen admits, 'as empty experiences go, it's one of the best.'

Sex, in the modern world, has been demystified. As we make sex less secretive, we may rob it of its power to hold two lovers together. Allen once said that his cousin, a mutual fund salesman, has provided for his wife through every kind of insurance, including 'orgasmic insurance': 'If her husband fails to satisfy her sexually, Mutual of Omaha has to pay her every month.' Allen's movies show a society in which the public impinges on the private: the celebrity who cannot meet his lover without being accosted by complete strangers ('I'm dealing with two guys named Cheech!'); the bedroom conversation that takes on the tone of the TV chat show ('Hey, what is this, an interview?'); the relationship which breaks up under the guidance of both partners' psychoanalysts ('you know, I trust her, because *my* analyst recommended her'). The pressures and sheer pace of modern urban life leaves sexual experience 'pinched and hide-bound': Allen's characters do not seem to have any time for foreplay or post-coital relaxation – a scene of the lovers on the street gives way to a brief sight of them in bed after making love, and then we cut to another street scene. Isaac's lover in *Manhattan* tells him she could imagine having a child with him; 'Hit the lights!' he gasps. Sex is explosive, evanescent, *fast*; as Allen says of life, 'such *small* portions'. Every reverie is interrupted, each embrace is soon followed by separation. How love begins and ends is as magical and mysterious as how a movie fades out in front of an engrossed spectator. Allen's lovers are driven by deadlines and decisions not of their own making and not to their liking. Allen considers the fate of authentic love in the face of modern, mass-produced, *mechanical* sexual images. The futuristic lifestyle found in *Sleeper* (1973) is a memorable example of the shallow, dispassionate, 'functional' sex which Allen finds so repugnant: in this ultra-modern world, everyone is frigid, foreplay is a subject one can major in at university, and physical contact has been replaced by the cubicle known as the 'Orgasmatron', which ensures that both partners reach the height of ecstasy in a matter of seconds. The disenchantment of the world has meant the deconstruction of love. The Kinsey Report reduced human individuals to biological units without any sacred or spiritual qualities; analysis has upset our integrity. Allen jokes that science 'has conquered many diseases, broken the genetic code, and even placed human beings on the moon, and yet when a man of eighty is left in a room with two eighteen-year-old cocktail waitresses nothing happens. Because the real problems never change' (Allen, 1981: 61). 'Sex,' says Allen, 'is a beautiful thing between two people ... between five, it's *fantastic*'. However, in an interview he has made it very clear that 'group sex' is one of the most unappealing activities he can think of. A traditionalist, he probably agrees with his character in *Manhattan* who says, 'I think people should mate for life, like pigeons or Catholics.' His dream involves nothing less than the transcendence of the opposition (as old as Plato) between erotic love and sexual desire.

He is anxious about 'self', concerned with its inward claim, and about 'mind', which may be our salvation or the real source of our suffering. At the same time he is driven by an irritable desire to recognize his relation to others, with society as such, with the felt texture of common existence, with nature and with the universe. Around such battles certain prime reminders occur: one is mortal, and death must be weighed; one is biological in process, part of nature, and one must find one's measure in it; one is consciousness, and consciousness is indeed in history; one is real, but so is the world in its historical evolution, and the two substantialities evade understandable relation. So Allen is drawn toward thoughts of extreme alienation, urgent romantic selfhood, apocalyptic awareness, while at the same time he knows himself to be in a post-romantic universe: Lenin's age of wars and revolutions, where his conditioning is inescapable. Social and historical existence may thus contend with mythical or metaphysical existence, but neither can finally outweigh the other, and the effort must be toward reconciliation.

Saul Bellow (1979: 192) has said that when critics 'knock at the door of mystery with the knuckles of cognition it is quite right that the door should open, and some mysterious power should squirt them in the eye'. Such a power is what Allen calls comedy. In 'The Whore of Mensa' (Allen, 1978), one of Allen's most effective short stories, the various parallels between intellectual and sexual curiosity are highlighted in a superb parody of the hardboiled detective genre styled by Raymond Chandler. The story opens with the private eye, Kaiser Lupowitz (King of the wolf-wits?), retelling the sordid story of the *femme fatale* and family man who lost everything. Lupowitz is a Bogart figure: he is the one man who is too self-controlled and dispassionate ever to give himself to another; thus, he is an intellect without a body, a man who can approach a woman with the cool responsiveness of a movie camera and the ruthless efficiency of a tape recorder. He is the Superman to whom real, mortal men turn in times of danger. Word Babcock is just such a mortal man: he tells Lupowitz that he is being blackmailed. It is a long story. Babcock has a mind that aches for intellectual improvement and adventure. He had met a young woman: 'Eighteen years old. A Vassar student. For a price, she'll come over and discuss any subject. Proust, Yeats, anthropology. Exchange ideas.' Babcock senses that Lupowitz is somewhat unimpressed by this recklessness, and he quickly attempts to defend himself: 'I mean, my wife is great, don't get me wrong. But she won't discuss Pound with me. Or Eliot. I didn't know that when I married her. See, I need a woman who's mentally stimulating, Kaiser. And I'm willing to pay for it. I didn't want an involvement – I want a quick intellectual experience, then I want the girl to leave. Christ, Kaiser, I'm a happily married man.' Babcock is being blackmailed by Flossie, the intellectual brothel-keeper, who will tell his wife unless he gives her $10,000. 'They bugged the motel room,' cries Babcock. 'They got tapes of me discussing *The Waste Land* and *Styles of Radical Will*, and, well, really getting into some issues.' 'I got caught reading *Commentary* in a parked car... I can get you photographs of Dwight Macdonald reading.' Lupowitz, intrigued, accepts the case. He calls Flossie and requests 'an hour of good chat'. He suggests Melville. '*Moby Dick* or the shorter novels?' she asks. Lupowitz inquires as to the difference. 'The price. That's all. Symbolism's extra.' Flossie proceeds: 'You want a blonde or a brunette?' 'Surprise me', drawls Lupowitz, and hangs up. As the action develops, Allen's prose style assumes a cheeky Chandleresque rhythm: the woman is 'a young redhead who was packed into her slacks like two big scoops of vanilla ice cream'. The discussion session begins. Lupowitz excites the woman with his request for 'Noam Chomsky explained to me by two girls'. Suddenly, he flashes his private-investigator's badge. 'I'm fuzz, sugar, and discussing Melville for money is an 802. You can do time.' She breaks down; it transpires that she has been trying to earn enough money to finish her master's degree. Lupowitz softens: 'She was every dame you ever saw ... pencilling the words "Yes, very true" into the margin of some book on

Kant. Only somewhere along the line she had made a wrong turn.'

Lupowitz, having established that the Hunter College book store is a front for illicit intellectual intercourse, decides to investigate. He poses as a customer, and is sent through to meet Flossie, who tells him of the diverse pleasures on offer; the *pièce de resistance* is mouthwatering:

> For one-fifty, you got the works: A thin Jewish brunette would pretend to pick you up at the Museum of Modern Art, let you read her master's, get you involved in a screaming quarrel at Elaine's over Freud's conception of woman, and then fake a suicide of your choosing. (Allen, 1978: 37)

Lupowitz, successfully cynical and thus unmoved, growls to himself, 'the perfect evening, for some guys. Nice racket. Great town, New York.' Yet it is Lupowitz's turn to be surprised: Flossie confronts him 'with the business end of a .38'. Behind a mask, Flossie is actually a man. He had been disfigured after plastic surgery to make him resemble Lionel Trilling had gone horribly wrong. Lupowitz outsmarts him and turns him in. Unlike the aesthete, who can (in Wilde's words), 'resist everything but temptation', Lupowitz is a sceptic who resists only that which truly tempts him. He celebrates the end of the case by spending an evening with Gloria: 'She majored in physical education. It felt good.'

'The Whore of Mensa' is one of Allen's most artful plays on the commodification of ideas and desire. The effect of fantasy is to 'commodify' the object of desire, and to replace the law of sexual relationship between people with the law of the market. Sex itself can then be seen as a commodity: something that we pursue and procure and possess in quantifiable form, and which comes in a variety of packages (in the form of a woman or a man, a movie or a dream, a fetish or an animal). Yet fantasy renders the world unsafe for self and other, and causes the subject to look on everyone, not as an end in him or herself, but as a possible means to one's private pleasure. Normally, the sexual act is regulated by a morality which enjoins us to respect the other person, and to respect the sanctity of their body, as the tangible expression of another self. The world of fantasy, on the contrary, obeys no such rule. 'The Whore of Mensa' plays with this thought in the context of its 'philosophical brothel' (significantly, Picasso's *Les Demoiselles d'Avignon* was originally entitled 'Le Bordel philosophique'). The connection of sex with the market-place is again made in *Annie Hall*, when, after making love, Alvy sighs, 'As Balzac said ... 'There goes another novel".' The labour of love has made love into a labour. In Allen's short story, the private investigator resists the promise of new ideas and new sexual experience; he protects his manhood through abstinence, a puritan solution. Lupowitz is a man who avoids any relationship in which he might become compromised, dependent on his partner. Hence, he has no lovers, only objects. He relaxes with a woman who studies *physical* education; the sex is for *him* ('it felt good'), and he remains invulnerable, impenetrable, impervious to the needs of the other. In the Hollywood *film noir*, the sexuality of the independent woman unsettles the middle-class man and causes his fall from grace. In 'The Whore of Mensa', a metaphysical lust makes the man pursue the intellect of the independent woman, and he meets a similarly humiliating fate. By substituting intellectual for sexual hunger, Allen exposes faddishness as a habit of mind as he presents characters who crave instant intellectual gratification: culture without commitment.

Perhaps a more accurate description of Allen's main concerns would be 'love, food and death'. Whereas Eliot summed up the life process as essentially nothing more than 'birth and copulation and death', Allen is also fascinated by the *material* basis of life, the stuff on which one feeds one's needs. The connections between eating and mating have been noted by Allen on numerous occasions:

> I love you, I want you in a way of cherishing your totality and your otherness, and in the sense of a presence and a being and a whole, a coming and a going in a room with great fruit...

Frequent allusions to the eating-as-intercourse metaphor from *Tom Jones* (see *Bananas*, *Sleeper* and *Love and Death*) emphasize Allen's interest in the life-enhancing possibilities of sex and food. 'Linda, your eyes are like ... two thick steaks'. Far from being an idealist, Allen is always aware of the material necessities without which love and learning would be worthless. When his character in *A Midsummer Night's Sex Comedy* (1982) hears a pretentious academic explain how Raphael had fainted upon first seeing the Sistine ceiling, he retorts: 'Had he eaten?' Broadway Danny

Rose, trying to placate a man whose wife has been put into a coma by a hypnotist, can only say, 'If your wife never wakes up again, I promise I'll take you to the restaurant of your choice.' The dream, for Allen, is a perfect state of harmony between mind and body, love and lust, and thus the view of eating as both basic (reproductive) and cultured (reflective) mirrors his view of sex as both animalistic and aesthetic. He once joked that for him the perfect mate is someone who can make love until dawn and then turn into a pizza. Yet hunger and reproduction have darker consequences: 'To me nature is big fish eating little fish, and plants eating plants, and animals eating ... It's like an enormous restaurant is the way I see it.' Hunger is not merely a disturbing sensation that can be assuaged by eating; it is an *attitude* toward edible portions of the external world, a desire to treat them in rather special ways. Chewing, savouring, swallowing, appreciating the texture and smell, are all important components of the relation, as is the passivity and controllability of the food. Like hunger, sexual desire has as its characteristic object a certain relation with something in the external world: another body, a person, and the relation is thus considerably more complicated. We still use many of our eating techniques: we smell the other, feel them, place our mouths on their flesh, sometimes even drink from them. What distinguishes *sexual* desire from hunger is the fact that it is founded upon an individuating thought. To satisfy one's hunger it is not necessary to eat a *particular* dish of food (one apple is as good as any); however, sexual desire for one person is not satisfied by making love to any other person. It is part of the very directedness of desire that a *particular* person is conceived as its object. Hunger leads to spontaneous interactions with food; sexual desire leads to spontaneous interactions with other persons, whose bodies are producing similar involuntary reactions and spontaneous impulses in them. One's sexual partner becomes more possessible through a process of physical contact, penetration, and envelopment. In Woody Allen's early movies, sexual desire is depicted as one-way: we observe *Allen*'s desire for sexual gratification, a form of *consumption*. This is the man who, when asked to accompany a woman to her bedroom, says: 'I'll bring the soy sauce.' This is the man who says that after death, unlike after sex, he does not feel nauseous. As Allen's work matures, his sexual desire leads to interactions with other persons, whose bodies are asserting their sovereignty in similar ways, eliciting similar impulses in them.

There is a more equal distribution of objectifying power: this version of Woody Allen is in as much danger as his partner of being regarded as an object (in *Annie Hall* his lover describes him as an 'island' and photographs him on several occasions; in *Manhattan* his lesbian ex-wife makes public his most intimate flaws and weaknesses; in *Stardust Memories* he is pursued by groupies who are in love with his image). With this increase in attention comes an exacerbation of the self, a heightened sense of the uncertain relationship one has with other people. Allen's is a vulnerable self, susceptible to the dreams and disappointments of one in love.

Allen's *schlemiel* often fails to manage even a priapic victory. He is frequently ignored or snubbed, rejected or abandoned by women he adores. In *Play It Again, Sam* his wife leaves him for a more muscular, active kind of man.

> I can't stand the marriage. I don't find you fun. I feel you suffocate me. I don't feel any rapport with you, and I don't dig you physically. *Oh, for God's sake – don't take it personal!*

She tells Allen: 'you may be very sweet but you're just not sexy.' 'Don't be so sure,' he says. 'You never said that when we were married.' The reply is devastating: 'I was thinking it.' In *Sleeper* his lover becomes infatuated with a tall, tough leader of political desparadoes. The Woody Allen movie retained the male point of view, but reversed the traditional male/female stereotypes: the man becomes the weak, irrational character whilst the woman is strong and assertive. 'I broke with Freud on the concept of penis envy,' says Leonard Zelig. 'He felt it should be restricted to women.' Allen's *schlemiel* is something of a first for American comedy: a man who is extremely vulnerable, inadequate, insecure, and often helpless. Watching this character we note how easy it is to hurt him: he is often pathetically dependent on his lover, openly begging her to stay with him, contradicting himself in order to match her tastes and interests, speaking entirely meaningless jargon in an attempt to match her intellect. While he is usually a social misfit, she is often a college graduate or an artist; she can easily better his intellectual and artistic abilities. Groucho Marx was a man who used women as objects for his derision; he would leer at some and insult others. Allen, on the contrary, mocks himself when he tries to mock women; after establishing his essentially weak and insecure personality, his attempts at *machismo* seem absurd. After soaking himself in cheap aftershave, spilling talcum powder down his shirt, and blushing uncontrollably, his sudden impersonation of Humphrey Bogart is laughable. It is pathetic when he snarls, 'I'm gonna come on to her later.... She wants me', when we have just seen the woman's appalled expression as he shovels Chinese food down his lap. This very insecurity is what makes Allen's man such a refreshing change from the traditional Hollywood stereotypes of the supremely self-possessed Cary Grant and the 'beefcake' (John Wayne, Rock Hudson, Sylvester Stallone).

Allen's *schlemiel*, although a remarkably original creation, does draw on several individual movie actors. Chaplin's tramp and Stan Laurel's archetypal *naif* are obvious early examples of the vulnerable man. These characters encourage us (men and women) to *empathize* with them: they are not men to 'look up to', men who are exceptionally charming, suave, strong, and successful. On the contrary, Chaplin and Laurel are figures whose inadequacies are most men's inadequacies (exaggerated but recognisable nonetheless): Chaplin popularized those aspects of men's personalities conventionally regarded as *un*manly – an eagerness to please and to be loved, a physical incompetence in the workplace, and a shyness with women. Laurel, in a similar sense, played on the so-called 'feminine' side of his character: he wept when criticized or in trouble, and he was so deferential to Oliver Hardy that he became a kind of wife – sometimes sharing his bed. However, the vulnerability that these two actors projected still lacked the sexual aggressiveness of Allen's character: neither Charlie nor Stan were the kind of men to go so far as to seek *physical* intimacy with a woman. They needed mothers rather than lovers. Their vulnerability is simply a given, they do not reflect on it or struggle to shield it. Allen's comic hero, Bob Hope, is rather nearer to the 'Woody' image: Hope usually attracted only derision as his partner, Bing Crosby, departed with the leading woman. However, Hope's was essentially an infantile image: he talked like a man but had the mind of a boy (he reads *Flash Gordon* rather than Freud). One never expects Hope to make love to the women he lusts after; he reminds one of a schoolboy who has heard that sex is naughty, but does not quite know why.

Allen's vulnerable, *Angst*-ridden lover is most reminiscent of the image of modern American urban man created by Jack Lemmon in a series of memorable movie roles (such as his characters in *Some Like It Hot*, *The Apartment*, *The Odd Couple* and *How to Murder Your Wife*). One can see much of Allen's future persona in Lemmon's C. C. Baxter from *The Apartment*. Baxter is a romantic who is struggling to survive in the big city. He is not an entirely honest man: he has weaknesses, moments of selfishness and envy. Yet he is a sincere little man, somewhat naive, good hearted and eager to be loved. He is the 'average guy', immeasurably committed to the 'right thing', and permanently insecure about the choices he has made. Like Broadway Danny Rose, C. C. Baxter has picked up second-hand language in a desperate effort to sound like the big men: 'percentage-wise', 'money-wise'. His clothes do not fit properly, he looks nervous and often spills drinks and drops things. He is physically *and* emotionally vulnerable: he catches colds after being locked out of his apartment, and quits his job after losing the woman he had loved from a distance. He tries to take but ends up giving. At the beginning of the 1960s, Lemmon's movie image showed a more realistic kind of man, far from being invulnerable and self-possessed; Lemmon is educated, but finds that life is still problematic. He *worries* his way into modern existence, trying to avoid compromises and searching for fulfilment in his work and in his life. Lemmon even sounds rather like Allen's *schlemiel*: gulping for air, speaking quickly with sudden changes in rhythm, hesitations and stuttering. Lemmon usually plays alongside a more traditional man, such as Walter Matthau, someone unemotional, hardened, cynical. Allen typically contrasts his febrile little man with the cool, amoral opportunist (Tony Roberts, Michael Murphy). Woody Allen thus follows Jack Lemmon in playing a lover who exhibits all the anxieties and sexual frustrations that Hollywood denied existed. Pauline Kael (1987: 90) makes the following point:

> In the forties and fifties, when Bob Hope played coward heroes the cowardice didn't have any political or sexual resonance, but in the late sixties and the seventies, when Woody Allen displayed his panic he seemed to incarnate the whole anti-macho mood of the time ... Woody Allen helped to make people feel more relaxed about how they looked and how they really felt about using their fists, and about their sexual terrors and everything else that made them anxious.

It is a characteristic of this type that failure forces the comic to enlist the understanding of the audience: Bob Hope is an example of the man who is funniest when recounting or reacting to his own humiliations, and Lemmon does the same thing in *Some Like It Hot* when his response to Joe E. Brown's concluding, sublime tolerance is to appeal despairingly to the unseen audience. Allen showed modern men that although they may be rejected, mocked and suffer sexual confusion and embarrassment, those failures do not undermine their manhood.

Typically, this image of the vulnerable outsider has been presented as part of Allen's 'Jewishness' (one recalls that nightclub story Allen told of the time his rabbi tricked him out of a date with a famous model). However, Allen eschews any attempt at seeing him as a 'Jewish' comic. 'I use my background when it's expedient for me in my work. But it's not really an obsession of mine and I never had that obsession with Gentile women.' Allen is justified in rejecting the 'obsessive' charge, but (like early Philip Roth) Allen certainly *has* explored the similarities and sharp differences between Jewish and Gentile people – *especially* women. *Annie Hall* radically accentuated the *Jewish* aspect of Allen's movie persona; it is not made into something comic or curious, but rather it adds depth to the character, drawing attention to another distinctive feature. Alvy Singer (and his later incarnations) is an outsider, critically examining the American Dream from somewhere off-centre. Alvy's character is not without its chauvinism, and his dismissive treatment of his two Jewish ex-wives surely prepares us for the *significance* of the All-American Annie Hall. Alvy practically pigeonholes her within a vulgar sociological category at their first meeting: 'What did you do, grow up in a Norman Rockwell painting?'; 'That's one of your Chippewa Falls expressions!'; and when Annie is in a delicatessen and orders 'pastrami on white bread with mayonnaise', Alvy lifts his eyebrows to comment on Gentile eccentricity. His fascination for Annie is compounded by his recognition of her cultural and ethnic otherness; she confirms Alvy's own sense of alienation simply by being herself. Her attitudes, mannerisms and colloquialisms strike him as exotic while reminding him that, in America, *he* is deemed the 'exotic' one, the Other, the 'real Jew'. The fascination, for Alvy, is akin to Alexander Portnoy's breathless voyeurism on the edge of WASP culture, gazing at the *shiksehs*:

> How do they get so gorgeous, so healthy, so *blond*? My contempt for what they believe in is more than neutralized by my adoration of the

way they look, the way they move and laugh and speak – the lives they must lead behind those *goyische* curtains! (Roth, 1986: 133)

Despite Allen's protestations that he is *not* an alienated Jew seeking assimilation through the love of a *shikseh*, his characters often exhibit just such a desire: think of Alvy Singer, acutely sensitive to anti-semitism and the 'classic Jew haters' in Annie's family; consider Isaac Davis, writing a book called *The Castrating Zionist* whilst he dates a young woman (played by Papa Hemingway's granddaughter!); observe Sandy Bates, making references to his entirely fortuitous avoidance of Auschwitz as he tries to find the 'perfect' (Gentile) lover. Only an ethnocentric critic would describe Allen's Jewishness as an 'obsession'; if one is Jewish or Black in the United States of America, one would have to be alarmingly insensitive *not* to reflect on one's identity. The Jew's attraction to Gentile lovers has been a major theme in modern Jewish literature. Again, *Portnoy's Complaint* encapsulates this cultural anxiety:

O America! America! it may have been gold in the streets to my grandparents, it may have been a chicken in every pot to my father and mother, but to me, a child whose earliest movie memories are of Ann Rutherford and Alice Faye, America is a *shikse* nestling under your arm whispering love love love love love! (Roth, 1986: 135)

The traditional, fevered search for the fantasy *shikseh*, the woman who can embrace Jewish insecurity and inherited melancholy and calm it with cool WASP self-possession, is shattered during *Annie Hall*. Diane Keaton's superbly conceived Annie, neurotic and mercilessly self-questioning, demolishes the old Jewish conception that Gentiles are people with frozen expressions and lobotomized emotions. Indeed, Allen sets up Alvy for a surprise which shatters his prejudices: after buying Annie books and sending her to adult education classes, she outgrows him. The man is left with his own fantasies, the woman has a new life.

Allen remarked recently:

There've been people over the years who say, 'Gee, he can only work with women' and 'He writes such good women', and they extol that, and then, you know, about the same projects there's been the other side of that. They say, 'I don't like the way he treats women'. And this happened, too, with Jewishness, where there've been people who've written over the years, 'This guy is too Jewish' and 'It's Jewish humor', and other people have written, 'He's anti-semitic, he hates Jews'. Why, I don't know. I never thought I was anti-semitic, nor did I ever think I was anti-feminist. (*Esquire*, April 1987)

Allen's comment is rather disingenuous; he has confessed elsewhere that his early movies relied to some extent on the depiction of women as objects of lust, because 'that's the easiest way to get laughs.' At times these early works encourage an extraordinarily warped view of women as predators, people who weaken men's self-control and trap them in marriage: thus, Fassbender in *Pussycat* shrieks, 'I hate you! I hate you! I've hated you from the moment we were first married!.' Generally, the tendency is for a Bob Hope style of boyish misogyny, with *double entendres* and tiresome scenes whose only function seems to be the celebration of various female bodies. Allen's characters tend to reserve their humour for private monologues or 'men's talk'. As Freud (1960: 99) observed, the jokes that individual men direct toward women are generally erotic, tend to clever forms (like the *double entendre*), and have a seductive purpose. The jokes that men tell about women in the presence of other men are sexual and aggressive rather than erotic and employ hostile rather than clever verbal forms, having as the purpose the creation of male group bonding. It is the latter kind of joke that occurs most frequently in Allen's early movies, showing that he is thinking essentially of a male audience. Indeed, his pre-*Annie Hall* work is often difficult to enjoy when viewed from a feminist standpoint (but then, it must be noted, audiences rarely view movies in such 'exclusive' ways).

Play It Again, Sam (1972) is Allen at his most shamelessly sexist, although he still manages to include a few shrewd observations on men's conceitedness. The story is basically a comic variant of the 'buddy' genre popular in the 1960s. The movie (based on Allen's play of the same name) concerns the extent to which popular cultural figures (such as Humphrey Bogart) have come to take the place of more traditional role models. We see Allen's *schlemiel* try to copy the masculine arrogance of Bogart in order to attract women. When he finally has an affair with his best friend's wife, he tells himself: 'Well, kid, she loves you. And why not? I was dynamite in bed last night. Lucky girl! I gave her my best moves.' Yet the Bogart fixation does not make him into a more appealing person. When his best friend tells him that he overheard his wife mumbling in her sleep about an affair, Allen is distressed: 'Did she mention any names?' 'Only yours. I woke her and questioned her and she said it was just a nightmare.' Throughout the movie Bogart is presented as the consummate manager of women. The end of the movie mimics perfectly the end of Curtiz's *Casablanca*: two men walking off together with not a woman in sight. In our context it evokes the male camaraderie movie of the past few years, and Allen's basic comic image as the ineffectual male is therefore revealed as only the contemporary reduction of the Bogart myth of masculine self-containment. Homage necessarily turns into implicit criticism; the veneration that many writers have expressed for the 'model' of the Bogart–Bacall screen relationship glosses over the defects of the kind of defensive self-sufficiency they always project when together on screen – hostility disguised as witty banter – because it also ignores the historical context wherein that hostility could have been an improvement on male-female relationships, but no longer is.

One of the most thoughtful interpretations of the role of women in Allen's work comes from Vivian Gornick. In a *Village Voice* article in the seventies she recalled Allen's night-club routines of nearly a decade before:

> What was most striking about Allen's humor in those years is that this Jewish anxiety at the center of his wit touched something alive in America at that moment, and went out beyond us ... It made Jews of gentiles, it made women identify with his myopic, dishevelled attempts at sexual success ... It meshed so perfectly with the deepest under-currents of feeling in the national life that it made outsiders of us all. (Gornick, 1976)

However, as Allen established himself in movies and made such works as *Annie Hall*, Gornick found herself 'identifying with the foil rather than the comic':

> God knows I could no longer find his ridiculing pursuit of women *funny*. The deep unspoken references vibrating in each of us at any given point in cultural time and from which all art – comic or otherwise – takes its life, no longer had wholeness or focus for me in Woody Allen's movies. (ibid)

Gornick here undermines her argument by uncritically assuming that one must identify with Allen's movie persona. Her disappointment serves to highlight the precarious nature of Allen's intensely personal humour: when he does not faithfully represent one's own impulses (innate or culturally determined) one feels betrayed. Joan Didion (1979) makes a similar mistake when critizing Allen's *Manhattan*; it is evident that she is reacting to the characters *as if* they were real, and as if Allen had been filming his autobiography. Yet it is misguided to assume that Allen approves of the central male characters in this movie: he is clearly criticizing much of their behaviour and values, and he describes the story as 'a metaphor for all that is wrong in modern society'. Significantly, it was this movie which marked the start of Allen's 'mature' period, when he began turning many of the jokes against himself and giving his women characters some of his most intelligent lines. Men's sexual vanity is satirized: in Allen's admissions of inadequacy there is a corrective candour, and his mock-heroic fantasies reflect the more familiar human trait of sexual vanity. The movie ends with the leading woman shown as blameless and wronged; what Didion ignores is the disparity between this sensitive work and Allen's early, slapstick comedies, which undoubtedly do contain some shamefully sexist moments.

One can identify three recurrent types of women in Woody Allen's movies:

1 *the castrator*: (the academic ex-wife in *Annie Hall*, the lesbian ex-wife in *Manhattan*). She ensnares, flattens and humiliates the Allen man, leaving him enervated and impotent;
2 *the free spirit*: (Annie Hall, Holly in *Hannah and Her Sisters*). She attracts, unsettles and fascinates the man, making him dissatisfied with his life as it is and encouraging him to break with convention;
3 *the tender realist* (Tracy in *Manhattan*, Hannah in *Hannah and Her Sisters*). She is methodical, protective, and unselfish. She sees things as they really are, and longs to rescue the Allen character for the sane world.

Traditionally, Allen's character begins his adult life with the castrator (who appears as the Jewish son's worst memory of his mother). In *Annie Hall* we see Alvy Singer looking back with horror at his two ex-wives – one a politically-motivated graduate student and the other a joyless academic groupie. In *Manhattan* Isaac recalls the unpleasant times he spent with his former wife, who left him for another woman. These women are sexless or rather 'mannish'; they are the nearest Allen gets to depicting the *Portnoy* negative image of the Jewish mother. The 'tender realist' is the woman Allen's men would want to live their lives with, 'in a cool hour', but whom they somehow manage to hurt. The problem is that this lover will not *quite* do, and this tiny, inexplicable omission is sufficient to allow sexual boredom to slip sniggering through the bedroom door. When this happens, the man is drawn towards 'trouble' – the eccentric otherness of the 'free spirit'. Alvy Singer finds Annie Hall, Arthur finds Pearl, Isaac Davis finds Mary Wilke, Sandy Bates finds Dorrie, Andrew finds Ariel, and Mickey Sachs finds Holly. This woman is the lover he cannot control: she arouses him, she unsettles him and she may eventually leave him. She is Allen's most positive woman, for he allows her to develop and change – often to the regret of her lover: Annie Hall 'graduates' and leaves her mentor, Holly becomes an impressive writer.

Comedy is by nature iconoclastic and it is inevitable that, when judged on grounds other than that of humour, it will sometimes appear insensitive or irresponsible. The comic does not observe any party line. This attitude has made Allen particularly unpopular with some women movie critics. Indeed, *Ms* magazine once described Allen's female characters as 'little more than projections of male lust'. Lee Guthrie, an American feminist, has argued: 'All right, Woody made it okay for the American male to be inadequate. All those beautiful young women he gets! No looks, but that's okay too. You can get yourself laid in a gorgeous Fifth Avenue apartment just like Woody Allen whatever your chest measurement. Even Diane Keaton is within range' (McNight, 1983: 160). This is an ill-conceived criticism, for it manages to uphold sexist values as it opposes them: certain women are accepted by Guthrie as particularly 'gorgeous' and 'beautiful', and her complaint seems to be that Allen ('no looks') is being vain and unrealistic (the most traditional of men could not have put it better). Joan Mellen (1978: 336) makes a similar mistake; after arguing that Hollywood has enforced entirely arbitrary standards of 'beauty' and 'ugliness', she proceeds to criticize *Play It Again, Sam* for failing 'to notice the incongruity of an ugly little man who always wants women who fulfill Hollywood's ideal for their sex'.

While one cannot absolve Allen of all accusations of sexism, it can certainly be argued in his defence that his work is unusually ambivalent in its treatment of women. Allen is working in an industry dominated by patriarchal values, and the comic tradition has (until recently) made women into objects of derision. Yet Allen's own character is a deconstruction of the male master comic. In place of the traditional male comic (who has exclusive ownership of such qualities as intellect, humour, and strength), Allen institutes the 'imperfectionist'. Responding to Gornick's critique, Allen said: 'I don't think of it as girl-chasing ... [Men] are lonely, they have difficulties with women, sex is a great area of human concern. I'm trying to show a guy caught up in all that' (Gornick, 1976). His movies are still indubitably male-oriented, in the sense of Allen's pseudo-autobiographical narratives, but there is no longer any distribution of qualities on the basis of gender. As Haskell (1987: 400) observes, Allen's mature work features strong, multi-faceted women characters, written with great care and even empathy:

> It's the kind of empathy we're more likely to find in European cinema: we're used to seeing Jeanne Moreau take on the years gallantly, her lovers, her disappointments, her *petits péché* etching gorgeous lifelines on her temptress's face. But who would have thought that actresses so defined by their youth as waiflike Mia Farrow or Barbara Hershey, the flaky sixties flower-child, could make the passage into womanhood so triumphantly, be more interesting without the little girl mannerisms.

His own movie persona has more in common with these women than with the other male characters; his sensitivity informs his relationship and acknowledges his vulnerability. Indeed, Pauline Kael has argued that Allen 'stands for the whole generation that was anti-Vietnam, he stands for all the people who are anti-macho'.

Woody Allen, interviewed during the 1980s, has claimed that the women's movement has permeated his life in many positive ways. He has spoken of the 'feminine' side to his personality, and has increasingly highlighted this in his acting.

> You know, my friends ... most of them are women. I mean, I'm not one of those guys who's at the fights with the guys and playing poker with the guys. They're females, my friends. And Mia [Farrow] kids me about that all the time. She thinks there's nothing I'd rather do then go out to lunch and dish with the gals. (*Esquire*, April 1987)

Yet the problem remains that Allen is simplifying all notions of gender identity (indeed, homosexuality is entirely alien to Allen's life and work). Allen is an unwitting dualist; he splits the world into two distinct kinds of thing – and this is the chief cause of his confusions. For Allen, the mind and the body are distinct, and he worries over how they can be united. Comedy and tragedy are distinct - hence his deferential approach to 'serious' drama. Men and women are each other's enigma – he allows no ambiguity within either sex. Allen splits his own characters in two – intellectuals or uncultured hedonists – and in doing so precludes their development. For example, the *schlemiel* Allen can say: 'I don't know much about Classical music. For years I thought the "Goldberg Variations" were something Mr and Mrs Goldberg tried on their wedding night'; on the other hand, the intellectual Allen can say: 'I'm really keen to learn new ideas and catch up on the philosophy and literature I didn't have time for before ... this culture really distrusts the importance of learning.'

Allen's *schlemiel* finally became an entirely believable, original character in *Annie Hall*. Drawing upon his own personal experiences, this movie managed to convey both Allen's commitment to comedy and his desire to move beyond it into a world of direct feeling. Dubbed 'a nervous romance', Allen's comedy captured many of the preoccupations and problems of lovers in the 1970s, a period in which the lessons of the women's movement and psychoanalysis were slowly taking effect in popular culture. The movie is clearly still a *man's* movie: the subjectivity is established at the outset, with Alvy Singer (Allen) ruminating directly into the camera, and continues the same perspective through to the end. However, although the man is at the centre of the story, it is a self-questioning man, a man slowly becoming aware of the misogynism within him. Like Roth's *Portnoy's Complaint*, *Annie Hall* is an intimate form of self-analysis. There is no 'solution', nothing is resolved; what we learn from the movie is that there are complex problems that Alvy Singer is only just beginning to deal with.

The movie opens with Alvy telling us two jokes which will act as *leitmotifs*:

> There's an old joke. Ah, two elderly women are at a Catskills mountain resort, and one of them says: 'Boy, the food at this place is really terrible'. The other one says, 'Yeah, I know, and such small portions'. Well, that's essentially how I feel about life. Full of loneliness and misery and suffering and unhappiness, and it's all over much too

quickly. The other important joke for me is one that's usually attributed to Groucho Marx, but I think it appears originally in Freud's wit and its relation to the unconscious. And it goes like this – I'm paraphrasing: '...I would never want to belong to any club that would have someone like me for a member'. That's the key joke of my adult life in terms of my relationship with women.

The joke immediately acknowledges a tension: a reluctance to conform or make a commitment (to an industrial organization, a political party, a marriage), yet the longing for assimilation (in a country, a city, a relationship) is a fundamental dialectic for the Woody Allen character. Alvy's monologue becomes circuitous and evasive. He resorts to his comedy skills, but a surge of sincerity causes him to confess:

> Annie and I broke up and I ... I still can't get my mind around that. You know, I, I keep sifting the pieces of the relationship through my mind and ... and examining my life and trying to figure out ... where did the screw up come, you know, and a year ago we were ... tsch, in love.

The rest of the movie reflects this search for lost love in its very structure: the past folds into the present, memorable conversations and sights and sounds impinge on current concerns as Alvy sifts through life, trying to read his own romance, inquiring into the nature of modern love.

We go back to Alvy's schooldays, when he expresses an unusually precocious sexual curiosity. 'Six-year-old boys don't have girls on their minds,' shouts a teacher. '*I* did' recalls Alvy. Suddenly we see the adult Alvy outside a movie theatre being pestered by two fans. When Annie Hall (Diane Keaton) arrives, she is scalded by Alvy for being late. The couple seem strained, and Alvy's clumsy attempt to interpret every sign of anxiety in his lover as due to 'a bad period' shows his own insensitivity. Later, when the couple are in bed together, Annie rebuffs Alvy's amorous advances with a slyly sarcastic reference to his overblown ego: 'I-I-I gotta sing tomorrow night, so I have to rest my voice.' She reminds Alvy that he also went through a phase of indifference to sex when he was married to Allison Portchnik. We see a flashback in which Alvy prowls around Allison's bedroom, expounding his theories on the Kennedy assassination (a sly twist – Mort Sahl was the comic who became obsessed with this subject). She says: 'You're using this conspiracy theory as an excuse to avoid sex with me.' The *naming* of the technique stuns Alvy; he turns to the camera and gasps,

> Oh, my God! She's right! Why did I turn off Allison Portchnik? She was beautiful .... She was willing. She was real ... intelligent. Is it the old Groucho Marx joke? That – that I just don't wanna belong to any club that would have someone like me for a member?

The contradiction is thus made eminently clear: Alvy yearns for the other yet fears the consequences of committing himself. Will devoting oneself to another entail a loss of one's independent identity (a death of one's authentic self)? The anxiety within Alvy is crippling.

In another memory of Alvy with Annie, the two lovers recall previous experiences with the opposite sex. These recollections introduce one of the movie's critical themes: the ways in which self-analysis kills creativity, with the gap between felt being and public image appearing as an unbridgeable chasm. We see Alvy being dragged around an academic cocktail party by his chillingly dispassionate wife, Robin. After a while she finds Alvy hiding in the bedroom, watching a basketball game on television. 'Alvy, what's so fascinating about a group of pituitary cases trying to stuff a ball through a hoop?' 'What's fascinating,' replies Alvy, 'is that it's *physical*. You know, it's one thing about intellectuals, they prove that you can be absolutely brilliant and have no idea what's going on.' He reaches for Robin and pulls her down beside him on the bed. 'No, it'll be great! It'll be great, because all those Ph.Ds are in there, you know, like ... discussing models of alienation ... and we'll be in here quietly humping.' Robin looks disgusted: 'Alvy, *don't*. You're using sex to express hostility.' He grimaces and sounds exasparated: ' "Why-why do you always r-reduce my animal urges to psychoanalytic categories?" he said as he removed her brassiere...'. Robin cannot have a physical relationship with Alvy; her 'monkish values' eschew spontaneity and simple pleasure. She says she cannot make love while there is any noise: 'What are you gonna do,' cries Alvy, 'have 'em shut down the airport, too? No more flights so we can have sex?'. The intelligentsia make Alvy seem, or, more accurately, *try* to seem incorrigibly ithyphallic. While it becomes clear that Alvy's private hell is not simply other people, professional intellectuals have undoubtedly played their part.

Annie enters into Alvy's life at a particularly barren moment.

He has just been telling his friend about his various conspiracy theories and he claims to be surrounded by Nazis. His friend calls him 'Max', underlining his current lack of self-esteem. Alvy's first meeting with Annie is full of awkward pauses and embarrassing small talk. Alvy, for once, is the one with the composure, self-confidence and the witty lines, yet he seems to be vaguely aware that this nervous, gauche woman possesses something that he lacks: the ability to enjoy oneself. This is perhaps playfully alluded to symbolically when Annie nearly thrusts the handle of her tennis racket into Alvy's groin. His matter-of-fact reference to his fifteen years in analysis is the first sign of his fatalism; he tells her he will 'give it one more year' and then pray for a miracle. Their conversation on Annie's terrace is a superficial discussion of her photography; the unspoken subtext is revealed by the use of subtitles on the screen:

Alvy: They're, they're wonderful, you know. They have ... uh ... a ... quality.
[*You are a great-looking girl*]
Photography's interesting, 'cause, you know, it's a new art form, and, uh, a set of aesthetic criteria have not emerged yet.
[*I wonder what she looks like naked?*]
Annie: Well, well, to me, I mean, it's all instinctive, you know. I mean, I just try to *feel* it ... I try to get a sense of it and not think about it so much.
[*God, I hope he doesn't turn out to be a schmuck like the others.*]

The technique is a neat play on small talk as foreplay. The unspoken wish to see the naked body is matched by the desire to see beneath the formal language. This is a something of a (strip)tease. Annie surprises Alvy with her confession that she does not have an active social life. She explains: 'Well, I mean, I meet a lot of ... jerks, you know what I mean? ... But I'm thinking about getting some cats ...'.

Annie is the Other: not so much because she is a woman or a Gentile, but because she seems uninhibited and ever-changing. She can express the emotions that Alvy keeps inside himself: she can sing, she is artistic, she is receptive to new ideas and images. Yet while Annie develops as a person, changing her appearance and tastes, Alvy stays a sceptic, unable to *engage* with anyone or any milieu. Annie embraces change, Alvy closes himself to it. Alvy is a master of language: he charms Annie with his amusing descriptions of passers-bys, he impresses her with his stand-up comedy act, and he influences her with his interest in literature and ideas. Yet this gift has its limitations: Alvy's words reflect on his world without touching it. He remains, in Annie's phrase, 'an island', a man closed off from outside influences. Alvy is constantly aware of his own mortality: 'It's a big subject for me,' he tells her. He buys Annie several books on death – his first attempt at making her appreciate his own attitude to life. When the couple eventually break up, she expresses her relief at being able to return all of his books about death. Upon hearing Annie's decision not to return with him to New York, Alvy's expression is one of mortification.

Annie breathes life into Alvy's meticulously ordered existence. After the first time they make love together, Alvy sighs: 'I'm a wreck .... Really. I mean it. I, I'll never play the piano again....' 'You really thought it was good?' whispers Annie. 'Tell me.' 'That was the most fun I've ever had without laughing,' he says. The scene is probably the single occasion in which Alvy's intellectual and sensual interests truly complement each other. Feeling undistinguished and weighed down by a technological culture in which things and spirit are equally real, he desires more contact with instinct than invention. When Annie asks Alvy if he loves her, Alvy refers directly to the inadequacy of language when expressing genuinely unique, intimate feelings: 'I-uh, love is, uh, is too weak a word for what I ... I *lerve* you. You know, I *lo-ove* you, I-I-I *loff* you. There are two *f*s. I-I have to invent ... Of course I love you!' Modern culture has devalued the language of love by mechanically reproducing its form, making the words colourless clichés. To *unperson* a word, severing its relationship with individual meanings and situations, is the modern habit which Alvy Singer is fighting. Language is everywhere; feeling is where personality is – and where is that? Ironies echo in a hall of mirrors. In the amorous passages of our lives, we lose the purchase on our states of mind that the categories of everyday language exert. The more vividly alive we are, the less able we are to commit ourselves to words worthy of that feeling. Our language is craven; and we are craven too.

The first tremor of doubt is felt when Annie suggests moving in with Alvy. She is incredulous at Alvy's negative attitude. He becomes visibly agitated (love and sex are once again drifting apart), and he struggles to defend himself: 'I ... we live together, we sleep together, we eat together. Jesus, you don't want it to be like we're married, do you?' His fear of making a commitment is made evident in his stubborn insistence on Annie retaining her own apartment: 'it's like a free-floating raft ... that we know that we're not married.' Annie's apartment meant apartness. No attempt is made to explain why co-habitation or marriage should be such frightening, destructive experiences. Alvy's anxiety is concerned with the evanescence of love: he cannot love Annie outside of time, but to love her *within* time would entail accepting her essential *changeability*, her constantly evolving self. The paradox unnerves Alvy: to love her is to accept that she will at some time be otherwise. Alvy seems to sense the death that lurks beneath the love affair. He prepares himself, almost from the first day, for that moment when he will discern, on the skin of the relationship, a certain minute stain, appearing there as the symptom of a certain death: for the first time he will do harm to the one he loves, involuntarily but without panic.

Allen has stressed the fact that *Annie Hall* was co-written with Marshall Brickman, thus warning critics against making lazy generalizations about the movie's correspondence to Allen's life and his recent affair with Diane Keaton. 'I was playing myself,' he admits, 'but not in autobiographical situations for the most part'. One situation that *was* based on personal experience was Alvy's dinner with Annie's parents, the atmosphere saturated with WASPish self-restraint; the scene was inspired by Allen's memories of Diane Keaton's parents:

> It was the quintessential kind of Gentile family. I was very conscious of my Jewishness when I met them originally, over Christmas dinner. They were very different from my own family. And there is a Granny Hall. That was Keaton's grandmother. She always had a dim view of Jews, as moneylenders and people who usurp all the good jobs and start wars and things.

'Love,' as Emerson wrote, 'is the bright foreigner, the foreign self'. Despite Granny Hall, Alvy and Annie are drawn to each other's *uniqueness*. As one finds in *Zelig* (1983), the denial of otherness is the death of love. 'It's safe to be like the others,' says the human chameleon. 'I want to be liked.' Yet by disguising his difference he ceases to be the object of anyone's love, and the trace he leaves in the newsreel is of a helpless flesh-and-blood person imprisoned within the dynamic imperatives of film. Love cannot live.

The most important theme in *Annie Hall* concerns the search for authentic love. Alvy Singer is uncompromising in his pursuit of authenticity: he has nothing but contempt for the commercialized *kitsch* culture of California, with its empty-headed attempts at avoiding unpleasant realities. What worries Alvy is the thought that life without 'bad faith' may be even more barren than life within it. The authenticity of confronting death exposes the inauthenticity of ordinary relations. Even Annie, apparently so joyous and carefree, turns out to be inauthentic: 'it ruins it for me if you have grass ... because, you know, I'm like a comedian, so if I get a laugh from a person who's high, it doesn't count. You know – 'cause they're always laughing.' When the intellect holds the heart captive, mediocrity prospers. Creativity involves the willingness to free-associate: those who are too determined to avoid making weak puns or poor jokes will never be truly funny, and those who are fearful of making fools of themselves will never be free to express their emotions. Alvy wishes to reach the heart *through* the intellect; he does not wish to bypass it by resorting to the bourgeois reliance upon intoxicating drugs.

Alvy's longing for the authentic, juxtaposed to his fear that it may not exist, leaves him unable to give himself fully to another. 'Alvy! Alvy! You're the one who never wanted to make a real commitment.' Alvy's lack of self-belief is projected onto Annie; he cannot believe that anyone could love him for his own sake. Thus, when he is *wanted*, he withdraws. The end of the relationship is rationalized by Alvy as the confirmation of this distrust. One cannot 'know' the love another feels for one – it can at best be an act of faith. Alvy cannot bear that uncertainty, that *trust*. He loses Annie, for the very quality that he loved in her was the quality he could never possess: her otherness, her integrity. His effort at controlling her ended in his alienating her. Everything he did for her (the foreign self) made her more like him – which made her too familiar to be interesting to him. The motivation had been to make the other over to confirm that 'who *he* is' is all right. Unconsciously, and unfortunately, Alvy manages to diminish what he most admires. He soothes himself by desiring what, being absent, can no longer harm him. It is a thin deceit. 'I can't believe this!' he cries. 'Somewhere she cooled off to me.' He stops an old woman on the street: 'Is it something that I did?' She looks at him, cooly, dispassionately: 'Never something you do. That's how people are. Love fades.' The worst of all possibilities has been articulated. Alvy is horrified. 'Love fades. God, that's a depressing thought.' He wanders the streets, hoping to find a couple who have experienced genuine intimacy. 'Now, with your wife in bed, does she need some kind of artificial stimulation like marijuana?' 'We use a large vibrating egg.' The search becomes increasingly desperate. He stops a healthy-looking couple and asks them how they have remained together. The woman says, 'uh, I'm very shallow and empty and I have no ideas and nothing interesting to say,' and her lover adds, 'And I'm exactly the same way.'

The cunning of desire, the way in which the one we love sometimes is the one we dislike, is Alvy's constant, obsessive worry. 'You know, even as a kid I always went for the wrong women. I think that's my problem. When my mother took me to see *Snow White*, everyone fell in love with Snow White. I immediately fell for the Wicked Queen.' Alvy's attempts at casual sex are disasters: 'Oh, sex with you is really a Kafkaesque experience. I mean that as a compliment.' 'I think there's too much burden placed on the orgasm, you know, to make up for empty areas in life.' He returns to Annie, confessing 'there's just something different about you. I don't know what it is, but it's great.' Yet although he comes to recognize the attractiveness of Annie's otherness, he is no closer to understanding her. They again agree to part: 'A relationship, I think, is like a shark, you know? It has to constantly move forward or it dies. And I think what we got on our hands is a dead shark.' Almost instantly, Alvy is despondent: 'I miss Annie. I made a terrible mistake.'

Although Alvy Singer is a more complex character than any of Allen's earlier movie incarnations, he remains a prisoner of his sex. Struggle as he may to bridge the distance between Annie and himself (even going so far as breaking the habit of a lifetime by *driving* to California to see her), he is still transparently self-centred. Annie rejects his proposal of marriage, and defends her decision to stay in Los Angeles: 'Alvy, you're incapable of enjoying life, you know that?' The movie was originally to be called *Anhedonia*, the inability to experience pleasure, and indeed his wit is shadowed by melancholy throughout the narrative. Alvy has failed to engage with life, and his recognition of his *own* bad faith makes the movie especially poignant. He wanted physical pleasure without artificial stimulation, yet he resorted to 'erotic artifacts' such as red lightbulbs; his justified critique of the shallowness of modern life was never accompanied by a practical

attempt at improving it. Crucially, Alvy's public display of intellectual and physical sincerity gives way to the private anxieties
of a man suspicious of anything beyond his control: 'Hey, don't
knock masturbation! It's sex with someone I love.' The movie
ends with two actors rehearsing a scene in which the characters
of Alvy and Annie end up united: 'Wait! I'm, I'm going to go
with you ... I love you.' We see the 'real' Alvy sitting in the
director's chair; he looks directly at the camera:

> Tsch, whatta you want? It was my first play. You know ... you know
> how you're always tryin' to get things to come out perfect in art
> because, uh, it's real difficult in life...

Alvy's art is, now, his only 'life-raft'; the photographs Annie
took of him when they were together are now a kind of epitaph.
That love will remain. Woody Allen did not conceive *Annie Hall*
as a study of a relationship (*that* was focused upon at the editing
stage); rather, he wanted to examine the character of Alvy
Singer, a man suffering from the inability to experience pleasure.
The movie is a reflection on 'dispriz'd love', and on the ways in
which one's body betrays one's intellect. The 'civilizing process'
has produced an individual who has found innumerable methods
of mentally dissecting himself, leaving him perhaps too disenchanted for such a strange, ambiguous, unsettling an experience
as love. Alvy's degree of condescension, his inability except at
rare moments to see the other in terms apart from those defined
by his pity and sense of responsibility, his unwillingness to let
them take sacrifices and choices or to carry the burdens, his
willingness to pretend and to lie to them, in short, his essential
failure to *respect* them, to say nothing of his own frequent
acknowledgement that he feels desire rather than love, are not
compatible with any relation we should easily or usefully call
'love'.

There is, nonetheless, a sense of hope at the end of *Annie Hall*.
The story is not unbearably bleak. Diane Keaton's awkward,
hapless character is eventually transformed into a secure, intelligent and independent woman. The *schlemiel* may still end up
alone, but his comic insights have contributed to the self-
education of another human being. Unlike in Shaw's *Pygmalion*,
Eliza does not need Henry Higgins, and she leaves him. Alvy is
left with his art, his seductive fantasies, to fill the space where
Annie once was. Death, the first question, is also the final

question: the movie began with an admission of the ageing process and the death of a love affair, and it closes with a haunting montage of memories from that affair. Only now, in her absence (a death of a kind), can Alvy love her; he is the projectionist, he conjures up the images. Alvy, having struggled to overcome the mind/body conflict for so long, belatedly comes to appreciate that this conflict is, perhaps, the grit that makes the pearl:

> I realized what a terrific person she was and how much fun it was just knowing her and I thought of that old joke, you know, this guy goes to a psychiatrist and says, 'Doc, uh, my brother's crazy. He thinks he's a chicken'. And the doctor says, 'Well, why don't you turn him in?' And the guy says, 'I would, but I need the eggs.' Well, I guess that's pretty much how I feel about relationships. You know, they're totally irrational and crazy and absurd ... but, uh, I guess we keep goin' through it because, uh, most of us need the eggs.

Allen's *Anhedonia* transformed itself into *Annie Hall* as his characters took on a significance which transcended the auto-biographical tone. As Allen explained:

> It was originally a picture about me, exclusively ... It was about me, my life, my thoughts, my ideas, my background, and the relationship was one major part of it. But sometimes it's hard to foresee at the outset what's going to be the most interesting drift. (Rosenblum and Karen, 1979: 283)

Marshall Brickman, who co-wrote *Annie Hall* with Allen, said of his colleague: 'Woody is not a frivolous person ... I think he's genuinely concerned with his philosophy, he feels advancing age, and he worries about death. And he's always intuitively tried to use his personal material in his work' (Brickman 1985: 274)

Interiors (1978) features the same problems of analysis versus creativity, love versus sex, and the appreciation of mortality, but the comic Allen character is entirely absent – thus making the movie an *ensemble* piece. Allen said that the movie was concerned with 'the floating unrest that can only be traceable to bad choices in life ... And how a lover can possess the loved one as an object he can control.' At the beginning, we find Arthur (E.G. Marshall), a sorrowful 60-year-old man, evoking an image of his estranged wife Eve:

I had dropped out of law school when I met Eve. She was very beautiful – very pale and cold in her black dress, without anything more than a simple strand of pearls – and distant ... At the time the girls were born, it was all so perfect – so ordered. Looking back, of course, it was rigid. It was like an ice castle.

The 'girls' Arthur alludes to are now adult daughters: Renata (Diane Keaton), a well-known poet; Joey (Mary Beth Hurt), an intelligent but uninspired middle child; and television star Flyn (Kristin Griffith). These three sisters (with obvious similarities with the sisters in *King Lear*, Chekhov and *Cries and Whispers*) are profoundly affected by several events: after years of marriage, Arthur requests a 'temporary separation' from Eve (Geraldine Page). Eve suffers a nervous breakdown and, as the movie gets underway, starts to recover by resuming her career. The title *Interiors* refers to Eve's interior decorating profession and, more significantly, to the characters' self-consciously inner preoccupations.

Renata speaks to her analyst about her impotence (sexual and artistic), brought on, she believes, by her recognition of her own mortality. She cannot even express this most personal of anxieties without employing an overly-mannered, 'rehearsed' form of expression: 'I can't seen to shake this ... the real implication of dying. It's terrifying. The intimacy of it embarrasses me.' Her husband Frederick (Richard Jordan), who is also a writer, feels overshadowed by his wife's fame and comes to interpret her encouragement as a form of condescension: 'I count on you for honesty, not flattery!' They have become two warring lovers who will not, perhaps cannot, leave each other alone, their fingernails so deeply buried in each other's wounds they cannot separate for fear of bleeding to death. Renata resents her sister Joey's artistic endeavours: 'She has all the anxiety of the artistic personality without any of the talent.' Joey cannot find a language that suits her feelings, and she is perplexed by her easy popularity with her father and her lover, Mike: 'Why do you stay with me? I don't understand you. I give you nothing but grief.' What she labours for she loses, and what she does not want comes to worry her. Frederick's artistic impotence breeds a self-contempt which he projects onto anyone whom he feels shares his inability to marry intellectual probity with sensual gratification: he lusts after the glamorous Flyn, whom he compares to his latest book – 'a perfect example of form without content'. These artists have anaesthetized themselves to the beautiful shock of their own imagination. There is an over-explicitness of intention in their language and actions which seems tired and achingly self-conscious. We see countless shots of characters looking at something (as though watching a movie): Renata puts her hand on a window-pane and gazes into the distance, Arthur stares through his office window, and, at the end, the three sisters position themselves by windows facing the ocean. Eve, on her first appearance, says: 'Would you mind closing the window? The street noises are just unnerving.' The city here is a city of interiors: things happen inside people's heads, inside empty cathedrals, inside lonely apartments. All the city's inhabitants seem lost within the bubble of their own preoccupations, the life they lead increasingly a life of mental operations: the body has become a mere pedestal for the skull. It is as if the world were partitioned off from these characters, as if it were screened off from them by something as transparent as glass and as unbreakable as people too afraid to lose control. Eve's suicide has an air of inevitability about it that suggests the character serves a symbolic function, referring to the refusal to truly experience life as a process (death seems the consequence).

The movie's only Jewish character (never explicitly identified as such but surely a significant choice) is Pearl (Maureen Stapleton), the second wife of Arthur. She enters into the Gentile family causing the same kind of cultural discomfort that Alvy Singer brought to the Halls' dinner table. Arthur's marriage, coming so soon after the suicide of his coldly proper wife, shocks his three daughters – who barely hide their dislike for Pearl. To the girls, she represents an outside force. They cannot see the life she gives their father, and the warmth she is capable of bestowing on the stuffy, New England family. 'She's a vulgarian,' Joey shouts at her father. Renata is offended by her spontaneity and her exuberance. Allen highlights Pearl's 'otherness' in a number of different ways. Her bright red dresses, for example, clash with the rest of the movie's frozen white interiors. Everything about Pearl and Arthur's first wife, Eve, is dissimilar: Pearl collects slightly erotic black ebony figures, Eve, grey vases; Eve wears tight, high collars, Pearl's dresses are open, loose and billowing; Pearl enjoys dancing, Eve, visiting old churches; Pearl reacts readily to her environment, sensing the numinous in the naturalness of things, Eve reconstructs her environment until it matches her preconceived standards of beauty. Allen even has

Pearl literally breathe life into the family. She gives Joey mouth-to-mouth resuscitation after the woman is dragged from the ocean. Indirectly, the movie continues Allen's concern for Jewish versus Gentile tensions and the role of the outsider in society.

'I think,' Joey had told her mother, 'you're really too perfect ... to live in this world.' Like Bergman's *Autumn Sonata*, *Interiors* revolves around a mother who is artistic, fastidious and impossibly overbearing. As one of her daughters tells her, 'You worship talent. Well, what happens to those of us who can't create?' Eve makes everything exterior into something interior: she craves the manageable indoors and eventually has a mythic confrontation between herself and the chaotic power of the ocean.

After Eve's funeral, the three sisters, dressed in black, gaze out at the ocean. 'The water's so calm,' says Joey. 'Yes,' replies Renata, 'It's very peaceful.' They now reflect on life with the knowledge of a death; a sense of mortality provides them with a more profound perspective. 'I saw the ending in a more positive way,' said Allen. 'I felt there was hope for the sisters that they had arrived finally at a point where they could communicate.' Allen said of Renata: 'She articulates all my personal concerns ... You have a sense of immortality that your work will live on after you, which is nonsense .... Renata comes to realize in the movie ... that the only thing anyone has any chance with is human relationships.' An exaggeration, of course, but it underlines the doubts Allen has about 'dispassionate' academic approaches to life.

Of *Interiors* Allen observed, 'There's something of me in all the characters.' In April 1987 he told *Esquire* magazine:

> I have a high feminine component, and I probably have that high heterosexual profile because of jokes I've made over the years. [Mia Farrow] is always kidding me in our relationship because I grew up interested in fashions. I grew up cutting out paper dolls and dressing Deanna Durbin in cut-outs, and Mia, now in her life, is the one who, up at her farm, drives the tractor and knows how to repair the television set when it breaks. She can do all that stuff. I'm the one who's always turning to the fashion page in the newspaper and saying, 'Look at this. Look at what Oscar de la Renta has come up with.'

Until recently, Allen's *identification* with women's feelings and interests has been translated in his movies into a more predictable voyeurism. Allen's character still looks at the fashion pages, but, unlike Allen himself, objectifies the women: 'I was just sitting around looking through the magazine section ... uh, no, no, no, I didn't read the piece on China's faceless masses. I was checking out the lingerie ads ... Yeah, I can never get past them. They're really erotic.' To miss the distance between Allen's character and Allen the writer would be to miss completely the critical edge that is crucial in such a scene. The old movie persona is increasingly treated in an ambivalent light. By 1988 Allen would say:

> I'm not interested in all the stuff that others like to direct. Action. Gangster movies. That's not my bag. I'm into human interest. And my main interest is what makes women tick ... psychologically. (*Hot Press*, 6 May 1988)

Unusually for a popular leading man, Allen is frequently seen as helpless until a woman deals with whatever is threatening him. *She* is not the threat; on the contrary, she is his protector, someone who possesses qualities he lacks. The scene in *Annie Hall*, where Alvy is unnerved by some live lobsters in his kitchen, is brought to a satisfactory end when Annie calmly puts them in the pot. Alvy sees her as almost magically gifted in the way she solves this problem: 'Look, one crawled behind the refrigerator. It'll turn up in our bed at night ... Talk to him. You speak shellfish!' In *Stardust Memories*, Sandy Bates is scared when a pigeon flies into his apartment, but his lover is able to think calmly:

> *Sandy*: ...Get it out of here. It's probably one of those killer
>   pigeons!
> *Dorrie*: No, get something for it to eat. We can coax it down!
> *Sandy*: You see, it's got a swastika under its wings.
> *Dorrie*: It's wonderful.

In his later movies, Allen begins to depict women as independent people with their own good and bad qualities, their own eccentricities and distinctive aspirations. His character no longer tries to dominate them. Allen observes but never stresses current social issues: he never posits feminism, for instance, as 'the reason why' something does or does not happen between a woman and a man. Annie and Alvy break up and immediately take on new mates. The temptation to blame the break-up on some idea or individual is resisted.

Manhattan is in some ways a more mature treatment of the

'love fades' theme of *Annie Hall*. Again, the story begins with Allen's character as a narrator: he talks of how hard it is to exist in a society 'desensitized' by various drugs and diversions. Isaac is in love with a woman (Tracy) and a city (Manhattan); both are constantly changing, evolving, and Isaac must eventually come to terms with this fact (which involves his coming to terms with his *own* transient nature). Allen said at the time of this movie that the person/place relation was one he was conscious of:

> I get angry and frustrated when I think of [the city], but it's the same kind of frustration that you get when someone you love disappoints you. But in *Manhattan* I'm not critical of New York: I question the roots of it. It's not a movie that says 'Clean up Central Park'. It's a movie that says 'Clean up your emotional life, or you'll never be able to clean up Central Park'. (Benayoun, 1986: 163)

Isaac, Yale and Mary are all writers, but they are so absorbed in their romantic problems that their work is postponed or deteriorates. Isaac's serious novel remains unwritten; Yale's critical study of Eugene O'Neill remains unfocused; and Mary descends from reviewing an edition of Tolstoy's letters for a prestigious quarterly to grinding out a 'novelization' of a popular movie. Tracy is still at school; she has not yet acquired the obligatory *ennui* of Manhattan's educated adults, and this is surely one of the reasons Isaac is so attracted to her. When Mary enters into the story, two relationships break down and Isaac is pulled into a community of neurotics in which someone complains, 'I finally had an orgasm, and my doctor told me it was the wrong kind.'

Isaac is hurt by all the women he knows except Tracy – that makes his betrayal of her so very hard to take. 'When it comes to relationships with women,' he says, 'I'm the winner of the August Strindberg Award.' Mary taunts Isaac about his ex-wife leaving him for another woman: 'that's incredible sexual humiliation. It's enough to turn you off women ... And I think it accounts for the little girl ... Sixteen years old and no possible threat at all!'. She is aggressive and deliberately intimidating: 'I'm beautiful, I'm bright and I deserve better!' When challenged about her attitude she replies: 'Hey, I'm honest. What do you want? I say what's on my mind. And if you can't take it – well, then, fuck off.' 'I like the way you express yourself,' Isaac replies. 'You know, it's pithy, yet degenerate. You get many dates? I don't think so.' Mary has not freed herself of masculine *hubris* – rather, she has learned its language. She knows how men distrust each other, how they hurt each other and debase language until it becomes little more than a cheap form of ammunition. Admirable though her strength and determination may be, Mary often behaves as badly as the most shallow of men: she devotes her time to drawing up lists of the most overrated artists (Kierkegaard, Mahler, Bergman, and so on), she attacks others for their creative lassitude whilst she labours over a vacuous movie plot, and her eagerness to mock her colleagues obscures a loneliness so chafing she allows herself to be duped by a self-seeking married man. Isaac, intimidated by anyone whose intellect holds desire in check, gradually realizes that Mary is no more 'rational' than he; her former teacher and ex-husband, Jeremiah, whom she has described as 'this oversexed brilliant kind of *animal*', turns out to be a small, balding man (Wally Shawn) whom Isaac describes as an 'homonculus'. When she recalls that Jeremiah failed her academic work when they were living together, Isaac's sense of unease increases.

In this narcissistic culture, people have come to substitute ideas for action. Isaac's ex-wife feels the need to attack him by publishing a book about his shortcomings; Mary and Yale avoid the reality of their situation by talking in portentous abstractions. 'My problem is,' says Mary, 'I'm both attracted and repelled by the male organ.' She 'deals' with the problem by hiding her insecurity behind an intellectual pushiness. Isaac is appalled by this solipsistic lifestyle, with its fetish for 'concepts' and its weakness for psychobabble and luxury drugs: 'You should abandon the show and open a pharmaceutical house!,' shouts Isaac to his TV colleagues. Yet his opposition to this community never goes beyond self-conscious parody: 'The brain is the most overrated organ,' he tells Mary. He is backing into a corner, coming on as the anti-intellectual whereas in reality he is *the* intellectual of all the New Yorkers. 'Gossip is the new pornography,' says Yale, and when Isaac hears his friends reading from his ex-wife's book about their marriage, he seems to have lost all sense of independence; he is now part of someone else's story, and his life seems at the mercy of the storyteller:

'He was given to fits of rage, Jewish liberal paranoia, male chauvinism, self-righteous misanthropy, and nihilistic moods of despair. He had complaints about life but never any solutions ... In his most private

moments, he spoke of his fear of death, which he elevated to tragic
heights when, in fact, it was mere narcissism.'

As the text refers to Isaac's fear of death, the camera halts,
allowing him to go beyond the frame and out of our sight (the
only truly cinematic *'petite mort'*).

The narrative, one feels, is not of Isaac's making; he does not
know how it will end. Isaac's fate is to be mangled in the
machinery of modern sexual desire. When Mary tells him she has
been seeing Yale again, he sits silently still, stunned and saddened.
'I wish you'd get angry so that we could have it out' says Mary,
but Isaac's vulnerability has drunk too deeply from his emotions.
'I don't get angry, okay? I mean, I have a tendency to internalize.
I can't express anger. That's one of the problems I have. I-I
grow a tumour instead.' When Yale and Isaac confront each
other over their desire for Mary, the cleverness and the carefully-
crafted language give way to the desperate gasps of two lonely
boys: 'Now we *both* like her!' 'Yeah, well, I liked her *first!*' ' "I
liked her first." What're you – six years old?.' 'Don't turn this
into one of your big moral issues.' Yet the meaning of Isaac's
attitude is that the ethical can never be suspended. Civilization
depends upon it. Nowhere is Woody Allen more Jewish than in
his constant insistence on this point. What he is struggling to
achieve is the dignity of the ordinary.

Isaac is perplexed by the contradictions inherent in modern
life, but he is also distressed by his own contradictions. He does
(in Wilde's words) 'all the foolish things that wise lovers do'; he
struggles to understand why, when love falls apart, the most
intelligent of people stumble and succumb to the most pointless
and inexcusably hurtful stupidities. When Isaac realizes that he
has always loved Tracy, and that all of his infidelities and
thoughtless remarks have been little more than attempts at
denying this love, a denouement is set up which is simultaneously
cruel and touching, bitter and moving – an ending worthy of
Salinger. Isaac runs across New York, arriving at Tracy's apartment house just as she is about to leave for the airport. His
breathless plea for her to stay is so shockingly remorseless one
feels embarrassed for him. 'You really hurt me,' Tracy replies,
sounding almost amused by his childish contrition as he begs her
to forget his past mistakes. Isaac is entirely denuded of his
defensive irony and verbal tricks, and his attempt at persuading

Tracy not to go to London for six months of acting classes is painfully irrational:

> ... you go to rehearsal and you hang out with those people. You have lunch a lot. And, well, you know, attachments form, and I mean, you don't wanna get into that kind of ... I mean, *you'll change*. You know, you'll be ... in six months you'll be a completely different person.

His pained yet hopeful expression reminds one of John Donne's famous line to his beloved: 'For God's sake, hold your tongue and let me love.' The actual question troubling Isaac – can he possibly wait six months for Tracy's return from London? – is terribly trivial, and represents Allen's comment on how modern life has become so ephemeral, superficial, and self-indulgent. When Tracy replies, 'Not everybody gets corrupted', the first suggestion of the possibility of *trust* has been made. No reply can yet be made: Allen's characters have not yet reached that level of moral strength, but Isaac is the first of Allen's movie personae for whom the *need* for trust is, potentially, overpowering. Isaac cannot turn away from Tracy, not even out of fear: while Alvy Singer can allow his lover to leave him and then 'retrieves' her in a play, Isaac appreciates that the contradiction is in life – it is not something that can be 'solved' in art. Isaac cannot hide himself from the anxiety of loving another; more pointedly, he does not *wish* to hide himself, any longer. This character is more open and vulnerable than Alvy Singer: he is not so self-protectively witty, and he makes (and admits to making) wrong decisions. At the end, when he asks Tracy to take him back, he is being selfish, unable to face up to the prospect of being alone, but it is clear that he really does care for her. Tracy, like Mary, is ideological, but she has a youthful beauty so fine that no cynicism can violate it. Tracy consoles, but hers are not the consolations of philosophy. Given the endless ambiguity of Isaac's relationship to Tracy – can body and soul live happily ever after? – this movie could not have ended happily in the conventional sense. The disjunction between the ideal and the real, the world dreamed and the world observed (increasingly problematic in Allen's work) reaches what must be a peak in *Manhattan*. What it offers is not the overcoming of our isolation, but the sharing of our isolation; not to save the world out of love, but to save love for the world, until it is responsive again.

'Not everybody gets corrupted': Allen has passed through the hell of profligacy and attained the seriousness of pleasure.

'Sex and romance', sighs one of Allen's characters. 'What we go through for a pretty face.' Time and again, Allen's lovers find themselves ambushed by their own desire. In the short story 'The Lunatic's Tale' (Allen, 1981), the man complains that he cannot 'find all the requirements one needs in a single member of the opposite sex'. He is married to a beautiful and intelligent woman who somehow does not arouse him sexually; he is infatuated with a photographer's model whose 'erotic radiation ... oozed from her every pore'. He attempts an experiment whereby he transfers the best qualities of both women into the body of one. His wife now makes him sexually aroused. However, after several months he 'inexplicably grew dissatisfied with this dream woman and developed instead a crush on Billie Jean Zapruder, an airline stewardess whose boyish, flat figure and Alabama twang caused my heart to do flip-flops'. Love fades; or rather, love never rests content within a single object, but moves between bodies through time. Desire has its own cunning, drawing us deeper into a puzzle that has no real solution. It seems that mental and physical provocation rarely turn up in the same person, and that the enigma of sexual arousal defies calculation. As Allen contemplates this theme, he subjects his characters to the cruelest twists of fate. In 'Retribution', Harold Cohen falls in love with WASP Connie, who prepares to take him to meet her family. She warns him that he might transfer his affections to her sister, who is intelligent, young, vivacious and exceptionally charming. The thought plays on Harold's mind. When he meets the sister, he acknowledges her great beauty and wit, yet he still prefers Connie. However, he *does* become fixated on Connie's mother, Emily: 'fifty-five, buxom, tanned, a ravishing pioneer face with pulled-back greying hair and round, succulent curves that expressed themselves in flawless arcs like a Brancusi'. Connie is pleased that her mother and her lover get on so well, but in time she comes to be reminded of her brother and thus cannot bear to make love to Harold anymore ('somewhere Freud, Sophocles, and Eugene O'Neill were laughing'). Connie starts to sleep with other men, and Harold marries Emily. After the wedding, Harold finds himself alone with Connie, and they laugh over the vicissitudes of their relationship. Suddenly, Connie seduces him: 'You turn me on like you can't believe.' 'It's a whole new ball game,' she explains. 'Marrying Mom has made you my father.' Harold is left to reflect on Connie's parting comment: 'Don't worry, Dad, there'll be plenty of opportunities.'

The lover is never in control of the love process, for what the mind fixes on is in constant motion. In *Stardust Memories*, Allen's Sandy Bates makes a movie in which he tries to subject the vagaries of desire to the power of logic, but he is outwitted by the non-rational qualities of love. Sandy has already announced that he is only content when he is in control of things ('art and masturbation'), and in his 'mad scientist' movie he tries to use science to solve the riddle of romance. The scene is a laboratory with two women lying unconscious on operating tables. The scientist prowls around the tables, connecting various wires and plugs:

> I've never been able to fall in love. I've never been able to find the perfect woman. There's always something wrong . And then I met Doris. A wonderful woman. Great personality. But for some reason, I'm just not turned on sexually by her. Don't ask me why. And then I met Rita. An animal. Nasty, mean, trouble ... and I love going to bed with her. Though afterward I always wished that I was back with Doris. And then I thought to myself, if only I could put Doris' brain in Rita's body. Wouldn't that be wonderful? And I thought, why not? What the hell, I'm a surgeon ... So, I performed the operation and everything went perfectly. I switched their personalities and I took all the badness and put it over there [*points at Doris*]. And I made Rita into a warm, wonderful, charming, sexy, sweet, giving, mature woman ... And then I fell in love with Doris.

Stardust Memories ends with Sandy Bates no nearer to understanding the two things that come instinctively to him: humour and sexual desire. 'You were always searching for the perfect woman,' says Dorrie in the sanitarium. 'You wound up falling in love with me'. An alien being steps out of a space ship and tells Sandy to forget about making 'socially significant' movies and concentrate on telling 'funnier jokes'. On the subject of Sandy's lovelife, the alien is no more enlightening:

Alien: Hey, look, I'm a superintelligent being. By Earth standards I have an IQ of sixteen hundred and I can't even understand what you expected from that relationship with Dorrie.
Sandy: I loved her.
Alien: Yeah, I know, and two days a month she was the most

exciting woman in the world, but the rest of the time she was a basket case.

The alien tells Sandy that his search for the definitive meanings of life and love is hopeless: 'These are the wrong questions,' he is told. When Sandy is told that his 'work will live on after him', he is horrified: 'What good is it if I can't pinch any women or hear any music?' As Woody Allen himself has said, 'I don't want to gain immortality in my works. I want to gain it by not dying.' The lover is forever prey to the decay that names us and claims us and shames us all, the 'other' that is the negation of one's life, the possession of which means the loss of everything. It is not actually death, but the *knowledge* of death, that creates problems for human beings. An insect caught between a person's fingers struggles as convulsively as a human being in the clutches of a murderer, but the insect's defensive movements when in mortal danger are an unlearned gift of its species; it knows nothing of death. Human beings know, and so for them death becomes a problem. Media advisers play on our fear of decay: Sandy Bates is told by his brother-in-law, 'I had two heart attacks before I got the exercise bike.' Since he got the bike: 'I also had two heart attacks.' The mother, in *September*, remarks: 'You study yourself in the mirror ... and you realize something's missing ... and then you realize it's your future.' Death, for Allen, is not something 'outside' of life; rather, it is an event which runs concurrently with the duration of that life, inexorable and undeniable. When Allen thinks of love, he also thinks of death.

Allen makes the movie idol in *The Purple Rose of Cairo* (1985) step out of the screen and into the movie theatre for his first experience of real love. Life in a movie is, literally, a living death; nothing changes, all is ordered. For genuine intimacy, the star has to forego his immortality. As Alvy Singer discovers, our visible fictions sometimes seduce us with their simplicity. Life in the actual world is difficult and embarrassing. Most of all it is difficult and embarrassing in our confrontation with other people, who, by their very existence, make demands that we may be unable or unwilling to meet. It requires a great force, such as the force of sexual desire, to overcome the embarrassment and self-protection that shield us from the most intimate encounters. It is tempting to take refuge in substitutes, which neither embarrass us nor resist the impulse of our spontaneous cravings. The habit grows of creating a compliant world of desire, in which unreal objects become the focus of real emotions, and the emotions themselves are rendered incompetent to participate in the building of personal relations. The fantasy blocks the passage to reality, which becomes inaccessible to the will. Allen (1978: 104) has written: 'To be loved, certainly, is different from being admired, as one can be admired from afar but to really love someone it is essential to be in the same room with the person, crouching behind the drapes.' Allen never surrenders the desire to be at home with the 'foreign self', yet he acknowledges that its very *foreignness* is at the centre of its charm. We love the private space beneath our roughened skins, the silence in which to shine out our aloneness, the separateness with which to contemplate the idea of unity, the chance to select a few other surfaces to tumble against. Yet we are also made anxious by the spaces between us, those unbearable silences that sometimes pass between us; the sense (a fear) that we have become imprisoned with ourselves. Allen desperately wants intimacy, but feels threatened by intimacy whenever it is offered. For instance, in *Play It Again, Sam*, Alan Felix goes shopping in preparation for a romantic candle-lit dinner; he mistakenly picks up some *yahrzeit* candles – which are used by Jewish families to remember their dead. The fear that love will fade gnaws at the hopes of Allen's characters, inviting the kind of thoughts expressed by Roth's *Professor of Desire*:

Oh, innocent beloved, you fail to understand and I can't tell you. I can't say it, not tonight, but within a year my passion will be dead. Already it is dying and I am afraid that there is nothing I can do to save it. And nothing that you can do. Intimately bound – bound to you as to no one else! – and I will not be able to raise a hand to so much as touch you ... unless first I remind myself that I must. Toward the flesh upon which I have been grafted and nurtured back toward something like mastery over my life, I will be without desire. Oh, it's stupid! Idiotic! Unfair! To be robbed like this of you! And of this life I love and have hardly gotten to know! And robbed by whom? It always comes down to myself! (Roth, 1985: 261)

Allen told *Time* magazine in 1979: 'I don't think it's right to try to buy your way out of life's painful side by using drugs. I'm also against the concept of short marriages, and regard my own marriages as a sign of failure of some sort.'

'Where did the screw-up come?' There is not enough time left to examine all the old times. In *Manhattan* there is a love scene that is also an observation on evolution; it is as though one thought is projected over the other, making a third meaning, a matter of love and death. Rosenblum and Karen (1979: 279) cites a particularly amusing scene from *Annie Hall* which was cut (for reasons of pacing) from the final version: Alvy Singer is on the bed watching a basketball game on TV – the New York Knicks against the intellectuals. Kierkegaard passes to Nietzsche, Nietzsche passes to Kafka, and Kafka and Alvy stand with the ball, both paralysed with anxiety and guilt, unable to shoot. 'I wanted to show the grace and beauty of the Knicks, and how what they do makes any accomplishments of the intellectual community look ridiculous and insignificant by comparison,' Allen told Brode (1986: 34–5). The cynicism of this satire is subverted by the fact that Allen plays for the *intellectuals*: he thus acknowledges that he plays a part in the very community he criticizes. He thinks that everything works out, but nothing will last. He feels that nothing works out, but everything keeps going on. As soon as he finds happiness, he catches himself thinking, 'when will it end?'

This tension continues to move Woody Allen as he tries to balance his love of truth with his appreciation of desire. Allen's lasting concern is with questions of the nature of our human contract, our eternality, the worth of our existence on this his-torically troubled planet, which has extended and grown more complex; but so, equally, has his concern with the definition of our late age, the darkening life of our century, the engulfing mechanisms of power and mass, the anxious performance of a consciousness ever more drawn toward excess and extremity. However far out Allen will go in quest of his version of the absolute, he is, above all, the artist and will always be right back. For, to paraphrase Blake, whether or not eternity is in love with the productions of time, it has to learn to live with them.

4

Celebrity and Integrity

If I was not born in Brooklyn, if I had been born in Poland, or Berlin,
I'd be a lampshade today, right?

Stardust Memories

You only live once: but once is enough if you play it right.

Interiors

Ralph Rosenblum has a favourite anecdote about Woody Allen's hatred of his celebrity status: the two men are sitting in a New York cafeteria, discussing some editing plans over lunch. Two middle-aged women pass by the table. They stop, whisper to each other, glance over at Allen, and eventually one of them retraces her steps and asks: 'Are you Woody Allen?' Allen, staring down at his plate, tense and still, mumbles 'Yes'. The woman smiles, and rejoins her friend. Allen slumps back into his chair. The two women are still in the mid-distance, looking increasingly agitated as they whisper to each other. One of them marches back to Allen's table, asking 'Are you *sure* you're Woody Allen?' Allen, now clearly undergoing agonies, mutters, 'Yes'. The second woman then arrives, saying, 'Can you identify yourself?'

Groucho Marx once pictured himself as 'a serious man with a comic sense'. This description also captures the central tension in Woody Allen's attitude to his work and its reception. He is a very private man who has made a name for himself in the most public of professions. He has a unique gift for comedy, yet his own interests are in philosophy, tragedy, and politics. He is probably the most popular contemporary Jewish entertainer, but he does not enjoy being reminded of his Jewishness. His critics are bemused by the shyness of a man whose movies so often appear to be about himself. His fans are surprised by the seriousness of the person who has made them laugh so often. His work is a fascinating series of visions of modern American life, but he is probably more admired and critically appreciated in Europe. Woody Allen is a complex, contradictory character; indeed, it is not clear who 'Woody Allen' is. Few of his friends and associates are prepared to talk about him, and those who do so only add to his mystique. Melvin Bourne, production designer on many of Allen's movies, says: 'Woody is totally prepared, always. He comes in and does his work, quietly and without fuss. He doesn't say much. And he's not much fun on set; no laughs.' Gordon Willis, the cinematographer who was responsible for the beautiful black-and-white images of *Manhattan*, can only comment: 'We never see each other off the set ... We're not close at all, on a personal level ... Working even as closely as we do, we don't socialise. None of the unit does.' When journalist Vivien Gornick went to interview Allen, she was surprised to find him 'in analyzed command of a personality that is direct, extremely sweet, and altogether kindly'. What *does* strike many people when they get to know Allen is his uneasiness about his own talent: 'He's incredibly modest, and he *hates* being told how great he is,' says his agent, Charles Joffe. Thus, he dismisses his finest movies as 'light conceits' or 'failures', and speaks in hushed tones about the 'masterpieces' of European cinema. He is described by his friends as an intellectual, yet he never misses an opportunity to satirize the world of ideas. Woody Allen is as much at odds with his times as he is a representative of them, a fascinating paradox for his audience to reflect upon.

Woody Allen's response to his celebrity status is in stark contrast to that of many other successful comedians. One thinks of Chaplin's frantic antics whenever any kind of camera was pointed in his direction, or Jerry Lewis' spasms of self-conscious 'zaniness' at awards ceremonies and television chat shows. Mel Brooks, who comes from a similar background to Allen, is perhaps the most obvious recent example of the extrovert comic. He displays an almost desperate need to be liked, to gain the acceptance and approval of others. He is never one in a crowd, rather he is always alone in front of an audience – a New York Jew who wants to play Puck. His colleagues describe him as constantly 'on', performing, as animated and inventive as he is on the screen; before shooting begins each morning, Brooks will ad lib in front of his crew. He has been known to jump out of his car in the middle of a traffic jam on the way to work, run over to a stranger's car, knock on the window, point to himself and shout: '*Mel Brooks! Recognize me?*' (Rosenblum, 1979: 193-

209). Allen, on the contrary, is remarkably shy and introverted. He is a man who craves the comfort of a familiar group of friends and colleagues, and he shuns any invitation to meet strangers. Rosenblum (ibid, 266) observes that Allen tries to avoid those people on the set whom he does not already know, and, when forced to shake hands, he is visibly uncomfortable: 'Those he gives – watery handshakes, no grip in them at all – seem to be moments of torture during which he won't know what to do with his eyes. He will either look away, or he will stare steadily into his opposite's eyes. Either way, the recipient will probably feel ill at ease.' According to Allen's oldest friends and associates, this reserve is quite genuine: Jack Rollins, Allen's manager since the fifties, insists, 'Now you've got to remember this is the shyest man I've ever met. To this day. *Truly* shy' (in McNight, 1983: 87). In New York Allen is an obvious target for the *paparazzi*, photographing him leaving restaurants and concerts, his hand in front of his face or thrust out towards the lens. 'My idea of a good time,' claims Allen, 'is to take a walk from my house to the office and not for the entire walk have to worry about hearing my name being called from a passing car or being spoken to at all. That would be perfect.' Allen's very anonymity as a public figure has been made into a new source of fascination by the gossip columnists and image-makers. He has been pushed into the category of the 'reclusive American author' alongside J.D. Salinger and Pynchon, his shyness being interpreted by many journalists as a kind of 'trademark'. Yet Allen regards this reputation as unjust:

> I'm certainly not a partygoer at all. I work 90 per cent of the time. But I'm not a recluse. People think because I don't want to get photographed by *paparazzi* all the time – I don't even mind that, if they don't follow me down the street for fifteen minutes, if they just take their pictures and go – that I'm a recluse. This is a thing that's been built up over the years for some reason, but it just isn't so. I go to Madison Square Garden for basketball games. I eat out every single night. I'm always at the opera or at shows. (*Esquire*, April 1987)

Far from being a gesture or a 'social comment', Allen's shyness is part of his personality – one which rests uneasily with his desire to perform. This tension in his character often causes him to appear contradictory and rather coy. There are famous occasions when Allen has surprised people by attending public events –

such as the evening he was the escort of Betty Ford. At other
times Allen will threaten to withdraw from all public activities:

> I see stopping making films at a certain point because it's hard work,
> and I'd like to write books ... I almost feel I'd like to do that now. It
> would be fun. People always say, 'You can't beat the hours'. To get up
> in the morning and not have to get picked up by the Teamster and go
> out to the set and deal with everybody. It'd be fun just to lollylag
> around the house, and practice the clarinet, and write. (ibid)

Allen's agent, Charles Joffe, claims that his client is 'not concerned
with fame, stardom, money – only work'. Even at the beginning
of his career, writing for television shows alongside the ebullient
Brooks, Allen preferred to work alone on material for himself.
'It's a need to work,' he said, 'to write. I'm *driven* to it. If I
don't write every free minute, I have this terrible guilt. It's like –
I don't know – if I don't write, I'll be sorry someday' (quoted in
Brode, 1986: 23). Allen's self-discipline is extraordinary: after
completing one movie he starts on the next without a single
day's break; during the making of a movie he will sometimes
spend the evening writing a short story or revising the screenplay. 'I have absolutely Prussian self-discipline when it comes to
my writing', he has said. Unable to relax, he attentively analyses
what he sees, carrying notebooks into museums and art galleries,
recording impressions, and writing down ideas. His unassuming
appearance facilitates his preparation for writing and acting,
allowing him to overhear conversations and observe gestures and
mannerisms. To be noticed, subjected to other people's attention,
is thus not just a threat to his sense of privacy but also a
violation of his role as observer. Allen's movies are full of references to this threat: for example, in *Annie Hall* Alvy Singer is
cornered by two burly men who refuse to leave him alone: 'You
were on the, uh, the Johnny Carson show, right? ... Hey! This is
Alvy Singer! This guy's on television! ... Can I have your auto-
graph? ... It's for my girl friend. Make it out to Ralph ... It's for
my brudder ... Hey! This is Alvy Singer! *Alvy Singer over here*!'
Alvy's anonymity has been prised open, and his reaction is only
superficially 'comic'; one can see that for Alvy (and for Allen)
this is a serious and painful problem.

Allen has done his best to shield his own background from the
prying eyes of the public. The biographical blurb inside his
books of short stories announces: 'His one regret in life is that

he is not someone else.' The playbill for *Play It Again, Sam* 'informs' us that Allen is the 'son of a Latvian prince' who once 'played Willy Loman in *Mr. Roberts*, to the consternation of many around him ... he is currently appearing on TV in *Mother Witwick's Porridge*, a psychological musical spoofing the evils of diabetes.' The idea of a press conference is distinctly unappealing for a man so keen to escape his star status; when he was obliged to attend these promotional events early on in his movie career, journalists found him evasive and frustratingly ironic. During a press conference for *Bananas* in 1971, Allen demonstrated his ability to shield himself behind a series of mocking wisecracks:

> *Question*: How do you get your ideas?
> *Answer*: They come to me all at once ... I see the opening credits unfold and then the first scene ... and then the rest of it.
> *Q*: You mean you see all of it at once?
> *A*: Yes.
> *Q*: How long does it take?
> *A*: In the case of *Bananas*, eighty-two minutes.
> *Q*: All of it at once?
> *A*: Yes.
> *Q*: You're not sending me up, are you?
> *A*: No ... Not at all.
> (*Rolling Stone*, 30 September 1971)

Much of this ill-disguised contempt for his media interrogators is a response to their eagerness to conflate his comic image with his private personality. For example, many writers (including some of his most sympathetic biographers) have made no distinction between Allen and his early movie characters. Allen himself is most definitely not a *schlemiel*; as he has said, 'I've never been that. It's an appellation for the unimaginative to hang on me.' Similarly, when journalists, starved of biographical material on Allen, try to draw on the many childhood references in his night-club act and his movies, Allen is quick to deny any correspondence: 'I really wasn't a scared and lonely child at all. I played at all sorts of games and was good at quite a lot of them. I wasn't poor, or hungry or neglected. We were a well-fed middle class family. We wore good clothes and lived in a comfortable house.' When he started his career as a stand-up comedian, he said: 'What I'm really interested in is creating an image of a warm person that people will accept as funny apart from the joke.' Not only did Allen succeed in this, but he also managed to make the character *believable* – and for an act based almost exclusively on the calamitous experiences and curious ideas of a New York Jewish comedian, this has caused tremendous problems for the author's own integrity.

Allen has come to regard his movie image as something of a burden and, possibly, a threat. As he has improved over the years as an actor, so the critics and the audiences have come to see him as identical with his screen persona: 'Woody' is confused with Allen. In movies, the manipulation of multiple selves is a highly *public* transaction, both calculated and commercial. This might, *a priori*, be considered an advantage in achieving control over the self, but more often it leads to diminished control. On screen, we have the movie star playing a character; off-screen, we have the person playing the movie star. All four of these 'characters' are present in the minds of the audience. Woody Allen has an existence in the world outside movies, whereas Alvy Singer does not. However, the Woody Allen who exists in movies, magazines, books and photographs, has only a complex relationship to the Woody Allen who exists apart from all these things. While there is necessarily a relationship between the two, it is not a given one and is always both a difficult relationship and one hard to establish. Allen is the writer of *New Yorker* short stories and a number of successful screenplays. Allen is the comic actor in several memorable movies. Allen is the clarinet player in the New Orleans Funeral and Ragtime Orchestra. Allen is the author who claims that he assumes his audience to be sophisticated enough to distinguish between fact and fantasy. However, his exploitation of his own identity means that the line separating fiction from reality is more blurred than it was with his comic predecessors. Chaplin dyed his hair black, put on a fake moustache and wore a tramp's outfit; Groucho Marx also sported a ridiculous painted moustache and hid behind joke names such as Otis B. Driftwood and Dr. Hugo Z. Hackenbush. Allen started his career with a similar openness about his character's artificiality: he called himself 'Woody Hayward Allen', 'Victor Shackapopolis', 'Fielding Mellish', and 'Miles Monroe'. However, with *Annie Hall,* all of this changed; 'Alvy Singer' was not only his most Jewish-sounding name, but it was believably ordinary. The names Allen now gives his characters sound 'right', they fit comfortably into a more realistic form of drama: 'Isaac Davis', 'Sandy Bates', 'Danny Rose', and 'Mickey Sachs'. For those who do not wish to see the gap between the actor and the character, Allen's movies have become progressively easier to interpret.

It is enlightening to look at Allen's 'personal' movies alongside the other introspective cultural work that enjoyed considerable popularity in America during the 1970s, for his success was not unconnected to a wider trend. American cinema came to acknowledge its own *auteurs*, with Robert Altman, Steven Spielberg, Francis Ford Coppola, Martin Scorsese and others being singled out by academics and critics alike. In popular music, the 'singer-songwriter' enjoyed unprecedented success: Carole King, Janis Ian, Paul Simon, Joni Mitchell, James Taylor and Carly Simon became celebrities who sang of their own (or what *seemed* to be their own) experiences – Joni Mitchell of her famous lovers, James Taylor and Carly Simon of their marriage. Their music was regarded as confessional, a reflection of their most intimate feelings and concerns. Paul Simon in this sense most resembles Allen in his background and themes. Another New York Jew, Simon has written lyrics dealing with the anxieties of modern city life ('Why am I soft in the middle/The rest of my life is so hard'), and the inexplicably trivial reasons for the collapse of a love affair ('I like to sleep with the window open/ And you keep the window closed/So goodbye...'). Both Allen and Simon deal with the contemporary problems and passions of Upper West Side intellectuals, drawing on psychoanalysis and local politics (Allen playfully cast Simon as a born-again Californian, the soporific Tony Lacey, in *Annie Hall*). The 'New Journalism' (in which the character of the narrator was one of the elements in the way the reader would finally assess the experience) that began in the 1960s, with writers such as Tom Wolfe and Hunter S. Thompson, had a profound effect on writing in the 1970s, the 'ME' decade, with authors becoming their own subjects in many of their reports.

Many successful contemporary novelists are deeply influenced by their own lives, and not least by the amount of praise, fame, and money their work attracts. Philip Roth's *Zuckerman* trilogy, for example, is a long meditation on the author after the successful novel. Norman Mailer rarely finds a topic that does not require 'Norman Mailer's' presence (although, showing rare self-restraint, Norman does not appear in *Ancient Evenings*). In movies, there are several obstacles to a similar thematic influence manifesting itself: most writers lose control of their story when the production begins and, more important, movie-making is a

group activity rather than an individual project. However, Woody
Allen is something of an exception to the rule, for he has
tremendous control over the entire process from beginning to
end. The ideas are his, as are the story, the screenplay, the direction,
the casting of leading roles, the choice of musical soundtrack,
and often the central acting role is played by him. It is something of a test-case for *auteurism*: if anyone today gets near to
the romantic idea of the 'creative artist', it is Woody Allen.

Indeed, Allen has encouraged this image in its most overblown
form by his reluctance to acknowledge any contemporary
influences. This is often clumsily signposted by Allen's rather
nervous lapses into the vernacular when questioned about similarities between his work and other writers: for example, when
told that Neil Simon was dealing with the same themes as *Radio
Days* in his Brighton Beach trilogy, Allen said, 'Is he? This I
didn't know'; when informed that *Stardust Memories* echoed the
narrative of *Sullivan's Travels*, Allen replied, 'This I haven't
seen' (can such a lover of movies *not* have seen the Preston
Sturges classic?); and when it was pointed out to Allen that
several of his contemporaries were now dealing with similar
issues and ideas, his response was, 'This I never heard.' While
such responses seem implausible, it is surely true that Allen does
lead an increasingly isolated professional life. He says that he
has not had the time to see many of America's new generation of
comedians, and his preference for casting old friends in his
movies is well known. Such familiarity facilitates Allen's control
of movie-making but, paradoxically, it undermines any control
he has over the *reception* of his movie image. Stars are recognizable – the narration need waste little time and space in explaining the character (audiences often laugh or applaud the
moment Allen's character first appears in *Hannah and Her
Sisters*). There is a rhetoric of authenticity: stars are presented in
various media in such a manner as to suggest a lack of pre-
meditation, an absence of privacy – generally a sense of 'seeing it
like it is'. Allen's use of his own memories and experiences as
'raw material' (in his words) for his movies has certainly
encouraged this effect. *Annie Hall* seemed to many people a
nostalgic return to Allen's old days as a stand-up comic and gag-
writer.

It was public knowledge that Allen and Diane Keaton had
recently had an affair, and thus art was perceived as very closely
imitating life. Alvy's 'stand-up' jokes are from Allen's old

routines; Alvy's appearance on the Dick Cavett show was identical to Allen's; we see Alvy having to write material for a dreadful comedian, thinking to himself, 'This guy's pathetic. If only I had the nerve to do my own jokes' (Allen also went through this experience). The well-known Allen themes are Alvy's themes: the Jewish background; the concern with sex and mortality; the love of movies; and the scorn for Los Angeles and intellectual pretension. Yet Allen co-wrote the screenplay with Marshall Brickman, who comes from a relatively similar background and drew on *his* memories and experiences when writing the movie. The 'perfect fit' between Allen and his movie persona is thus illusory.

As a writer and an actor, Allen may use some of his own habits and mannerisms to create a character, but he is under no obligation to treat them respectfully; authors and actors can *lie*. However, it does seem that Allen exploits his past to a remarkable degree: Diane Keaton is Diane *Hall*; Eudora Fletcher taught Woody Allen at school, and 'Dr. Eudora Fletcher' is the psychiatrist in *Zelig*; Allen's father was once a cab driver, and so is the father in *Radio Days*; Allen's own movie character usually has the same talents as himself; Allen's lovers – Louise Lasser, Diane Keaton, Mariel Hemingway and Mia Farrow – have been cast as his screen lovers. An old acquaintance of Woody Allen and Marshall Brickman, Susan Braudy, heard that some of her characteristics had been incorporated into both Meryl Streep's and Diane Keaton's characters in *Manhattan*. Streep's character writes a post-divorce book called *Marriage, Divorce and Selfhood*; Braudy had written one called *Between Marriage and Divorce*. Braudy wears her hair in the same shaggy style as Keaton's character does, and their speech habits are very similar. For instance, Braudy once said to Allen, 'I'm from Philadelphia, where they still have moral standards.' In the movie, Keaton's character says: 'I'm from Philadelphia ... We believe in God.' As we watch movies such as *Annie Hall*, *Manhattan*, and *Stardust Memories*, we seem to be looking at real people rather than actors: the crowds waiting to enter the cinema; the celebrities and groupies at Elaine's; above all, a man named Woody Allen, a nervous Jewish intellectual who looks like a *schlemiel* but is really a very shrewd person. Many of the interior scenes in *Hannah and Her Sisters* were shot in Mia Farrow's apartment on Manhattan's Upper West Side. Allen does not feel the need to explain why the children of the fictional Hannah look oriental: it is taken for granted that everyone knows all about Mia Farrow's adopted Vietnamese children, who 'play' themselves on the screen. The movie-goers can feel they have been admitted to the inner sanctum of Woody Allen's glamourized reality through his *cinéma vérité*. Although Allen protests, he must realise what a fragile argument he is making; his first wife, Harlene Rosen, was moved to sue him after her lawyers had failed to persuade Allen to cut out the more 'damaging' jokes about their marriage in his night-club routine. Indeed, there is something rather wilfully naive about Allen's attitude. His friends are asked to call him 'Max' whenever they are in public, in order to preserve his anonymity – yet this continues even after *Annie Hall* made that pseudonym very public.

Early in his movie career Allen bought an ivory-coloured Rolls Royce and was chauffered around Manhattan, stopping a block away from his destination in order not to cause a 'scene'. Soon he realized that cars were superfluous to his needs ('I don't find them pretty'). Nonetheless, the controversy that his Rolls caused has left Allen feeling, once again, very misunderstood:

> much was made of it because people always associated me with Greenwich Village and sweaters with holes in them and things like that. And I've never been that kind of person. Never. I never lived in the Village. I always lived on the Upper East Side of Manhattan. I always ate at good restaurants. When I went to buy a car I said, 'what's the best car?' Just automatically. But people always found that at odds with my image. They thought, 'This is the guy who's a regular guy and who wears jeans to formal dinners and who must live in the Village someplace'. (*Esquire*, April 1987)

Allen's complaints would sound more serious if he could explain some of the many contradictions in his attitude: for instance, he told me:'I don't read criticism, good or bad, because I find it distracting', yet he often makes a point of writing to the major critics to thank them for a good review; he says he has 'very frugal tastes and needs', yet his apartment is imaginatively decorated and is situated near Central Park; he says, 'I am very happy in my shell', yet he dines out 'nearly every night'; his casual jeans, shirts and jackets are often made by well-known tailors. The contradictions are far from crippling, but Allen's silence encourages his critics to portray him as a devious mis-anthrope.

Most discussions of Woody Allen uncritically conflate the

person with the characters he plays. As Jarvie (1987: 348) observes:

> Since the fans are in love with 'Woody' they make two mistakes: (1) that whenever Woody appears on the screen he is going to play 'Woody', the 'Woody' they love, the comic, the clown, the nebbish; (2) they operate under the delusion that 'Woody' is actually the real Woody Allen. Thus they yap for him to go back to making us laugh, and not spring these new films on us that get further and further away from the 'Woody' they know and love.

In a culture that is accustomed to a steady flow of information about the 'private lives' of its celebrities, the reticent star is seen as a contradiction in terms. Thus, Salinger is dragged out of hiding to take legal action against his biographer; John Lennon's five-year 'retirement from showbusiness' encouraged the wildest and most extravagant news stories of his entire career (and encouraged one psychotic admirer to 'punish' him for his reported inactivities). Allen is seen as a challenge to the biographer; if they cannot get through to *him*, they will pursue him by other, indirect means. Popular biography moves from public images toward private information; it seeks to pierce the curtain, to see backstage into the secret life of its subject. The private realm twice triumphs over the public: first as being regarded as more 'real', and second by being accepted as ultimately dominant over public events. Biographies thus make the discrete personality their pulsating centre, from which emanate the shaping forces that guide events, articulate doctrines and generate art. Potential biographical figures are eminently capable of simulating a specious personality for the benefit of writers and reporters. Is the real Nixon the man who self-consciously recorded himself on a concealed tape recorder? Is the real Sophia Loren the woman described in her autobiography? Such accounts may only be a tour into surrogate back regions, 'films within films', manufactured by the subject. The 'intimate' interview has been known to imbricate a desirable fiction; the more gifted the performer, the more anxious the analyst – how can one trust an individual who appears able to effortlessly contrive 'sincerity' on cue, take after take? Allen has constructed a screen 'Woody', an artfully constructed character that obscures as much, if not more, than it clarifies about its real life counterpart.

Movie stars go from role to role, but each role is assimilated to their cumulative presence until, as mature players, they carry with them into every part they play echoes of their own screen pasts: James Stewart, for example, embodies a number of memorable characters, including honest George Bailey from *It's a Wonderful Life*, the courageous little man from *Mr. Smith Goes to Washington*, the eccentric Elmer P. Dowd in *Harvey*, and the brooding photographer from *Rear Window*. Each character is imbued with the star's personality, but each character has in some sense changed that personality; acting is not (or ought not to be) a mechanical activity, but rather a complex *experience* whereby one 'becomes' another for a certain period. After the performance, that other self is not *entirely* erased – a trace remains, a memory of another way of thinking and behaving. As Morin puts it:

> The star is more than an actor incarnating characters, he incarnates *himself in them*, and they become incarnate in him ... Once the film is over, the actor becomes an actor again, the character remains a character, but from their union is born a composite creature who participates in both, envelops them both: the star. (Morin, 1960: 38–9).

It is almost impossible to think of any one of Allen's performances in isolaton from the others, so that one has less impression of invention and impersonation than an idea of a contemporary who has grown older with oneself and has changed in appearance and character only on his own terms. Like a public figure, he has passed into a popular contemporary mythology. However, although Allen has become a universal archetype, he possesses the personality to sustain and develop his image. Whatever Allen's insistence that his screen image is not *him*, he certainly believes he *owns* it: he once tried to sue a look-alike for $7 million, claiming that actor Phil Boroff wrongfully impersonated him in adverts. Allen's lawyers claimed that it caused their client 'distress and harm'. Boroff argued: 'I posed as myself. Can I help looking like Woody Allen? It's genetics or something.'

A star, such as Woody Allen, is someone whom the audience is ready to see doing and thinking certain things, someone who sums up, through a series of cumulative performances, an approach to contemporary reality which the audience can share. A star (in part) is a *social* construction. For successful 'personality stars' there are restrictions on the kind of acting that is possible. Stars must be partially predictable; they can show off different facets of the 'persona' they have come to represent, but they cannot easily abandon the persona altogether. It is the persona, or public face presented in performance, to which the public become attached. When Allen appears in a new movie, the public know what kind of character to expect (perhaps one reason for people's anxiety when confronted with *Interiors*, or *September* or *Another Woman* is the absence of Allen's screen image). He needs the media attention that accompanies the release of each 'Woody Allen movie', but he is careful to protect his work from the more exploitative aspects of the publicity process: he personally selects excerpts from his movies for screening on television review programmes, he chooses restrained, small advertisements, and he only grants interviews to magazines he regards as 'serious'. Allen is deeply suspicious of the media and the cult of celebrity; he regards the recent wave of 'celebrity' magazines as a sign of the trivialization of every cultural figure and event.

Because of modern communication technology, society's capacity to transmit images has grown a thousandfold. Movies, radio, television, cable, magazines, billboards, satellite dish receivers – all facilitating the world-wide diffusion of images. Inspired by the modern notion of universal distribution, enabled by transportation and sophisticated communication and marketing tools, society has developed the ability to create, in Daniel Boorstin's terminology (1961: 47), *well-knownness* – and to blanket the world with it. When Boorstin first proposed his theory of the power of communication technology to inculcate 'artificial fame', the practical knowledge about how it could be accomplished was far less sophisticated than it is today. By the 1980s the manufacturing and marketing of people into celebrities had become an institution fuelled by an army of consultants, mentors, advisers, agents, managers, and promoters. Moreover, an entire industry has evolved whose very existence depends upon producing – and profiting from – highly visible celebrities. It is an industry that virtually all other industries have come to depend upon, because celebrity has developed into an asset with an independent identity and function, a propellant invigorating a wide variety of activities: selling movie tickets; generating charity donations; promoting political and social causes; and selling religion, jeans, food, health club memberships, and virtually everything else. What the star obscures is not so much the performer as the celebrity industry, which has a vested interest in maintaining its own invisibility (Horkheimer, 1979). It is an

industry with few laws mandating what it must tell consumers –
the fans who admire its products. It is this very industry which
Woody Allen abhors so. In movie after movie, he includes some
stinging criticisms of the false values and cynical practices of the
image-makers (the turning point for his characters is often the
moment he decides a career in 'showbusiness' is no longer
tolerable). By assuming such control over the production and
marketing of his work, Allen is able to retain a degree of artistic
and moral independence that is rare in any sphere of modern
culture.

The more successful Allen's movies became, the less free he
was to experiment with his screen persona. The characters
whom stars play in movies are written, directed and acted to stir
deep feelings of recognition within us. The fan, from the Latin
fanaticus (meaning 'someone inspired to frenzy by devotion to a
deity') identifies with these characters and the star who plays
them. Allen's uneasiness when forced to deal with this heightened form of admiration has been evident throughout his career.
Linda Hersch, the teenage president of Allen's first fan club in
the early 1970s, recalls: 'To tell the truth I was in awe of him
most of the time. There was something a bit scary about him to
me at that age, though he was always very courteous and nice;
very considerate even' (in McNight, 1983: 144). Although Allen
has since eschewed the idea of his own fan club, and generally
avoids coming into contact with his admirers, nonetheless the
intensity of his fans' devotion is remarkable. Dee Burton, a New
York psychiatrist, discovered that so many individuals had
unconscious fixations on Woody Allen that she collected several
case-studies in a book entitled *I Dream of Woody*. Burton
discusses the 'Woody' dreams of over one hundred people living
in New York and Los Angeles. In these dreams, Allen emerges as
a larger-than-life hero (or, sometimes, villain). Dispensing bene-
dictions and favours, the dream 'Woody' is sensitive, kind, warm,
and romantic. Some of the male dreamers want to *be* Woody
Allen; many of the women want to be *with* him. Burton notes
that these dreamers are typically drawn to Allen's honesty about
his feelings and anxieties, his willingess to be different, and his
perseverence and determination: 'He's helped men realize they
can express their fears, admit their insecurities about women and
their lack of athletic prowess and still feel good about themselves as men. Men see that women respond positively to the
vulnerability of the Woody film persona and they realize they

can relax and be themselves a little more without fear of seeming weak to the opposite sex' (Burton, 1984: 192). One woman told Burton: 'Woody and I are on the same wavelength. There'd be an equal understanding between us if we ever spoke.' Significantly, the dreaming is thought of as a means of bridging the gap between themselves and the intensely private Allen; many dreamers say their 'dream Woody' is distinct from the real Allen image – 'It may show the way he really is,' they conclude. Allen's screen image is sufficiently sharply defined to polarize audiences into intense admirers or intolerant critics. His characters are endowed with the shades and contradictions of real life, and the sum of all these countenances makes up a kind of portrait of a particular person, at a particular time, in a particular society.

In 1977 Allen became the subject of a syndicated comic strip, 'Inside Woody Allen', read in over sixty countries. Drawn by Stuart Hample and written occasionally by Allen (who monitored the series), the cartoons simplifed the 'Woody' image, focusing on the early *schlemiel* with the identity crisis. The mythological status of 'Woody' was encouraged by this cartoon image, sandwiched as it was between Snoopy and Doonesbury. It was said at the time that Allen hoped this obviously cartoon characterization would help to distance the image from his own personality.

The late 1970s were the years in which Allen's aversion to celebrity was most evident and widely discussed. His devotion to his jazz performances at Michael's Pub means that he never attends the Academy Awards in Hollywood – not even in 1976, when *Annie Hall* won him Oscars for Best Director and Best Original Screenplay. The statues were passed on to Allen's father, and Allen himself is open in expressing his dislike for the Hollywood awards. When asked if he would ever patronize the event, he replied:

No. There'd be no chance in the world. Not out of any big drive or anything. It's just not my interest, or not my bag, not an area I function in. You'll probably think this is being over-cute, but I don't mean it that way – I will probably be playing jazz that night, as I take that very seriously. I've rarely missed an evening in fifteen years. It's one of the pleasures of my life. We play on Monday evenings, and the Academy Awards are Monday evenings. (*Esquire*, April 1987)

The success of *Annie Hall* made Allen into a social phenomenon, crossing over into the newspaper gossip columns, academic reviews, and popular magazine 'profiles'. His private life was now deemed public property, and he became the subject of several hastily-written biographies. Allen spoke of his envy of J.D. Salinger for being able to write without publishing his stories or accepting any interviews: 'But that demands an almost Oriental discipline, of which I'm incapable.'

The shy celebrity, the unassuming public figure, has become something of a minor theme in Allen's work, with the elusive Leonard Zelig and the prickly Alvy Singer, who is so desperate he will admit to any name but his own. In Allen's written essays, identity is a constant problem. His persona never assumes one character name, his narrators rarely name themselves – they are various critics, book reviewers, scholars, or authors. As soon as something familiar and plausible intrudes on one fantasy, Allen constructs another. In the early movies, Allen tries on a number of borrowed personae – Groucho Marx, Bob Hope, Chaplin, Keaton – and what becomes unmistakable is Allen's anxiety about his own elusive identity, and this in turn provided the scheme for *Zelig* (1983). This movie, one of Allen's most original jests, is in the tradition of Max Ophuls and *Lola Montes* (another conundrum about the real and the sham), and to the work of Ophuls' son Marcel, who has specialized in documentaries. For Allen's inspiration here is to tell a story that *looks* like a documentary, a patched-together, black-and-white case-history of the life and times of one Leonard Zelig (Allen), a non-person extraordinary, an actor in history's pageant precisely because he has no reality himself. Zelig is – in exaggerated form – what David Riesman (1976) called the 'other-directed' personality: the personality whose whole being is attuned to catch the signals sent out by the consensus of the community and by the institutional agencies of the culture, to the extent that he is scarcely a self at all but, rather, a reiterated type. Zelig (that surname perhaps a learned play on *seelisch*, meaning 'psychic' or 'spiritual') is the self dissolved into the role-player. Zelig takes on the personality of whomever he happens to be with: a black, an Asian, a Gentile, a Greek, a boxer, psychiatrist, doctor, rabbi. He is glimpsed beside Eugene O'Neill, Scott Fitzgerald, Chaplin, Calvin Coolidge, and Herbert Hoover. He slips, unnoticed, into the cultural spotlight; even Cole Porter tried to write a song about him – 'You're the tops, you're Leonard Zelig' (alas, the reference had to be excised when no word could be found to rhyme with 'Zelig'). Zelig is shown, masked, as Pagliacci; during analysis, he removes his glasses and resembles, for a moment, Stan Laurel. Allen, as Zelig, seems to comment on the clown image. The idea of the mask, the unchanging dominant expression, calls to mind the classic device of actually using a mask, a false face that obliterates the clown's own features. In respect to comedy it provides the Pagliacci pattern, implying that two realities exist in the representation: art and life, laughter and tears. The 'documentary' has Susan Sontag, Saul Bellow, Bruno Bettelheim and Irving Howe reflecting on the prismatic nature of modern celebrity. Zelig's 'condition', of course, is the basis of all Allen's humour – the plight of the little guy, the nobody who wants to be like Bogart or Brando, but is always catching himself out. *Zelig*, then, ostensibly a parodic documentary, is also an amusing and challenging conundrum on other levels, about someone becoming famous as a nonentity, about a movie that poses as the record (a mini-*Citizen Kane*) of a disappearing hero. Allen has declared that the movie does not deal with a character so much as the reactions which society makes to the stimulus which Zelig represents. 'Otherwise,' Allen remarked, 'this would be nothing more than the pathetic tale of a neurotic.' He added: 'I thought that desire not to make waves, carried to an extreme, could have traumatic consequences. It could lead ultimately to fascism.' Zelig tries to acquire what Emerson described as 'the courage to be what you are'. 'Be yourselves,' Zelig tells his audience, but we witness the pressures that threaten to overwhelm him again.

Rosenblum (1979: 263–4) has described his working relationship with Woody Allen, providing one with a fascinating insight into a director whose aloofness appears at once both as weapon and shield:

> With colleagues, silence is his primary tool both for protection and control, and it works an unsettling devastation whether in a room full of smooth executives at United Artists or a group of garrulous production people on the set. ...[D]espite his power, Woody has a fade-into-the-woodwork manner that becomes more and more incongruous the more famous he becomes.

Allen claims that he can only work in a very quiet, studious manner; indeed, he once told Kenneth Tynan (1980) how astonished he was to hear that Mel Brooks could tolerate such a relaxed and happy atmosphere on the set. As Allen's celebrity has increased, and the expectations have grown higher, his insecurity has become a genuine problem. He is very open about his feelings of self-doubt and nervousness in any public place:

> When I was 19 ... I won a Sylvania Award ... and there was a dinner given ... a big honor for me. And I went up to the door and I couldn't go in and I never did go in. I went home, and I felt so relieved when I got home. And I've repeated that problem or syndrome or symptom many times. (McNight, 1983: 193)

Allen's avoidance of public appearances has usually been interpreted by critics as evidence of his contempt for his fans and his fellow celebrities. In fact it is much more a consequence of his personal sense of inadequacy; it is not something Allen is satisfied with, but rather a problem he has struggled with throughout his career. Jack Rollins recalls the traumatic period when Allen made the transition from a humorous writer to a comic performer:

> Woody was a guy who lived purely by his intellect, his brain. He would go into his room, shut out the world and write jokes which he'd conceived in his mind. But getting him to express these was like asking a piano to speak. Even on a personal basis, you know, he found communicating difficult ... He didn't like coming out in the open. Not at all. But I'll tell you that this guy has the guts and courage of a second-storey man. And the self-discipline he has I've never seen in any other human being. (McNight, ibid: 87–1)

Allen's friend and co-star, Tony Roberts, has said:

> He is never 'on' in a room the way most comedians are driven to be. I'm not sure he ever really enjoyed performing his 'act' all that much. But by cloaking himself behind his screen character... or, better still, as the author-director of a carefully controlled progression paraded before an audience without his actual presence even required, he is able to perform his real magic. (Roberts, 1988:52)

Discussing his acting with me, Allen remarked: 'It isn't therapeutic, nor is it all that comfortable for me ... it's okay, I guess.' Acting, far from always 'solving' one's shyness, sometimes only serves to complicate it. Marlon Brando, a performer whom Allen greatly admires, has said: 'I just put on an act sometimes and people think I'm insensitive. Really, it's like a kind of armour because I'm too sensitive. If there are two hundred people in a room and one of them doesn't like me, I've got to get out' (in

Bates, 1986: 186). Allen's character on screen – animated, noisy, argumentative, often charming, sometimes arrogant – may actually *exacerbate* his off-screen introspectiveness. Far from being a simple fiction, his screen appearance may be as 'true' a reflection of his personality as is his private behaviour. What a gifted performer offers to the camera is a buried and sometimes paradoxical part of him or herself; a fragment turned into a whole. As an actor, consciously drawing on his own charac-teristics and memories, Allen must draw on a vast emotional reserve, making himself articulate previously unspoken feelings and summing-up considerable physical expressiveness. As a per-formance it is not so much living a lie as the discovery of another truth, and, for any actor, the experience can be both physically and mentally draining. Away from the camera, away from a role, an actor may sometimes give people the impression of somnambulism. Peter Sellers described his off-screen personality as 'sponge-like', as he spent evenings listening quietly to people, studying their mannerisms and speech patterns. As the British actor Simon Callow observed, recalling his own 'withdrawn' behaviour when engaged in a long-running play: 'The more ex-perience one has, the more one learns to husband energy, to use exactly as much as is needed and no more and above all, to use it on the stage, and nowhere else' (Callow, 1985: 100). It is not clear why Allen should be regarded as more 'real' when he is *not* acting; indeed, Allen's own comments about his need for analysis and his sense of inner turmoil suggest a person very aware of the ambiguous nature of a far from static identity. This indeterminacy is also evident to the audience at an Allen movie; there is no uniquely correct reading. What passes between spectator and image will in detail be idiosyncratic, and, in the fine grain, unique.

A star outside the confines of the movie world is potentially the most stylish and artful of liars. An actor can fool us because we are unsure of how to 'read' someone who makes a living manufacturing believable but fictional selves. We may fear the attenuation of selfhood that results from impersonation, like Rousseau's belief that the actor's art of 'counterfeiting himself, of putting on another character than his own', is an unworthy deception (Rousseau, 1960: 25). Our feelings of insecurity and suspicion are heightened when we hear of actors who have political ambitions (the 'Great Communicator', Ronald Reagan, is the obvious example, with his effortless show of detachment during Irangate). We have a deep-seated suspicion, and fear, of the power of transmutation, the talent to make us believe in the innocence of masks. The star, as an actor, has the ability to do something at once deeply disturbing and very frivolous: to appear, and feel, as other than they are.

If an actor wishes to step away from his or her image and make a sincere statement, a different kind of trust needs to be won. With comedians, the frustration is particularly evident: the American public came to accept Ronald Reagan as their President, but would they have accepted Bob Hope (who was just as politically motivated and ambitious)? Stan Laurel, Jerry Lewis, Charlie Chaplin and many other comedians have been fascinated with 'culture' and self-improvement. The thirst for a more 'civilized' image has often appeared rather pathetic: Chaplin learning his new words each morning, Jerry Lewis reading dictionaries, Bert Lahr building up his vocabulary by doing crossword puzzles, Tony Hancock pursuing Bertrand Russell, and Groucho Marx breathlessly describing his meetings with the Great and the Good. Allen's retiring, rather modest personality means, paradoxically, that his interviews shy away from any controversial subjects, leaving us with a collection of comments about himself and his work:

> I'm not great on interviews. I'm really not. I just hate boring people. Interviewers are busy people: I just don't know why they want to listen to me. I really hate letting people down. I mean ... well, you know, somebody comes here and expects some terrific quote or overview of the world. Like, is Armageddon about to come and if so will it be before or after dinner? Then you get me, standing here like this ... I never was terrific at this sort of thing. (*Hot Press*, 6 May 1988)

Allen avoided political material in his night-club act, but he has made several very public gestures to show his Democratic allegiance, campaigning for Adlai Stevenson, Mayor John Lindsay and Michael Dukakis, opposing American involvement in Vietnam and Latin America, apartheid, and the Reverend Jerry Falwell's Moral Majority movement. Indeed, Allen managed something of a first by including a pre-Watergate joke in *Sleeper* about Richard Nixon being written out of the history books for doing 'something really terrible'. However, when Allen tried to use his comedy as political satire, he seemed to lose all subtlety and originality. His PBS tv special *The Politics of Woody Allen* (1970), which has never been seen by a general audience, featured a very half-hearted spoof on Harvey Wallinger

(Kissinger) and Richard Dixon (Nixon):

If you want something done, you have to be in good with Harvey. If Mrs Dixon wants to kiss her husband, she has to kiss Harvey first ... Attorney General John Mitchell has many ideas for strengthening the country's law-enforcement methods and is hampered only by lack of funds and the Constitution.

Until fairly late in his career, Allen found it almost impossible to combine his serious concerns with his comedy techniques. The isolated, iconoclastic wisecrack is Allen's most successful weapon against the pompous and the self-righteous (on one memorable occasion during a television special he asked Billy Graham which was his favourite out of the Ten Commandments). In one of his *New Yorker* pieces, Allen imagines a debate about an Italian restaurant carried out in the style of the letters column of the *New York Review of Books*, and the lit-crit name dropping is hilarious: 'As Hannah Arendt once told me,' one letter goes, the restaurant's prices are 'reasonable without being historically inevitable'. Certainly his most notable 'political' jokes have been kept quite wilfully obscure. For example, many New York Jews argue that the most memorable political joke is the line in Allen's *Sleeper* about how the Third World War broke out when a madman named Albert Shanker got his hands on an atomic bomb (Shanker was the volatile and controversial head of New York's teachers' union during the 1960s).

The Austrian satirist Karl Kraus once said, 'If I must choose the lesser of two evils, I will choose neither.' Woody Allen undoubtedly sympathizes. The unflinching integrity of his heroes leads them to break the chain of complicity and rebel against the falseness and hypocrisy of contemporary society. 'Is that all there is?' is the invariable *envoi*. Having broken out of bad faith, the Allen hero finds himself at a nodal point, a crossroads, inviting that imaginative leap into the unknown that both excites and unnerves: Should Alvy marry Annie? Should Isaac trust Tracy? Should the *Purple Rose of Cairo* fan choose the actor or the role? The anxiety, and exhilaration, of the freedom to choose is something Allen's hero craves. The old world, the ordered world, the world of orders, has dissolved, leaving ambiguity – questions where once there were only answers. Enlightenment begins anew, this time on Allen's own terms. As Mickey Sachs says in *Hannah and Her Sisters*, 'I gotta get some answers.' What Mickey discovers is that the bedrock of all ideas is faith, and nothing 'harder' or more telling than this can help us to 'prove' that we are loved or needed or cared about. 'Mr. Big' (1975) is a short story in which Allen satirizes the disenchanted thinker, the sceptic who seeks certainty beyond belief. A Philosophy major at Vassar has to write a paper on Western religion, so she hires a private eye to find God for her. 'All the other kids in the course will hand in speculative papers. But I want to *know*. Professor Grebanier said if anyone finds out for sure, they're a cinch to pass the course!' The private eye only discovers that the student has 'fixed' the result, God is found dead, and the metaphysical explorations of past centuries come to resemble a *film noir* plot:

> You got rid of Socrates easy enough, but Descartes takes over, so you use Spinoza to get rid of Descartes, but when Kant doesn't come through you have to get rid of him too ... You made mincemeat out of Leibniz, but that wasn't good enough for you because you knew if anybody believed Pascal you were dead, so he had to be gotten rid of too, but that's where you made your mistake because you trusted Martin Buber. Except, sugar, he was soft. He believed in God, so you had to get rid of God yourself. (Allen, 1975: 149–50)

The lesson is: 'When the Supreme Being gets knocked off, *somebody's* got to take the rap.' Those who try to deny ambiguity, suggests Allen, will be forced to embrace either nihilism or dogmatism. All of Allen's heroes, especially from *Manhattan*'s Isaac Davies onwards, are moved to come to terms with the position expressed, memorably, by Wittgenstein (1968: 217): 'If I have exhausted the justifications I have reached bedrock, and my spade is turned. Then I am inclined to say: "This is simply what I do" '. Despite his efforts to unravel and disentangle that skein of anxieties we feel wrinkling the surface of our convictions, the Allen hero eventually comes to accept the uncertainty of life, and to struggle against any attempt to enforce any dogma. 'Hey,' he says, '*trust* me!'

In the mid-1970s, Allen decided to register his opposition to any form of witchhunt in the movie industry by agreeing to star in Martin Ritt's *The Front* (1976). It was a sensible and rather courageous move by Allen, stepping outside the limitations of his comic, personalized work and appearing in a movie written and directed by other people. *The Front* is set in the early 1950s, with McCarthyism taking hold of Hollywood. Its main characters are several black-listed writers, comedian Hecky Brown (Zero Mostel), a well-meaning but spineless TV producer (Herschel

Bernardi), his idealistic assistant Florence (Andrea Marcovicci), and 'front', Howard Prince (Woody Allen). Howard works as a night cashier in a bar; he is an under-achiever who lives from day to day, optimistic but lethargic, ambitious but constantly in debt. His immediate responses are rarely subtle: 'I know some people ... well, they're not exactly people, but for 50 bucks or so they'll break a few legs ...'. His writer friend, Alfred Miller (Michael Murphy), is blacklisted, and he asks Howard to act as a 'front' (e.g. putting his name to scripts Alfred cannot otherwise get accepted). Welcoming this opportunity simultaneously to help an old friend *and* acquire some lucrative profits, Howard readily agrees, as he will subsequently agree to front for several of Alfred's friends. He takes 10 per cent of their earnings and 100 per cent of their professional reputations. Howard makes it clear that he does not wish to know about these writers' political affiliations. However, after several scripts have been produced on television, 'Howard Prince' becomes respected as a humane and talented dramatist, and attracts the admiration of Florence. She falls in love with a false impression of Howard Prince the writer, and thus is horrified when he continues to wallow in his success while the most gifted network employees are placed on the blacklist. Inevitably, Howard himself is eventually called for routine scrutiny by the House on Un-American Affairs Committee. After the shock of Hecky Brown's suicide, and encouraged by Florence, Howard decides to take a stand and defy the Committee. Howard is the uninvolved Everyman who eventually is awakened by the murderous obscenity of the blacklist.

The Front was made by people who were themselves blacklisted twenty-five years earlier: as the final credits roll, they not only identify the producer, director, writer and actors, but also list the year in which each was blacklisted. Even in the 1970s, it was not a movie the Hollywood establishment wanted to see made, and some subtle pressures were placed on all concerned to drop the project. Allen's involvement was the stimulus the movie needed, and he made it clear that his decision was a gesture of solidarity with the victims of McCarthyism:

> I remember hearing about blacklisting when I was in public school, not really understanding the implications of it all. But in retrospect, what I know now historically, it was a horrible time. The script expresses me politically even though I didn't write it.

'I didn't look at *The Front* as my chance to play *Hamlet*,' he added. 'The reason I did *The Front* was that the subject was worthwhile.' The movie stresses the need for personal and political commitment in a time of social unrest: 'You know you're always looking for a middle you can dance around,' Alfred tells Howard, 'this time there's no middle.' When Howard finally gets to testify, he says what many blacklisted artists had longed to say to McCarthy's henchmen: 'Fellas, I don't recognize the right of this committee to ask me these kinds of questions... And furthermore, you can all go fuck yourselves.'

Although *The Front* is a disappointing movie (overlong, poorly paced and, in tone, preaching to the converted), Allen's acting is remarkably impressive. Many of Howard Prince's best lines are delivered with such perfect timing it is impossible to imagine them coming from anyone but Allen: 'Buy them off,' he says of the witchhunters, 'How expensive can they be? I mean, they're just Congressmen.' Florence tells him he writes about 'people': 'Well,' he replies, 'I feel if you're going to write about human beings, you may as well make them people.' When Howard, full of self-confidence, decides to give his writers a lecture on the art of drama, he stresses, 'The key word here is *substance*.' Flirting with Florence, he says: 'In my family, the biggest sin was to buy retail.' Allen needed to find ways of making his distinctive screen persona illuminate the character of Howard Prince, rather than submerging his identity beneath the written role, because the movie needed his star profile to attract an audience. The delicate balance between Allen as celebrity presence and Allen as actor was achieved with considerable alacrity by someone who had never before appeared in someone else's narrative. Screenwriter Walter Bernstein remarked: 'It would be very tough for Woody to act in a completely serious film ... the audience comes prepared to see WOODY, and they have a response to *him*.' Bernstein's comment, although to some extent correct, misses the uncharacteristic aspects of Allen's portrayal of Howard Prince: the contrast with the clever, genuinely gifted Alvy Singer (Allen's other movie persona of 1976) is considerable – particularly in a scene that has a bewildered Howard slumped over a typewriter, (arms wrapped around it as though it were an art deco radiator), unable to think of a single word and wondering how he can escape being uncovered as the imposter he is.

The Front managed to combine its indictment of McCarthyism with a more subtle appreciation of the fact that so many of those blacklisted were Jewish. Howard Prince has more than purely political reasons for opposing the witchhunt. 'The Jew,' as George Steiner put it, 'is a living reproach'. One of the central themes in the culture of the 1970s was the rehabilitation of ethnic memory and history as a vital part of personal identity, with modernists acknowledging that such a recovery was essential to the depth and fullness of self that modern life opens up and promises to all. Allen's portrayal of such characters as Howard Prince and Alvy Singer highlighted the trend in 1970s cinema toward greater self-consciousness, with movies and characters being tailored for specific audiences (such as the 'black heroes' following *Shaft*, or the more liberal treatment of Jewish characters in such movies as *The Heartbreak Kid*). 'I'm not a "Jewish" comedian,' Allen insists; he resents the imposition of such an 'ethnic' label, a safe category for his highly individualistic personality. However, his Jewishness *is* indubitably an essential aspect of his personality and a particularly sharp edge to his wit. 'For every ten Jews who suffer and complain,' goes the proverb, 'God creates an eleventh to make them laugh.' Certainly when Allen *does* draw upon his Jewish background, the results are rarely less than striking: 'The concentration camp is the real test. There are some who betray their best friends, and there are others who behave with incredible courage.' Allen is *not* an uncomplicatedly 'ethnic' artist; indeed, his non-denominational character has often displeased orthodox and practising Jews, and the biting references here and there in his work have often aroused resentment and earned him the odd epithet, 'Jewish anti-Semite'. In 1988 this controversial aspect to his position on Jewish affairs became particularly pronounced when Allen wrote a letter to the *New York Times*, criticizing Israel's policies towards the Palestinians in the Gaza Strip and on the West Bank. New York's right-wing Jews were outraged that Allen's liberal Jewish voice should have spoken out on such a sensitive issue. One Jewish militant demanded to know why Allen had not used his talents to indict the Austrian leader Kurt Waldheim. Another claimed that Allen was intent on somehow minimizing the Holocaust by his carefully considered words of warning to Tel Aviv. Allen loathes being entangled in political controversy, but he felt that he had no alternative but to speak out on this issue. The Middle East and what can be done to resolve its crisis became his major concern as the 1980s drew to a close, and he started using his authority and prestige to try and encourage such a resolution. It was an eminently courageous move by Allen, and one that did nothing to make his work any easier; the US movie industry is conservative and, traditionally, controlled by people sympathetic to Israel. Allen was one of the few celebrities who believed it was necessary to make a public statement about the Israeli government's conduct: 'All those beatings, those shootings. What are people , who have suffered so much, doing all that for?' he asked. The question was asked with great dignity, showing a man whose compassion has left him highly sensitive to all forms of injustice.

In *Annie Hall*, Alvy Singer is haunted by Auschwitz: his frequent, ritualistic visits to *The Sorrow and the Pity* are doomed attempts at some kind of absolution. Comedy is not the place to discuss the Holocaust, but the Holocaust has come to haunt comedy; after the death camps there are at least six million reasons not to laugh anymore, and at least six million reasons to try and laugh again. Jewish humour, in particular, has acquired a particularly ironic quality in the post-war years, reflecting the knowledge that laughter (although necessary) has to coexist with the saddest, the most hellish of memories. There is a tremendous tension in contemporary Jewish humorous writing between the authors and their Jewish identity, and between their defiant, isolated intellectual protagonists and the indelible ethos of the part-nurturing, part-negating Jewish community in which they grew up. Woody Allen, despite his claims about the 'irrelevance' of his background, is clearly conducting an ongoing dialogue with his Jewishness as a state of mind and a way of life. He draws much of his strength from an irritable energy of dissent and an artistically vigorous view of Jewish metaphysical perception, which attempts to pursue connectedness and moral responsibility in a world that insists either on bland incorporation into society or else self-preservation. 'His lack of education,' said Allen of a notorious racist, 'is more than compensated for by his keenly developed moral bankruptcy'. For Allen's characters, opposition to the 'banalization of evil' is probably *the* essential moral stand; those people who are content to live in a kind of ethical numbness are incomprehensible to the Allen hero. Allen's heroes *de*banalize evil; evil exists to them, people are again held responsible for their actions, and little Alvy Singer and Mickey Sachs walk around saying to people, 'How on earth could people have done such things?' This capacity for shock is one of the most admirable qualities in the Allen hero. In *Hannah and Her Sisters*, Mickey Sachs asks his parents, 'But if there's a God, then wh-why is there so much evil in the world? Just on a simplistic level. Why-why were there Nazis?' 'Tell him Max,' shouts his mother (who shuts herself away, both mentally and physically, when confronted by such questions). 'How the hell do I know why there were Nazis?' mutters the father. 'I don't even know how the can opener works.' In his short story, 'Remembering Needleman' (1981) Allen satirizes an academic (playfully reminiscent of Martin Heidegger) who writes a cut-out book on the Holocaust: 'Needleman had always been obsessed by the problem of evil and argued quite eloquently that true evil was only possible if its perpetrator was named Blackie or Pete.' Needleman finally decides that the only thing that exists is 'his IOU to the bank for six million marks' – this precise sum marks Needleman's irresponsibility. The evasiveness and flabby immorality of those former Nazis (such as Albert Speer) who sought to rewrite their past are the target of Allen's most open contempt. 'The Schmeed Memoirs' (Allen, 1975) features the pathetic apologies of Hitler's former barber: 'I did not know that Hitler was a Nazi. The truth was that for years I thought he worked for the phone company. When I finally did find out what a monster he was, it was too late to do anything ... I did contemplate loosening the Fuhrer's neck-napkin and allowing some tiny hairs to get down his back, but at the last minute my nerve failed me.'

The references Allen's own movie personae make about Adolf Hitler always have a very poignant quality about them, with Allen's delivery acquiring a noticeably more passionate, more biting tone. It is immediately following Annie Hall's final rejection of Alvy Singer that he comes to think of Hitler; Annie says that she must go with Tony Lacey to the Grammy Awards, and Alvy explodes with anger – 'Awards! They do nothing but give out awards! I can't believe it. Greatest fascist dictator, Adolf Hitler!' Fame triumphs over content, and Alvy rebels. In his stand-up routine, Allen recalls a wife with Nazi recipes who cooks him 'Chicken Himmler' for dinner, and he refers to a *very* reformed rabbi ... a Nazi'. In *Play It Again, Sam* Allen's wife leaves him for 'a Nazi', and in *Bananas* Fielding Mellish complains that his lover is leaving him for 'a leader ... Hitler'. Alvy Singer cannot feel safe anywhere: there are, he suspects, Nazi record salesmen, television producers, and policemen. In *Manhattan*, a group of Gentile pseudo-intellectuals condescendingly advise Isaac that a satirical piece in the *New York Times* is the most effective way to counter anti-semitism; Isaac replies, 'We-e-elll, a satirical piece in the *Times* is one thing, but bricks and baseball bats really get right to the point ... true physical force is always better with Nazis, why, because it's hard to satirize a guy with shiny boots on.' He confides to his friend: 'There must be something wrong with me, because I've never had a relationship with a woman that's lasted longer than the one Hitler had with Eva Braun.' In *Stardust Memories*, when Sandy Bates is asked by a policeman to explain why he keeps a gun in his car, he says:

> Yeah, that's mine ... I carry a pistol ... it's ... uh ... I've a ... thing about Nazis. It's a little paranoid weakness that I have ... I-I don't need a permit. I never shoot the gun or anything ... It's strictly a Nazi thing.

In *Hannah and Her Sisters*, Mickey concludes a disastrous evening with Holly by saying: 'I had a great time tonight, really. It was like the Nuremberg Trials.' The ascetic artist, Frederick, tells his lover:

> You missed a very dull TV show about Auschwitz. More gruesome film clips ... and more puzzled intellectuals declaring their mystification over the systematic murder of millions ... The reason why they could never answer the question 'How could it possibly happen?' is that it's the wrong question. Given what people are, the question is 'Why doesn't it happen more often?'

The monologue is unsettling, not just for the sharpness of the views, but also for the detached manner in which they are expressed. Allen agrees with Frederick's argument, but abhors the mundane manner in which it is articulated; fascism has become one more topic to be discussed on TV chat shows, 'consumed' like the sandwich Frederick munches at. Fascism is the spectre that haunts Allen's humour, and understandably so. As Adorno (1978: 49) has written: 'The expression of history in things is no other than that of past torment.' Against the one-dimensionality of *kitsch* culture, the passivity of modern representations of tragedy, the moral blindness of much 'comedy' *per se*, Allen repeatedly brings one back to an historical, moral appreciation of local indignities. Sometimes this tactic is clumsily executed, but it is always done with feeling. Mel Brooks has also commented on comedy's 'black spot', with his 'Springtime for Hitler' from *The Producers* and his remake of Lubitsch's courageous *To Be or Not to Be*; however, when Brooks makes his references to fascism and its inhumanity, the story pauses – the comment is made *ex cathedra*. When Woody Allen invokes the memory of the Holocaust, life, on the contrary, goes on; the very *impotence* of his remarks (nobody takes much notice of them) shows up the seriousness of the recent banalization of horror. *This* memory, in fact, is too horrible to occur occasionally; on the contrary, it is ever-present, it is in the present, the present is a different place for its presence. Thoughts of the Holocaust follow one into the supermarket, the office, the bathroom, the bedroom – it is this coexistence, of the tragic with the routine, that Allen works to show up. The offensively smug intellectuals in *Manhattan* are not disturbed in the least by Isaac's insistence that Jews are *not* adequately protected by a newspaper column (or, implicitly, by a Woody Allen movie). The hurt that occasionally reveals itself in these comments from Allen is both memorable and moving; they are glimpses of wounds, reminders of the fact that there is nothing purely or simply 'funny' anymore. As Allen suggests in *Stardust Memories*, surely only alien beings could seriously expect him to content himself with his 'early, funny films'.

If serious thoughts and themes become muted within a comedic form, one might either move to tragedy, or redefine the boundaries of comedy. Allen told *Esquire* magazine:

> I would like to make both kinds of films, serious films and comic films. *Interiors* was my first attempt at a serious film, and I plunged right in there. I think I made a number of mistakes in it, as I did, though they're less apparent, in my comic films ... When I first started making films, I was concentrating on getting laughs exclusively and trying to make laugh-machine films. And then over the years – well, *Annie Hall* was the first one where I said to my manager, 'I'm not going to go for one crazy laugh after another, but modify it, and see if I can get the audience interested in the people' ... I don't dislike comedy. People think that because you don't want to do it all the time, you have contempt for it. But it can be a dead end for a person ... It's a very safe thing to get into that relationship with an audience where they depend on you for something and you fulfill it all the time ... You want your films to be successful, but every now and then, when one doesn't work at all, it's a sign of life. (April 1987).

This is one of Allen's most mature accounts of his own position; he has not always been so thoughtful. The example set by Chaplin, who took chances and experimented (with *A Woman of Paris*, a dramatic movie, the social commentary of *Modern Times*, and

the clumsy satire of *The Great Director*), is one Allen refers to in
many interviews. *City Lights*, with its blend of ironic observation
and pathos, has been a clear influence on Allen's later movies.
'Maybe I'll get lucky,' he says, 'and come up with a *Bicycle Thief*
or something one day'. Allen's dissatisfaction with the constraints
imposed on him by the comedy genre is, to some extent, a
consequence of a more profound concern with the most urgent
and disturbing issues of his society. Alvy Singer says, near the
close of *Annie Hall*, 'I can't enjoy anything unless I ... unless
everybody is. I-you know, if one guy is starving someplace,
that's...you know, I-I ... it puts a crimp in my evening.' If
anything, the offscreen Allen is far *more* anxious and prone to
depression. There is an anecdote about a man who seeks help
from a psychiatrist, pleading for a solution to his terrible melancholy: the psychiatrist reassures him – 'My friend, go to see the
Great Grimaldi, the funniest clown alive, and you will be cured
through laughter.' 'But I *am* the Great Grimaldi...'. Allen has
never been entirely comfortable with comedy: he cares too much
about the great problems of life ever to simply mock them. He is
the intellectual whose intellect only gives him reason to mistrust
himself. His humour satirizes the pretentious ways in which
some people may discuss mortality, inequality, intolerance or the
unpredictability of romantic love; he is appalled when it is said
(as it frequently is) that he 'jokes' about these issues themselves.

There is a scene in *Manhattan* (perhaps the first Allen movie to
transcend the categories of 'comedy' and 'drama') where Isaac
(Allen) is in a deserted classroom with his old friend Yale. Yale
has told Ike that he has secretly been having an affair with the
women he loves. Isaac's reaction includes some of the views one
associates with Allen: a demand for sincerity and personal
integrity, a loathing of immorality and hypocrisy, and an uncompromising determination to refuse the lesser of two evils:

You're not honest with yourself. You talk about ... you wanna write a
book, but-but, in the end, you'd rather buy the Porsche, you know, or
you cheat a little bit on Emily, and you play around the truth a little
with me, and-and the next thing you know, you're in front of a Senate
committee and you're naming names! ... What are future generations
gonna say about us? My God! He [*points to a skeleton*] You know,
someday we're gonna-we're gonna be like him! I mean, y-y-y-you
know – well, he was probably one of the beautiful people. He was
probably dancing and playing tennis and everything. And-and-and
now – well, this is what happens to us! You know, uh, it's very

important to have ... some kind of personal integrity. Y-you know, I'll-I'll be hanging in a classroom one day. And-and I wanna make sure when I ... thin out that I'm w-w-well thought of.

Allen's most 'serious' comedies are subtle studies of human beings struggling to control their own psyches, their own slippery sense of self amidst the babble of modern existence. Self-consciousness and insecurity are the novel features of Allen's comic personality, providing depth to the humour, forcing it into the audience's world. Groucho Marx, for example, never examines his own character: he is the outsider, the asocial figure who remarks on everyone else. 'How did I get in this lousy movie?' he sometimes mumbles as he looks out at us; he is not even responsible for his own movie, and this irresponsibility is part of his appeal – but it has its limitations. Allen, in a radically new manner, includes *himself* in the comedy: whatever is absurd is also absurd for him (and, by implication, for us). Where Groucho plays, Allen probes: Groucho, like Olivier, deals in illusion; Allen, like Brando, deals in life.

It is important to respect Allen's seriousness. He is a master of the comic touch, he knows how to catch the humorous light as it shines on the surface of a saturnine being, but he *never* simply translates misery into amusement. An example is the insecurity felt by Alvy Singer in *Annie Hall*: he is presented in a fairly comic light as he worries about anti-semitism, academic insularity, television, decadence, drugs, the fading of love, and so on. Allen acknowledges the funny side of the character's behaviour, yet this, he insists, is but one perspective amongst several: 'I think the character's complaints are all completely legitimate. The degree to which he obsesses over them in the movie gets to be seen as neurotic, but to me that's not neurotic' (Rosenblum and Karen, 1979: 275). A tension emerged after *Annie Hall*, with Allen seemingly torn between the challenge of combining comedy with the dramatic, of transcending the industrial constraints of the comic genre, and the seductiveness of making 'serious' movies. In a perverse way, *Annie Hall* was such a success that it upset Allen's plans. He told Robert Benayoun (1968: 157):

it's very hard to be as serious as you want to be within a comic film. People only see the laughter and don't remember the rest – they exit laughing and ignore the content. But if you do a completely serious film, you don't have to hide behind your laughs; it becomes a totally different experience.

A similar reaction from Allen was recorded after the popularity of *Hannah and Her Sisters*; in a BBC TV interview (13 November 1987) he explained:

> I wanted *Hannah* to be a melancholy film for the most part. But for some reason, incompetence in the directing or the writing or something, the emphasis shifted so that it was perceived by audiences as more up and optimistic than I had intended. And consequently was very popular.

Interestingly, Allen tends to discuss his work in terms of *consumption* rather than production. He has made the notorious comment: 'There is something second-rate about comedy. It's like eating ice-cream all the time; after a while you need to take in something more solid.' 'Serious' drama represents the great challenge for Allen. His ability to inflect the everyday event with a humorous tone is now so sharp, so swift, he regards it as instinctive. As Allen told Jacobs (1982: 117–18):

> What so many people don't understand is that comedy is impossible if you can't do it, but it's no big deal if you can – it's just good luck. I can sit down in an afternoon and do a couple of pages for the *New Yorker* and start a script and write some jokes. If I'm on the film set and I have to revise a scene to make it funny, that's easy for me. But revising *Interiors* was very, very difficult. I was in completely unfamiliar waters.

Jerry Lewis reacted against comedy by making an awkward, self-conscious movie about the concentration camps (*The Day the Clown Cried*); Allen sometimes seems to crave the supposedly uncomplicated *gravitas* of the 'serious' movie. 'Popular' carries negative connotations when spoken by Allen: 'There does seem to be this correlation generally between this enormous popularity and a quality of movie I wouldn't want to make' (*Esquire*, April 1987).

Even as Allen's first major success, *Annie Hall*, was about to be released, he told Douglas Brode (1986: 179) that his *next* movie would be 'a totally serious one, that I won't appear in. My presence is so completely associated with comedy that when the audience sees me, they might think it's a sign for them to begin laughing.' In another comment which is especially intriguing for its use, yet again, of the food analogy, Allen said:

'Comedy just pokes at problems, rarely confronts them squarely. Drama is like a plate of meat and potatoes, comedy is rather the dessert, a bit like meringue.' This is an extraordinary *non sequitur*: for Allen's argument to be convincing one would be obliged to define 'comedy' in such banausic terms that it would be synonymous with slapstick. The either/or dichotomy of 'funny' *or* 'serious', useless *or* useful, is a suffocating one for a genuinely mature artist. Allen's reasoning is as follows:

1 with serious, dramatic works, we put ourselves in the mood to explore only strongly meaningful linkages between the trains of association emanating from the poles of each incongruity;
2 with comedy, on the contrary, the incongruities encourage us to explore the trains of association not in search of truth, but pleasure;
3 comedy, and the frame of mind it encourages, are a mockery of the whole costly process whereby we experience and interpret reality and pay for our knowledge and mastery. Moreover, so this argument goes, we are encouraged to feel no guilt for our killing, because the humorous context tells us it was all a joke.

Allen's argument is needlessly exclusive. His view of 'serious' work as unfunny would struggle to comprehend the humour in Beckett's *Waiting for Godot*, or Ionesco's *The Lesson*, or Welles' *Citizen Kane*, to say nothing of the work of Lichtenberg, Nietzsche, Karl Kraus or Kafka. Allen seems unwilling even to consider any alternative view: his dogmatic insistence on the rigid boundaries of each category is not only unrealistic but is also something he, above all others, has contradicted in such works as *Manhattan* and *Hannah and Her Sisters* – movies which move in and out of both comic and dramatic perspectives with unprecedented subtlety and sophistication. Struggle as Allen may, he cannot maintain his view of drama as more 'true to life' than comedy: life is both comic and tragic, it combines the two in an inseparable unity. For Allen to stand guard at the gates of his art, denying entry to anything 'comic', is tantamount to a kind of self-inflicted masochism.

Interiors was, in Allen's own words, his first attempt to 'sit at the grown-ups' table' and make a 'serious' (i.e. non-comic) movie. 'I have always felt tragedy was the highest form,' he said at the time. 'With comedy you can buy yourself out of the problems of life and diffuse them. In tragedy, you must confront them and it is painful.' *Interiors* is intense chamber-drama, an examination of family breakdown. The three sisters are struggling for personal fulfilment, with varying degrees of success: one is an actor, one is a writer, and the other is a brilliant young person with no easily categorized talent. This sister, special without being specialized, is ultimately the pivotal character in the narrative. Allen seems especially drawn to the plight of a person who has the ambitions and *Angst* of an artist but, paradoxically, none of the recognized creative skills. One may recall Allen's own remark: 'Art doesn't save you. The sense of being immortal through your work is as illusory as the Catholic idea of an afterlife and a heaven.' The movie received some of its best reviews in Europe, but in the US it was savaged as both 'pretentious' and 'ponderous'. Allen responded with the following argument:

> One of the criticisms of *Interiors* was that all serious works that are worth anything have humour in them as well: they're leavened by wit. But that's simply not true. Bergman's *Persona* is a truly great film, and there's not a comic moment in it. So this was, I thought, a clichéd phrase which sounded meaningful, but in fact wasn't. (Jacobs, 1982: 127).

This remark by Allen sounds extraordinarily defensive and needlessly accommodating. In his desire to 'eat at the grown-ups' table', Allen seems determined to preserve a crude separation between 'solid' and 'light', 'serious' and 'comic'. To claim that *anything* substantial and true to life is therefore devoid of any humour is either a wild lapse of judgement or an attempt to be as perverse as possible. When Allen is in this frame of mind he is marked by a spirit of denial, a stubborn insistence on a non-ambiguous, one-dimensional conception of drama. *Interiors* is, at times, a moving work, but it could have achieved considerably more, on several levels, if Allen had not been carefully avoiding certain ironies like a former alcoholic avoids alcohol.

Manhattan was introduced with Allen's comment that 'It's like a mixture of what I was trying to do with *Annie Hall* and *Interiors*.' He added that the movie concentrated upon 'the problem of trying to live a decent life amidst all the junk of contemporary culture'. In the constantly changing city of New York, where fads fade before many people have even heard of them, where 'relationships' undergo analysis from the moment they are made, Allen's character is trying to hold onto a sense of self, of truth, of personal and social worth. Whilst his intellectual friends compile their 'Academy of the Overrated', Allen tries to list his 'things that make life worthwhile'. He comments at one point: 'People in Manhattan are constantly creating these unnecessary neurotic problems for themselves because it keeps them from dealing with the terrible, unsolvable problems of the universe.' It is a tendency which Allen is known to sympathize with; in 1987 he told an interviewer:

> I've always felt if one can arrange one's life so that one can obsess about small things, it keeps you from obsessing about the really big things. If you obsess about the big things, you are impotent and frightened, because there's nothing you can do about ageing and death. But the little things you can spend days obsessing about. (*Rolling Stone*, 9 April 1987)

Nothing is allowed to undermine the careful constructions in Woody Allen's narrative. He controls his movies with a firmness of grip reminiscent of Fritz Lang or F.W. Murnau. Gene Wilder, who worked with Allen on *Everything You Always Wanted to Know About Sex...*, has stressed the systematic nature of Allen's approach:

> Working with Woody is what it must be like to work with Ingmar Bergman. It's all very hushed ... The way Woody makes a movie, it's as if he was lighting ten thousand safety matches to illuminate a city. Each of them is a little epiphany, topical, ethical, or political. (Tynan, 1980: 259)

Woody Allen is not averse to giving interviewers comments which contribute to his image as a highly-disciplined movie-maker who believes that, with a little more or a little less light, or better acting, or different locations, he still might succeed in translating the *written* story into its accurate visual counterpart. Allen cannot bear to watch his own movies; he says that they fall so short of his original ideas. One might compare this experience to the one of the movie-goer in *The Purple Rose of Cairo* who longs for the star to step off the screen and into her life: Allen's increasingly meticulous weaving of his web, in which the reality of his script will be caught, is equally hopeless. In practice, Allen has transcended his scepticism and directed some superb movies, works which could only be imagined *as* movies (such as *The Purple Rose of Cairo* or, indeed, *Annie Hall*). In his own mind, he seems unaware or unwilling to acknowledge how gifted he is.

'None of my movies has been very enjoyable experiences,' said Allen. He claims that his 'least unsuccessful' work has been most poorly received. He was referring to his belief that only *Stardust Memories* – his least popular movie with critics and public alike – is even *near* to being satisfactory. Is this false modesty or genuine diffidence? He said that *Stardust Memories* was intended as a parody of celebrity 'social awareness' (thus reminiscent of Preston Sturges' *Sullivan's Travels*) rather than as a critique of fandom:

> I caught a lot of flak on that picture. I think that was unjustified. Some people came away saying that I had contempt for my audience. That was not true. I never had contempt for my audience; if I had contempt for an audience, I'd be too smart to put it in a picture. I'd grouse about it at home. I've always felt that the audience was at the least equal to me or more. I've always tried to play *up* to the audience. (*Esquire*, April 1987)

Sullivan's Travels (1941) features a movie director who wants to make a 'significant', socially conscious film, *Oh Brother, Where Art Thou?*, and his producers, who want to keep him making the escapist fluff at which he excels, such as *Ants in Your Pants of 1941* or *Hey! Hey! In the Hayloft*. Sullivan rebels, and goes off to film 'real people' with serious problems. Eventually, through a series of bizarre accidents, Sullivan winds up truly wretched and helpless, an inmate of a brutal Southern prison. In the midst of his misery, he goes to the movies; the prisoners are guests of a black congregation on its movie night. The down-trodden prisoners and the poverty-stricken blacks are suddenly laughing at a Walt Disney cartoon. Sullivan concludes (after he gets out of prison just as bizarrely as he got in) that *Oh, Brother, Where Art Thou?* is not worth making (at least not by *him*). He directly proclaims, 'There's a lot to be said for making people laugh. That's all some people have. It isn't much, but it's better than nothing in this cockeyed caravan.' Allen insists that he had no knowledge of this movie when he made *Stardust Memories*, but the sentiment it expresses is echoed in many of Allen's later movies. In *Hannah and Her Sisters*, the suicidal Mickey Sachs is 'saved' after watching a Marx Brothers movie. In *Stardust Memories*, there is a similar tension between the comic with the serious concerns and the producers and fans with the need for comedy. However, unlike *Sullivan's Travels*, there is no simple closure, no suggestion that the director will settle for the role set out for him. Another movie with similar themes to *Stardust Memories*, Fellini's *8½*, told of the contradictory, disorderly, Dionysian aspects of creation. The problem afflicting Allen's Sandy Bates is, however, more prosaic than the one from which Marcello suffers. Bates does not doubt for one moment his own ability to create; it is simply that he gets exasperated when he is told that his creative ability was greater when he was a comedian. The movie explores *movies*: successful director Sandy Bates suddenly realizes the 'bad faith' involved in 'making stupid movies', and he resolves to do something more meaningful and helpful to others. He is at the centre of an industrial structure which is imprisoning him, closing him off from everything except the suffocating sycophancy of his producers, co-stars, and fans. When he finds an opportunity to escape from the movie set it is only in order to attend a movie convention dedicated to his own *oeuvre*. His lovers are movie actresses, his dreams are like movies, his movies are dream-like, his critics and colleagues are keen to categorize him according to old movie traditions. This character is desperate to find a way out to the other side of the screen, but (unlike *The Purple Rose of Cairo*) no such escape is available. Why, everyone asks him, can he not be content with making people laugh, as in his early *funny* films?

Whereas *Manhattan* presented the central character's liberal views in a fairly sympathetic manner, *Stardust Memories* questions the moral stance of the bourgeois intellectual whose sensitivity to human suffering is often matched only by his inability to alleviate any of it. Forgiveness is rarely found in this world, for any of the characters. 'I'm doing this piece on the shallow indifference of wealthy celebrities,' says a student, 'and I'd like to include you in my piece.' In Sandy Bates' words, his 'metaphor for life is a concentration camp'. Wit has rarely been closer in spirit to self-disgust. If there is one consistent refrain in this movie, it is that, for Woody Allen, love is never easy (yet it has never been needed more urgently).

September (1987) showed that Allen learned from some of his mistakes with *Interiors* and produced a much more balanced, mature dramatic work that underlined how much he has outgrown his own 'serious'/'funny' dichotomy. The story takes place at the end of summer, and a group of characters – all complaining about loss and failure – prepare to leave Vermont and return to the city. Lane (Mia Farrow) has done nothing for two years but nurse a broken heart and recuperate from a nervous breakdown.

Howard (Denholm Elliott) is a lonely widower who is hopelessly in love with her. Lane is obsessed with Peter (Sam Waterston), who has taken the summer off from a Madison Avenue job to write a novel. He, in turn, is attracted to Lane's married friend Stephanie (Dianne Wiest). Then there is Lane's loud, flamboyant mother (Elaine Stritch) who is a faded movie star, terrified of old age; and her latest live-in lover, Lloyd (Jack Warden), depressed about nothing less than the universe, which he finds 'haphazard, morally neutral and unimaginably violent'. Peter's role as the prospective biographer of Lane's mother is full of contradictory possibilities: Lane sees it as a form of vampirism, denying her future for the sake of her past, while her mother regards it as a rejuvenating tribute. Peter moves from being a liberating figure to an exploitative one, as mother and daughter become increasingly antagonistic. Allen portrays these characters with an irony that was so lacking in *Interiors*, gently mocking their cliche-ridden language and their inconsistent attitudes. Nothing is as it seems: the country drama was conceived and shot in the city, the intimate account of the storms and confusions of six people also has the abstract playfulness of billiard balls clicking against one another (a frequent aural reminder of the Humean anxiety). This is put into words by one of the characters, a physicist, who remarks on the randomness of the universe and the helpless mortality of its inhabitants. The characters live in a closed and airless world. Allen's cameras never stray outside Lane's house (we never so much as glimpse the sky, and the light is filtered through lace and slatted shutters). Yet although the characters are physically so close, there is no intimacy between them. Each is locked into private anxieties, and when they talk about love they are talking about their own needs and fantasies. Indeed, the characters simply talk too much about themselves, acting as unconscious narrators of Allen's story: Lane gasps 'I'm suffocating', but really we should be allowed to discern this for ourselves. Allen's writing is still woefully unsure of itself when it addresses 'serious' drama: the introduction of a loud, shallow couple as prospective house buyers provides entirely unnecessary and clumsy light relief – as though Allen were trying to please the critics who found *Interiors* unremittingly somber. With *September*, the comic moments seem remarkably weak coming from such an exceptionally gifted humorist. A diet of meat and potatoes has its own problems – it can lead to heart failure. Overly concerned with his own identity as a 'comic' artist, Allen again seems to lose his confidence by respecting the rigid distinctions between comedy and tragedy.

Allen avoids self-scrutiny whenever it threatens to disrupt his creativity. When he interviwed Groucho Marx for Charlotte Chandler's *Hello, I Must Be Going* (1980), he behaved as if he was entirely ignorant about the art of laughter. Chandler recalls that Allen (whom Marx described as 'an absolute genius') 'was one of the few people seeing Groucho who never tried to be funny'. During the interview, Groucho struggles to explain precisely why he found an early Chaplin routine so amusing, but he can only express the fact that it is inexpressible. Allen, remarkably for a fellow comedian, seems unable to understand Groucho's problem:

Groucho: It was the greatest thing I'd ever seen.
Allen: Why was it the greatest thing you'd ever seen?
Groucho: He was so funny.
Allen: What was he doing?
Groucho: Crazy things.

(Chandler, 1980: 461)

It is hard to imagine Allen tolerating such blunt journalistic questions being asked of *him*. Indeed, Allen's impatience with his interrogators is probably a sign of a more general anxiety amongst artists when asked to analyse their own creativity. 'Great humor,' says Allen, 'is intellectual without trying to be' (quoted by Gilliatt, 1974: 42). Although Allen has been in analysis for many years, he eschews any public request for information about his motivations and anxieties. Whenever he can, he chooses to pose as an entirely 'instinctive' artist, an individual who has very little self-knowledge: for example, when asked why he choose 'Woody' as his pseudonym (some of his contemporaries had claimed it was either 'borrowed' from Woody Herman or else a playful offshoot of Midwood school), Allen claimed the name was 'entirely arbitrary'. It is difficult to believe that a man who changed his name from Allen to 'Woody' would sincerely mean, after decades of psychoanalysis, that there was *nothing* significant or interesting in that transformation. It is rather easier to believe that Allen, who has found his work pawed over, picked at and searched for every trace of autobiographical symbolism, does not wish to encourage this investigation further by offering genuine insights into his background, interests, hopes, and fears. Indeed, as a comedian Allen would contend (with some justification) that his humour cannot be appreciated simply by critical analysis; one may recall the scene from *Annie Hall* when Alvy tries to joke with his new date:

> *Alvy*: I'm not myself since I stopped smoking.
> *Girl date*: Oh, when'd you quit smoking?
> *Alvy*: Sixteen years ago.
> *Girl date*: Whatta you mean?
> *Alvy*: Mean?
> *Girl date*: You stopped smoking sixteen years ago, is that what you said? I-I don't understand. Are you joking, or what?

It is impossible for a comedian to make a joke funny to someone by means of explanation, and it would be just as unreasonable to expect the comedian to know what the joke 'really' means (note Lenny Bruce's agony during cross-examination in court). The point is that the laughter of the comedian is a more mysterious response to the world than is the anger of the satirist. We might be able to 'deconstruct' a simple joke, but what does it *mean* when Allen's mother 'knits a chicken' or polishes a pith helmet, or when an Allen character makes that distinctive smile? We know the 'point' of Allen's comment that as a political gesture he 'once didn't eat grapes for twenty-four hours' – but what does he mean when he writes that a man is chased by an irregular verb? Most of us offer more uniform and more confident opinions on satire than on comedy. It is this uncertainty about *why* we laugh that probably accounts for the difference in the way society treats satirists and comedians, as well as for the fact that the satirist has at his or her disposal a much more clearly defined and socially respectable justification for his or her art than has the comedian. Allen's appreciation of this fact may go some way towards explaining his coyness.

His judgement of his own work shows an insecurity which has often distressed his executive producers, Jack Rollins and Charles Joffe. Allen remembers: 'When I finished *Manhattan*, I went to Rollins and Joffe and said, "Do you think there's any way I could buy this from United Artists and not have them release it, and then I would do one free film for them or something"' (*Esquire*, April 1987).

> When I get the idea for a film and I'm just walking around flushed with the idea, it's magic – it's Renoir and Fellini. It's just

great. Then I start to make the film, and the truck rolls in every day with fresh compromises. You can't get the actor you want, and you don't have enough money to do this, and you're not as good as you thought. And by the time the film is finished, it's 50 or 60 percent of what I had envisioned. (in McClelland, 1987: 329).

Renoir and Fellini, Allen seems to be implying, begin with an idea for a film that is 'magic' and they finish making the film with that magic undiluted – masterpieces from conception to reception. To an extent, Allen's response is understandable; because people have intentions, we tend to interpret what people succeed in doing as a *consequence* of their intentions. However, although people know what they are doing, the consequences of what they do characteristically escape what they intend (see Schelling, 1984). For example, we do not passively react to a movie, but rather we actively interpret it, using our own personal set of prejudices and interests. What we get out of a movie is not necessarily what the movie-maker puts in. It is conceivable that our favourite moments from a movie were quite unintended by its makers. The aesthetic wholeness Allen finds in a work by Fellini or Renoir is no more or less likely than the aesthetic wholeness many people see in, say, *Hannah and Her Sisters*. For all his talk of wanting to make a 'masterpiece', Allen does not yet possess the self-confidence to acknowledge (even to himself) the fine things in his work. His romantic notion of greatness belittles his own achievements. During an interview broadcast by the BBC in 1980, Allen said: 'I never feel any obligation to be funny. It astonishes me what a lot of intellectualising goes on over my films. They're just films. Yet they treat me like a genius at times, at other times like a criminal. Because I've produced "bad art" '. Allen's insecurity and isolation is, perhaps, connected to his relationship with American culture in general. European artists may be equally alienated from their societies, but they seem able to draw confidence from the artistic traditions behind them. It is this kind of confidence which seems unavailable to many American artists. 'Art', as far as Allen is concerned, means European cinema and, especially, literature. In *Love and Death*, Boris hears from his father that (according to one of the Karamazov brothers) 'that nice boy next door', Raskolnikov, murdered a woman:

Boris: He must have been *Possessed!*
Father: Well, he was *A Raw Youth*.
Boris: *Raw Youth*! He was an *Idiot*! I hear he was a *Gambler*.
Father: You know, he could be your *Double*.
Boris: Really? How novel.

In Allen's movie worlds, the Book is the highest form of cultural achievement. Everyone seems to be reading, writing, or trying to write, the Big Book: Alvy Singer starts his relationship with Annie Hall by giving her *Death and Western Thought* and *Denial of Death*; *Manhattan* has Isaac and Yale in the process of writing their books, Mary preparing herself to begin one, and Isaac's ex-wife has already published one; *Interiors* and *Another Woman* feature professional writers; in *Hannah*, Lee says to Elliot: 'Oh, I love that book you lent me. *The Easter Parade*? You were right. It had very special meaning for me'; *September* features a prospective biographer. Perversely, as Allen becomes progressively visually literate he dwells increasingly on the writing classes.

Any attempt at *placing* Woody Allen, positioning him within our own scheme of things, is greeted by him with a curt contradiction. Confronted by the description of him as the comic of the intelligentsia, Allen immediately seeks to pour scorn on the idea:

> People over the years have always thought I was appreciated by an intellectual audience, but I've always felt the exact opposite was true. I never found myself appreciated by the so-called intellectual critics. The more intellectual the critic, the worse I've done with them over the years. I've never been a favorite of Pauline Kael's or Dwight McDonald's or Stanley Kauffmann's or John Simon's or those people that you think of as the more erudite critics. (*Esquire*, April 1987)

Clearly, Allen is ready to contradict some other aspects of his public image when he feels it is expedient: for an artist who 'rarely reads the critics', Allen here shows a remarkable knowledge of their long-standing views on him. He continues:

> I don't know who my audience is, but it hasn't been the intellectual press. I just don't know who it has been. When I was a comic they used to say to me, 'You do college concerts; they're gonna love you, they'll eat you up', and I would do college concerts, and I would have to give back the money because nobody would come. (ibid)

Jack Rollins for one has contradicted this assertion, insisting that Allen was very popular with college audiences and with the intellectuals who read the *New Yorker* and visited clubs such as the hungry i.

Such autobiographical guile has only further antagonized Allen's most notorious critics. For example, Pauline Kael's *New Yorker* critique of *Stardust Memories* bases itself on the implicit belief that Woody Allen's movies are straightforward reflections on his own life and personality. Kael writes: 'Woody Allen calls himself Sandy Bates this time, but there's only the merest wisps of a pretext that he is playing a character; this is the most undistinguished of his dodgy mock-autobiographical fantasies' (Kael, 1987: 87). When Sandy Bates brushes past his sycophantic admirers, Kael argues he 'degrades the people who respond to his work and presents himself as their victim'. Certainly there is much to criticize about Sandy Bates: his repeated expressions of anguish and horror over other people's suffering are made to seem self-serving diversions when we see his apartment decorated with pop art poster blow-ups of such obscenities as an execution in a Saigon street during the Tet offensive. Is *this* what Sandy Bates means when he says he sees human suffering everywhere he looks (alongside a microwave oven and a rubber plant)? What is far more ambiguous than Kael allows is whether or not *Allen* means this. How would Kael react to Sandy Bates if Allen re-shot the movie with another actor in the role? It is surely more plausible to regard Sandy Bates as one of the characters Allen depicts in a largely *critical* light. Indeed, if there *is* any conscious identification with the character, then Allen might just as well be questioning his *own* moral position – the director who photographs human suffering rather than alleviates it. Kael argues that Allen's movie, with its aliens telling Bates to go back to the 'early, funny films', has woven dubiety into its text, anticipating all criticisms: 'you may feel you're being told that you have no right to *any* reaction to Woody Allen's movies.' You *may* feel this, obviously, but then again you may feel any number of other things; viewing is not the passive pastime Kael suggests. Kael's critique grows more and more provocative: 'He's trying to stake out his claim to be a serious artist like Fellini or Bergman – to be accepted in the serious, gentile artists' club. And he sees his public as Jews trying to shove him back down in the Jewish clowns' club.' This is a clear example of a critic taking the movie director's biography as a subtext for the movie; Kael's 'reaction' to a movie is sometimes so immediate it precedes the movie, *imposing* her meanings rather than uncovering the movie's meanings. Allen told Jacobs (1982: 147–8):

> So many people were outraged that I dared to suggest an ambivalent, love/hate relationship between an audience and a celebrity; and then shortly after *Stardust Memories* opened, John Lennon was shot by the very guy who had asked him for his autograph earlier in the day. I feel that obtains. The guy who asks Sandy for his autograph on the boardwalk and says, 'you're my favorite comedian' in the middle of the picture, later, in Sandy's fantasy, comes up and shoots him. This is what happens with celebrities – one day people love you, the next day they want to kill you. And the celebrity also feels that way toward the audience; because in the movie Sandy hallucinates that the guy shoots him; but in fact Sandy is the one who has the gun. So the celebrity imagines that the fan will do to him what in fact he wants to do to the fan. But people don't want to hear this – this is an unpleasant truth to dramatize.

Kael employs a rhetorical device which suggests an unusual degree of insecurity on her part; whenever she wishes to make a personal judgement, she tries to project it onto her reader: '*You* may feel...', '*You* can't respond...', '*You're* not sure how to react', '*You* can't laugh at the nightmarish melancholy...', and so on. Serous criticism is of the form: 'what you say cannot be true because of...'. Without sustained reasons to support her reading of Allen's movie, Kael succumbs to the temptation to use the narrative as a pretext for taking issue with Allen's off-screen behaviour.

The critical community has contributed to the pigeon-holing of Allen's talents; whenever Allen threatens to deviate from the identity the critics imposed on him, he receives the kind of response found in Kael. Ironically, critics famous for their aversion to *auterism* have had no trouble in teasing out Allen's personal obsessions in almost every frame of each movie he makes. They manage to explain his 'deviations' on *their* terms, by labelling his 'non-Woody' work as 'Bergmanesque', 'Fellinesque', or 'Chekhovian'. When *September* was reviewed, the common approach was to deny that the work was a 'real' Allen movie: 'If this sounds like a Chekhov play you have a point' (*New York Daily News*); 'The play is Chekhovian' (*New York Times*); 'Neo-Chekhovian' snaps Vincent Canby; 'True to Chekhov' (*Downtown*); 'A Chekhovian house party' (*New*

York); 'Chekhovian seriousness' (*Guardian*); 'No Woody Allen, no laughs, and a whole load of Chekhovian pining' (*The Sunday Times*); 'this time, he's giving us his version of Chekhov' (*The Listener*); and Marcelle Clements, chewing her pencil and daring to be different, if totally incomprehensible, with 'para-Chekhovian' (*Premiere*). The 'Woody Allen comedy' has come to be seen as a genre in itself, and a consequence has been the critical denial of Allen's attempts at any other kind of movie (drama is a foreign country, they do things differently there). *September* does involve some fine evocations of straining emotional states inhibited by physical constraints, and one of the movie's themes is the search for physical and intellectual intimacy, but to label the work as 'Chekhovian' reveals a barren imagination and a disturbingly limited critical vocabulary (if anything, the drama reminds one more of O'Neill and Arthur Miller). This attempt to enclose Allen in a comedy straitjacket has, if anything, only exacerbated his negative evaluation of his own humour.

'Nobody likes to write in a vacuum,' said Allen. Despite his apparent alienation from the critics, and his claim that he does not know who goes to see his movies, he is nonetheless an artist who wishes to communicate certain ideas to his audience. His screen persona, with his anxious self-questioning and occasional impassioned arguments, articulates in comic form a concern about political and social issues (the individual is helpless as the state continues to trample over what should be preserved) and sexual and emotional problems in the context of modern urban living. Allen told Benayoun (1986: 162):

> I think popular culture in America has become another kind of junk food; our television, our music, most of our films, our politicians, our architecture, most of it is very mediocre and junky. And it is too bad, because we have the money, the technical knowledge. We could have had the greatest culture, but people are drugged by television, by cocaine, by whatever...

'They don't throw their garbage away,' says Alvy Singer of California. 'They make it into television shows.' 'Waste' has come to be a key word in American culture as writers try to trace out what America has made of its unparalleled resources, and from Henry Adams through Scott Fitzgerald up to Norman Mailer, Thomas Pynchon, Saul Bellow, Don Delillo and many others, one can hear a doomed sense of America transforming its natural plenitude into a heap of 'waste' which can neither be recycled nor disposed of. *Manhattan* follows in this tradition, with Isaac Davis seeing his city as a metaphor for the decay of modern culture.

Allen has said, 'Groucho has told me that the Marx Brothers films were never consciously anti-establishment or political. It's always got to be a funny movie first.' '*First*': Allen here acknowledges his role as a humorist, but he also suggests that none of his movies need ever be *merely* funny. *Annie Hall*, for all its wisecracks and hilarious observations, leaves us with the memory of a profoundly alienated, melancholic man. *Manhattan* closes with a question none of us would find easy to answer (how deeply do *you* trust other people?). *Zelig's* interaction of parody and satire (combining the story of the little man who transformed himself in order to fit in with newsreels of the rise of Hitler and the horrific demise of those who did not fit in) is almost Brechtian in its ideological effectiveness. Allen has come to use humour as a means of objectifying personal experiences and private obsessions into comic works that can be publicly performed for others. He does not deal in messages but rather in *ways of thinking*, humane responses to modern dilemmas.

Allen regards his audience as a loyal one; he seems to take for granted the fact that the majority of the people who go to one of his movies are familiar with his *oeuvre* and its development. He has said that he will not go back to playing the *schlemiel* of his early movies because 'the audience wouldn't believe in it any longer.' The problem is where he can go from here as a performer: the 'Woody' image is so powerful and so popular that the moment Allen appears on the screen, people expect him to conform to the familiar identity. This immediacy will also continue to have its effect on Allen's private life; as he says, 'Before, when I was shy and unknown, I thought that if I could only make it in some way, it would really help relieve me socially and I could relax and go to parties and do things. But then, as soon as I did become known, *that* became the problem – I thought, "My God, *I'm well-known* – I can't go out" '.

Allen's anxieties over his identity – his uneasy relationship with his comic image, his Jewishness, and his celebrity – continue to inform his movies and their meanings. If there is one aspect of modern culture that he can be said particularly to dislike, it is the tendency to redescribe the unique in generalised terms: everything must be immediately comprehensible – movies must fit neatly into genres, stars must conform to stereotypes, sexuality must be straightforward and relationships permanent, ideas must be simply true or false, governments honest or corrupt, people good or bad. In opposition to this, Allen offers a creative kind of ambiguity – mixing comedy and tragedy, intimacy and aloofness, desire and revulsion, introspection and social awareness. '*I gotta get some answers.*' What matters most to him is his independence, and the freedom to try to understand himself and his society:

> I never think of being 'Woody Allen Inc', of being a 'mini mogul', or whatever they are now called in Europe. I just think of the old Puritan work ethic: a day's work. My day is my own. I get up when I feel like it. I take a break when I want to play my clarinet. I write when it is all in my head, buzzing along. But it has all to be there in my head before I start. I have to see the last shot before I begin to set down the first one. It may not be the most perfect of lives – but I don't know a better one. (*Hot Press*, 6 May 1988)

5

Stardust Memories

Perhaps being old is having lighted rooms
Inside your head, and people in them, acting.
People you know, yet can't quite name.

(Philip Larkin, 'The Old Fools')

The opening image of *Play It Again, Sam*: the movie lover watching *Casablanca*, enraptured, gazing up at the screen with a look of wonder draped over his face. This is the archetypal Allen film buff, luxuriating in the beauty of the moving image. As time goes by, his face replies to the action on the screen: a wry remark from Bogart elicits a twitching of the mouth and a sly wink of an eye, while Bergman's anxious plea makes the eyebrows rise with fear and the mouth gape open. His face reacts to the black-and-white lights that dance on his lenses; his expression is one of perfect awe. It is the 'look that hides the eyes', the appearance of wonder, the sight of enchantment: it is the magic of the movies. We see that look of awe in countless Allen movies, and each time it serves to emphasize the power of the movies, and the hope and the promise that lurk within such peculiar, spectacular games. The very idea of the movies fascinates Woody Allen: a uniquely modern cultural form that makes a collection of fragments appear to be a seamless whole, an invented place where imagined ideals are invoked as a structure for reality, a dream-like experience that impinges on our everyday lives. Indeed, Allen insists that, so thoroughly have we assimilated the methods and manners and effects of the movies, they are determining our understanding of the present and our discovery of the future. Ours is the Movie Age. Since the advent of the motion picture, we cannot but think, write and act differently: we need forget nothing, for every event can be stored on film; the plasticity of film makes all its content information until there is no real distinction between its personal and public significance; the elliptical nature of film, composed as it is of a montage of images, has affected the way we tell stories, report observations and interpret a sequence of events. Allen is a notable product of the movie age – he grew up enthralled by its magical aura; he is also a major contributor to that age, creating some of its most distinctive images. To understand Allen, one needs to appreciate his understanding of movies.

Allen is a movie lover who loathes movie 'experts'. He always depicts the professional film buff as a humourless figure whose fanatical breaking down of a movie into trivial 'facts' renders all movies equally uninteresting: 'Libby just did a definitive cinematic study of Gummo Marx. Interestingly, he's the one Marx brother that never made any movies'; 'Sandy, Sandy, you know this is exactly like one of your satires. It's like we're all characters in some film being watched in God's private screening room.' People have become servants of signals, compelled to decipher, decode, deconstruct their culture; Allen is disturbed by the excesses of this approach, how it distrusts everything it encounters. The academic in the cinema queue in *Annie Hall* encapsulates all that is cynical and selfish in this attitude: 'I found it incredibly ... indulgent ... I admire the technique but he doesn't hit me on a gut level.' What is so devastating about Marshall McLuhan's magical appearance is not his actual presence but the pathetic submission of the bore when McLuhan talks complete gibberish at him: 'You know nothing of my work. You mean, my whole fallacy is wrong...'. In contrast to the analysts' method of breaking movies down and examining their parts, Allen tries to remember old movies, drawing his memories together in a process that is both constructive and cumulative; the more he remembers these movies, perhaps the nearer he will come to recovering his past.

Allen, as he readily admits, was profoundly influenced by the movies of his youth ('too many to mention,' he told me); when he remembers his youth he recalls certain movies and special stars, and how and when he first saw them. He was born in the mid-1930s, when America was saturated with movies, movie stars and movie talk. In 1939 there were more movie theatres (15,115) than banks (14,952) in the United States. Approximately four hundred new movies were released annually and over fifty million Americans went to the movies every single week of the year. Movies were the nation's fourteenth biggest business in terms of assets ($529,950,444) – more successful than the supermarket chains (see Rosten, 1941: 3–4, 378–9). The movies achieved the zenith of their popularity and influence during this period, culminating in 1946 when attendance reached its peak with net profits of $121 million. Allen recalled his visits to the movies as a teenager:

> the movies that we were watching were all coming out of England. There was a spate of great black-and-white comedies we all used to adore, which is one of the reasons I actually like making films in black-and-white myself. Sometimes you can do so much more with the look of it, like those films did. They were the trendsetters for me in those days. (*Guardian*, 11 August 1988)

One would imagine that these comedies included the rather black, idiosyncratic films that came out of Ealing during this period, such as *Kind Hearts and Coronets* (1949), and *The Lavender Hill Mob* (1951). With the end of the Second World War, Hollywood movies reflected the anxiety of society, with stories of role reversal, deception, alienation, and sudden insecurity. William Wyler's glutinous *The Best Years of Our Lives* (1946) dealt with the return home of three war veterans and the psychological and economic problems of readjustment that they confronted. The movie was a subtly manipulated tribute to the American way of life – to institutions such as the small town, the family, liberal corporate capitalism, and to Hollywood's belief in the redemptive power of love. The movie was one of the most popular pictures of the post-war period, assuaging the fears of the American public. Frank Capra's *It's a Wonderful Life* (1946) featured his archetypal common man, George Bailey (James Stewart), struggling to prevent his small town from being destroyed by selfish materialism. The two ideas at the heart of the movie, said Capra, were that 'no one is born to be a failure', and 'no one is poor who has friends.' James Stewart's superb performance as the unlucky hero was remarkably affecting, making his eventual magical redemption rather less convincing than perhaps Capra envisaged. Other movies acknowledged the shift in concern from the dangers of war to the problems of peace. The *film noir* featured heroes who were frequently weak and confused men who were morally equivocal, sexually promiscuous, and who did not know (or could not commit themselves to), what was good and moral. One can see some of the future Allen preoccupations in these forties movies: the doubts expressed dealt more with the nature of identity (sexual, economic, political) and self than with society in general. Had the past, the cherished traditions, been lost irretrievably? Hollywood had never seemed so unsure of itself and its values. Women, having entered the labour market during the war, had undermined their filmic image; America, once so insular, had assumed international responsibilities. The anxiety of the time came through in the use of 'magical' solutions to seemingly insurmountable problems: thus, George Bailey's life is saved by an angel, and every financial crisis was driven out by the Hollywood musical's indomitable *brio*. Gene Kelly and Stanley Donen's *On the Town* (1949) was one of the most popular of these acts of wish-fulfilment. It featured three sailors on a three-day pass in New York City, and used real locations – Brooklyn Bridge, the Statue of Liberty, the Empire State Building. The soldiers, as though by magic, transformed the City into a place where one could realize all one's dreams, especially those of love and success: 'New York, New York, it's a wonderful town.'

The 'magical' resolutions of some movies of the period surely would have appealed to the teenage Allen. At thirteen, he became obsessed with magic and illusions, and would spend three or four hours a day teaching himself card tricks. As Orson Welles and Bergman loved the very *idea* of illusion, so Allen grew enchanted. Nearly forty years later, he said,

> I still do a few card tricks. When I was a boy I planned to become a professional gambler or make a career in crime! It seems all comedians can do a number of things like sleight of hand, photography, or play an instrument. Groucho played the guitar, Jack Benny played the violin like Chaplin, Sid Caesar the saxophone. I play the clarinet and soprano sax. There's a pattern it seems. (Benayoun, 1986: 159)

We can see the magic tricks performed in *Sleeper* and *Stardust Memories*, but there is a more profound way in which the fascination shows itself – in the construction of the movies. Like Welles, Allen delights in the power of movies to transgress conventions of reality and fantasy. His characters can hold conversations with horses (*Annie Hall*), visit the future (*Sleeper*), relive old relationships (*Stardust Memories*), meet old idols (*Play It Again,*

Sam), and, most beguilingly of all, survive death (*Love and Death*).

Allen's appreciation of his past is also, to some extent, an appreciation of the movies of his past. This sensitivity to the impact of the visual media on the way history is studied is something Allen shares with many of his contemporaries. Since the mid-1960s, an extraordinary number of movies have depended on their audiences' ability to recognize them as overt parodies, revisionist genre pictures, or exaggerated camp versions of Hollywood's traditional mythology: examples include *In Like Flint* (1967 – James Bond parody); *Bonnie and Clyde* (1968 – revisionist gangster movie); *The Long Goodbye* (1973 – revisionist *film noir*); *Young Frankenstein* (1974 – horror parody); *Airplane!* (1980 – disaster movie parody); *Dead Men Don't Wear Plaid* (1982 – *film noir* parody); and *Who Framed Roger Rabbit* (1988 – cartoon satire). The sheer number of these movies suggest American culture's increasingly ironic attitude toward its own traditional mythology. A key factor in the culture's growing self-consciousness has been television. The networks' commitment to Hollywood's old products turned every household into a private movie museum. The effect on how Americans watched movies was enormous. With so many people being able to watch so many old movies, it became easier for the more stylistic aspects to be well appreciated and analysed: movies were quotable. Billy Wilder's *The Apartment* (1960) has its hero watching *Grand Hotel* on television, and Stanley Donen's *Charade* (1963) makes its imitation of Hitchcock's romantic thriller appear as a knowing wink to the audience. Indeed, this self-conscious plundering of the past was highlighted by the presidency of Ronald Reagan in the 1980s; his most seemingly spontaneous moments – 'where do we find such men?' (about the American D-day dead), and 'I'm paying for this microphone, Mr Green', (during the 1980 New Hampshire primary debate) – are not only preserved on film but also turn out to be lines from old movies. He left the 1988 Republican Convention with the familiar quote from his own *Knute Rockne-All American* (1940): 'go out and win one for the Gipper.' Reagan became at once the viewer of the object and the object viewed; his behaviour showed us the extent to which movies and reality have merged in some people's minds. He knew the Holocaust had happened, he told a group of survivors, because he had seen films of the camps (*San Francisco Chronicle*, 13 July 1985: 8). A self that sees itself from all angles fragments and disappears into its own image. Such is the danger of believing in the reality of movies. One may recall *Taxi Driver's* Travis Bickle, alone in his room, imagining dramatic encounters: 'Are you talkin' to *me*? You must be, 'cause I'm the only one here.' Movies may reflect society, but they also mould one's view of it. What one sees in a movie assumes a special significance; film validates reality. This is why the quality of movies is not just an aesthetic question: it is also a political and social problem.

The break-up of the studios (effected by the rise of television and the anti-trust rulings) made possible not only the emergence of new young movie-makers, but also their relative independence. These new directors had varying backgrounds: film criticism (Bogdanovich, Schrader), theatre (Nichols, May), film school (Coppola, Lucas, Polanski, Scorsese), television (Altman, Spielberg, Mazursky, Peckinpah) and acting (Beatty, Hopper). In effect, they began as obsessive buffs who learned about film-making from going to the movies. Above all, the period's defining self-consciousness arose from a new awareness of the inescapable interrelationship of media, audience and historical events. Where cameras, tapes and commentators had once seemed only to record the news, they now clearly helped determine it, with many of the period's most crucial incidents becoming inconceivable without the guaranteed media presence. In every transaction between the self and the world, cultural images perpetuated by the media intervened. This recognition altered irrevocably the relationship of American Cinema's determinants. If movies in the 'Golden Age' of Hollywood had resulted from a triangular configuration of industry, audience and the culture's collective perception of historical developments, the new arrangement had become curiously circular.

Woody Allen has worked to understand this sense of a world mediated by the movies. His ambivalent view of the impact of movies is well expressed in *Zelig*, which was largely constructed from fragments of film history, and satirized its effect on the audience that experienced it. Allen's *Zelig* is a seamless imitation of a television documentary, including interviews with people who knew the enigmatic Leonard Zelig and comments from experts about what the subject 'symbolized' to the public (to the French critics, we are told, Zelig symbolized 'everything'). All is as it would be in a genuine documentary film, except the subject, who never existed. In fact, *Zelig*'s use of documentary footage makes the point that every movie has a documentary basis – at least in the camera's ineluctable interrogation of the natural endowment of the actors, the beings who submit their being to the work of film. President Woodrow Wilson, upon seeing his first movie, is said to have exclaimed: 'It's like writing history with lightning.' From its inception, the American movie absorbed history or, rather, took its place and at the same time took the place of the inner life. The size of the image and its reproducibility, the close-up and the film cut, the magical transformations on-screen, and movies' documentary pose – all these, it seemed, dissolved the boundaries that separated audiences in darkened theatres from the screen. *Zelig* shows the dangers implicit in such illusions of intimacy, with the American public discovering, ignoring, rediscovering and eventually forgetting the odd little character called Leonard Zelig.

Allen's direction shows a keen eye for the way people looked, and tried to look, and imagined they looked, in the 1920s and 1930s: the nervous way they glanced at cameras, posed themselves for photographs, or invented 'business' for newsreels. 'Everything in the jazz age moves too quickly,' the narrator insists, 'like Red Grange', as the camera cuts to a newsreel shot of the football star in action; lethargic political and social reform is thus obscured by the entirely inconsequential metaphor of the fleet-footed footballer. The technical brilliance of *Zelig* is undeniable: Allen has *engrained* himself in the old movie images. Fitting into fifty-year-old frames, Zelig appears to hug Josephine Baker and James Cagney, pose alongside Eugene O'Neill and Calvin Coolidge. The concern for authenticity is abundantly evident: the lighting is set in the style of the period, there are 'rain-type' streaks to give the effect of worn film, the sound is metallic, and the still photographs are often creased or scratched. What is most poignant and haunting about these particular photographic images is their lack of motion, their deathly stillness. Zelig stares out at us, his face registering a hunted look, as though he senses that now, at this moment, we have pinned down a part of his fugitive self. In contrast to the newsreel images of Zelig, clowning for the camera and constantly moving and gesturing, the still images come as a shock, a mortifying glimpse of a figure flattened out by history. In one of these photographs he looks petrified, staring straight ahead, expressionless; it is like a freeze-frame of the drama, a still picture of a painful moment, in which the fatal trajectories have a seductive clarity, and even, shockingly, a kind of beauty – we are almost dazzled and disturbed enough to take it all as truth. The movie manages to capture the transition undergone by the movie camera from an ornament to a central component of consciousness, with newsreels of Hitler addressing huge crowds being seen by millions of movie-goers (in Walter Benjamin's memorable formulation, 'History breaks down into images, not into stories'). *Zelig*'s parodic gifts are immense: as the character assumes a multiplicity of personalities, so too does the 'look' of the movie. One of the wryest moments occurs when we see an imaginary clip from the Warner Brothers' screen version of Zelig's life story, *The Changing Man*, the Hollywood 'biopic' beautifully parodied in visual style (the soft focus, the 'improved' looks of the central characters) and arch dialogue (studded with awkward little clichés). Leonard Zelig is a figure caught up in the flow of film; he changes with the lighting, the focus and the final cut. Fidel Castro said, 'History will absolve me'; Zelig seems to say, 'History will dissolve me.' All that remains, all that is present, is film.

The movie allusions within Allen's movies suggest his sense that America is a nation that has been shaped by its experience of movies. Allen's characters are all children of the movie age, thinking and acting in ways inconceivable to a pre-movie world: in *What's New Pussycat?*, when the fully-clothed hero joins his lover in the shower, she asks, 'Shall I get dressed, or is this foreign movie time?' In *Play It Again, Sam*, Allan Felix, instead of dealing directly with his own emotions, retreats into film-based fantasies. Eventually, he realizes the absurdity of identifying with the mythic Bogart – 'I have one thimbleful of bourbon, I run out and get tattooed.' The title is mythic (Bogart never said 'Play it again Sam'), the hero is mythic (Bogart was not the screen Bogie). In the futuristic world of *Sleeper*, Allen shows how images can be subjected to entirely misleading narration, with Miles Monroe identifying Charles de Gaulle as a famous television chef and misremembering Bela Lugosi as a mayor of New York City. Life consists of varieties of reality that include fantasy, fictions, and even fictions about fictions. We may notice the unreality of *Play It Again, Sam*'s Bogart, but do we recognize the differences between Alvy Singer and Woody Allen? Indeed, does Woody Allen understand the effect his own movies have had upon his own sense of self? Many of his stories involve a return to his character's formative years, and a recollection of his first experiences of women, anti-semitism, authority, adventure, and movies. It is as though Allen were trying to run the film backwards, in an effort to catch sight of some authentic self.

In *Radio Days*, Allen looks back with fondness, in a warm, amber-toned reminiscence of what the wireless meant to him and his family at the start of the Second World War. At the centre of this community, the radio crackles like a fireheath, cleverly used by Allen to interweave a series of wry tales and anecdotes. One is moved to recall the opening monologue from *Annie Hall*: 'I keep sifting the pieces of the relationship through my mind and examining my life and trying to figure out, where did the screw-up come...?' Ten years later, Woody Allen (on the verge of fatherhood) was trying to figure out where the happiness came from, how it survives, why it lurks in the memory. The movie is a work from the heart, a moving and amusing reflection on nostalgia and the afterglow of stardom. *Radio Days* is a conscious recollection, not of the past but of one individual's *image* of the past, a past that assumes conviction and colour and clarity only during the casual, carefree time of the daydream. It is, literally, *whimsical* – a sudden, passing fancy – as, perhaps, all movies are. The movie is perfectly evoked, visually accurate and imbued with an emphatic love of the lost days of childhood. One watches and remembers what it feels like to be a kid to whom a few coins were windfalls; what it is like to grow up in the warm cocoon of a family full of eccentric relatives, sisters on dates, parents caught in the balancing act of bringing up children in hard times. With an eye on the gutter and an ear to the wireless, these people dream of a charming community of stars. Rabbi Baumel is appalled by little Joe's slavish devotion to the 'Masked Avenger' show. The radio, he tells Joe's parents, corrupts the spirit. The boy replies, 'You speak the truth, my faithful Indian companion.' Horrified, the rabbi slaps the boy. Pop says *he* is the authority figure (*slap*); Mom says he is too soft on the brat (*slap*); the rabbi repeats his argument (*slap*); Mom responds (*slap*). 'Enough, enough!' cries the rabbi, 'you'll hurt the boy!' Despite the warning, Joe returns to the magical sound-pictures, listening and imitating, content to play in a state of unrestrained amusement. We are shown that, in reality, there is no barrier separating dreamer from star, and the distance between them is measured with the hopes of silent, private fantasies.

Several critics saw the movie as a 'sketchy', self-indulgent rag-bag of incomplete short stories. No reaction could be more blind or insensitive. When Allen's voice-over speaks of old songs suddenly making him experience 'instant memory flashes', we hear him express the most important point of the movie. *Radio Days is* fragmented, the characters *are* often inadequately developed, for nothing returns for very long, save the sense of having gently brushed-up against one's past. There is a leading character in the story, and he is the narrator, describing each glimpse of a half-forgotten milieu, ordering and re-ordering the many impressions and insights. The pleasure lies in the process of recollection, the novel experience of reconstituting a delicate reading of the past, of what was lost but is still loved. Walter Benjamin (1950: 152) remarked, 'Like a mother who holds the new-born infant to her breast without waking it, life proceeds for a long time with the still tender memory of childhood.' What Allen is moved by in *Radio Days* is a consuming interest not in the 'useful' memory one summons up in answer to particular questions, but rather the memory which unaccountably and unexpectedly takes hold of one's thoughts, sometime somewhere conjuring up images from earlier days. Joe's recollection of his first trip to Radio City Music Hall is an enchanting illustration of this theme, managing to focus the narrator's mind on all the significant figures and forms of the era: his family, the movies, the celebrity of James Stewart and Katherine Hepburn, and the voice of Frank Sinatra. *Radio Days* is open in its affection for people and places and for the ability to recall them. Diane Keaton's brief appearance as a singer has her end her song in precisely the fashion she did in *Annie Hall*: eyes glancing down and to the side, an embarrassed 'thank you ... thank you'. It does seem like old times for a Woody Allen movie, but never have they been explored with such pleasure and such care. As the radio stars celebrate New Year's Eve, the camera leaves us on the rooftops with neon lights and the fall of snow, colours and shapes losing their sharpness, fading gently into someone else's memory. The hands of the clock repossess their old positions, every day and every night, the images are rapidly reshuffled, yet we now share in their allure, they are now fragments in our stardust memories.

Little Joe's first magical experience of movies captures Allen's nostalgia for a certain atmosphere the cinema once had. Bruno Bettelheim recalled:

The moviehouses to which I went as a youth were true pleasure domes, very different from those of today, which are characterized by their spareness and cold functionality. As soon as one entered these old dream palaces, one felt transposed to another world. Inside, there were nooks and crannies and boxes with heavy curtains which suggested privacy and intimacy. Here one could escape the watchful scrutiny of one's parents and all other adults, and do nothing constructive whatsoever – but daydream. (Bettelheim, 1981)

This is the kind of playful, whimsical experience we find Allen's characters seeking, and sometimes finding, in the movie theatre; the screen becomes an extension of the spectator in the same sense that the dream embodies the dreamer. The movie begins, it captures our attention, it commands our involvement. We focus upon the movie screen. Unlike the television screen, which seems to lack depth, the movie screen invites us to gaze into it, to project our private thoughts and desires onto the characters in the narrative. We are still, silent, and in suspense: we cannot control what is happening before our eyes – this is part of the attraction, part of the anxiety. Upon leaving the movie theatre, one may catch oneself trying to remember moments from the movie, and sometimes certain moments from a movie may suddenly make their way back into one's consciousness. The reason for our conscious searching of our 'stardust memories', or the thoughts of actual events or people or ideas which these memories may nag one into recalling and re-examining, point to the ways in which a movie awakens us as much as it enfolds and entertains us. To revive the space wherein we watched the movie, we need more than the mere act of memory: we require an act of imagination, we must re-create the scenes we are struggling to recall. Talking about movies, trying to remember them clearly, is a similar experience to describing and recalling dreams; Buñuel once wrote, 'A film is the story of a dream. A dream recalled because of the realistic nature of the cinema.' Each person possesses the knowledge of certain movies – irretrievable except in memory and evocation. Our responses to movies are thus never really shared. Allen's characters are drawn into the movie theatre for an intensely personal experience which sometimes leads to renewal (*Hannah and Her Sisters*) but which may occasionally encourage introspection (*Play It Again, Sam*).

Allen's early movie appearances encouraged him to continue his rather detached, ironic narrator role he played so well in night-clubs. Because he was disaffected after seeing his screenplays tampered with, he could only wander through these stories, half-heartedly joking his way through scenes he clearly does not believe in. In his early directing work he undertook a variety of technical experiments that enabled him to learn his craft while he parodied established forms. *What's Up, Tiger Lily* manages to subvert both 'high' and 'low' film forms, satirising the subtitles of the 'Art' movie and mocking the machismo of the James Bond bed-hopper. *Take the Money and Run* parodies the *cinéma-vérité* documentary trend of the 1960s, which characteristically tried to convey the impression of recording life 'as it happened', without staging or distortion by editing. Allen neatly undermines this in a number of ways: by contrasting his incompetent subject with an heroic commentary; by using an 'invisible' hand-held camera that is even, inexplicably, present in Virgil's bedroom on his honeymoon night; and by interviews with 'innocent' bystanders who prove to be grotesque camera hogs. The movie's central tension derives from the juxtaposition of the specious realism of *cinéma-vérité* with the romanticism of the gangster movie tradition. Allen, directing his first full-length feature, is over-eager, 'quoting' classic movies whenever he can; before shooting began, he had some 'model' movies screened for himself, including *Blow-Up*, *Vivre pour vivre*, *Elvira Madigan*, and *I am a Fugitive from a Chain Gang*. Such preparation was not unique (Orson Welles did the same before making *Citizen Kane*), but it surely contributed to the cumbersome self-consciousness of these early works. Allen even manages to revive the old gag concerning the bathrooom in which the plumbing is mischievously erratic – a close copy of a scene from Laurel and Hardy's *Saps at Sea* (1940). *Bananas* was, in a way, a rather laboured reprise of the 1923 Harold Lloyd two-reeler, *Why Worry?* At this stage, Allen's reliance upon his comic predecessors was beginning to seem a problem.

Everything You Always Wanted to Know About Sex (But Were Afraid to Ask) was described by Allen as 'the first picture where I've cared about anything but the jokes. I wanted to do something where the color was really pretty and controlled, and the moves contributed and everything worked.' The movie is divided into discrete sections, and each section parodies a particular kind of movie or television show. The movie is thus not about sex but rather a movie about movies about sex: mass-mediated sex. In the medieval sketch, the awesome awfulness of the television comedian is mocked: 'TV or not TV, that is the congestion.' A sketch on frigidity features Italian newly-weds Fabrizio (Allen) and Gina (Louise Lasser), and their plight presented in the style of Antonioni. As the unsuccessful lovers reflect on their impotence, the screen fills with empty white walls, then a variety of plastic and chrome furniture; abrupt shifts of perspective and tone recall the narrative habits of Antonioni's most memorable work. One shot of Venetian blinds, purple flowers, and shadows was intended by Allen as 'a totally satirical Bertolucci shot'. Such subtitles as 'Go easy on my hymen' deflate the stylish images in a manner Allen will use again in *Annie Hall*. The most audacious parody of all is 'What happens during ejaculation?', referring back to Richard Fleischer's *Fantastic Voyage* (1966), with the inside of the human body being explored in the language of the science-fiction genre. The set design is suitably Kubrick-cool, and the casting is highly appropriate, with the officious Tony Randall as the technocrat inside poor Sidney's brain. Allen's ability to parody stylized forms of discourse had been evident in the earliest of his *New Yorker* pieces, and here he employs it to ridicule the dehumanizing effects of using scientific jargon to describe evanescent emotions: 'Roll out the tongue', 'Maintain hands on breast.'

The short sketch format of *Everything...* afforded Allen an opportunity to control every aspect of the images, with meticulous care being spent on ensuring that the clothes, furniture, make-up and *mise-en-scène* looked exactly as Allen wished them to look. Although the movie undoubtedly bears the mark of Allen's night-club routines, with little narrative continuity, it would be wrong to see it purely in this light. Rather, the movie reflects Allen's admiration for the compendium movies of the 1940s, such as *Tales of Manhattan* (1942). The format continues to appeal, with *New York Stories* (1989): 'I must say I'm quite happy the way it [Allen's contribution] came out, but then 40 minutes is a very *controllable* length. We shot it in three weeks' (quoted by Walker, 1988: 25). *New York Stories* is evidence of Allen's development as a writer and director; it is a conventional movie triptych, with Allen's contribution beautifully conceived and performed. *Everything...*, on the other hand, is the work of an impatient, rather insecure man; it fails to exploit the arbitrariness of its topics, and avoids any opportunity to transform its sketches into more challenging short stories.

By the time of *Sleeper*, Allen's concern for *visual* felicity had distinguished him from other 'comic' directors, and intrigued the critics (Pauline Kael remarked, 'To have found a clean visual style for a modern slapstick comedy in color is a major victory: Woody Allen learns with the speed of a wizard. *Sleeper* has a real look to it, and simple, elegant design'). Indeed, the anachronisms in *Sleeper* concern not only the content (Miles Monroe wakes up in the year 2173) but also the form: the beautifully-shot scenes, rich in colour and sharply-lit, feature Keatonesque routines one instinctively associates with the grainy black-and-white shorts of the 1920s; the images of a 'brave new world' are accompanied by a Dixieland score. *Sleeper* proved to be very difficult to edit, and Allen's distributor, United Artists, insisted on a prompt release; the pressure caused Allen to part company with his long-time associate, Jack Grossberg. A major problem had been the movie's ending; indeed, the problem of the ending had been a recurrent one for Allen during this phase of his career. *Love and Death* is again replete with movie quotes: Chaplin's *Soldier Arms* (1918) and *The Great Dictator* (1940) being two of the most notable points of reference. Directing himself, Allen resorts repeatedly to the classic comic gesture of defiance: the direct address to the camera. Bob Hope's movies are full of sly asides to the audience ('Did you see *that*?' 'You think Crosby's going to pick up this check?'). Groucho Marx made the cinematic taboo of the direct address into his trademark: in *Horsefeathers* (1932), Groucho turns to the camera just before Chico begins a piano solo and mutters, 'I've got to stay here, but there's no reason why you folks shouldn't go out into the lobby until this thing blows over...'. Allen echoes his predecessors when, as Boris, he looks out at the audience and says, 'He's got a great voice, eh? I should have shot him.' *Love and Death* now appears curiously torn between Allen's old comic irreverence and his more recent cinematic sobriety. The treatment of Boris is cavalier in the great tradition of movie clowns: the role flaking away to reveal 'Woody Allen', joking his way through every scene. Other aspects of the movie reflect Allen's interest in visual coherence and symbolism; for example, the final scene features a close-up of Sonia's and Natasha's faces, blending them together in a manner reminiscent of Bergman's *Persona* (1966). Ghislain Cloquet's stunning cinematography of the French and Hungarian countrysides throughout the movie serves to highlight the 'strangeness' of Allen's character, with his Hope-like patter and self-conscious asides to the camera. The speculative digressions on such topics as God, poetry, Kantian ethics and the nature of history, are visual signs of Allen's expectations concerning his work: 'What really concerns people,' he said, 'are the motivations and the subtleties of psychological anxiety ... and these are not subjects for the traditional cinematic comedian.'

Allen has often explained his concern for control over his movies by citing Malraux's remark that art is 'the last defence against death'. In that sense, his frustrations when making *What's New Pussycat?* went beyond a simple desire to protect his own screenplay: he was alarmed at being in someone else's story, subject to someone else's decisions and directions. Jack Rollins and Charles Joffe, since the beginning of Allen's independent career, have protected him from the Byzantine bureaucracy of movie-making, giving him a degree of power over his projects that is virtually without precedent (with only Chaplin coming near to Allen's autonomy – but Chaplin was more sensitive to the box-office). Before and during production, Allen's movies are shrouded in secrecy; they rarely have titles, but instead are referred to by the studio as 'the Woody Allen (Fall/Winter/Spring or Summer) Project'. His working relationship with Rollins and Joffe is, Allen says, 'very nice. There is never an argument, ever,' not even when he announces that his next movie will not feature himself. 'I have an absolutely wonderful working situation. I have no friction whatsoever.' Such a remarkably straightforward approach to his work is necessary not just because of Allen's desire for coherency but also because of the rapid pace at which he makes his movies. Once again, Allen stresses that his brisk schedule is in accordance with the way movies were made when he was a child:

> It's funny when you think back to the old Hollywood days. Mia's mother [Maureen O'Sullivan] was telling me that she would do something in a Tarzan film early in the morning and then she would change her costume and walk three studios down the road and do something in *The Merry Widow*. And maybe that afternoon she would do something else. And it worked. They turned out so many wonderful movies. Now, one or two a year seem to be enough, and sometimes they are not so wonderful, are they? (*Guardian*, 11 August 1988: 21)

It has been estimated that Allen has ideas, treatments, and even scripts, for his next twelve movies (Navacelle, 1987). Certainly, his productivity is channelled only into his own projects; he rarely contributes any material to other movies or magazines, and his lifestyle has evolved out of his work schedule.

Charles Joffe and Jack Rollins have always given Allen their personal backing and encouragement; they helped him to become one of America's highest paid writers during the early 1960s, and they subsequently negotiated his movie deals. Joffe has come to accept Allen's singlemindedness: 'He's always saying to me, "If I make a dollar profit, then I can go on to the next picture." ' Describing his arrangement with United Artists at the beginning of his movie career, Allen said: 'I have a nice gentleman's agreement ... I've traded the idea of making millions in return for artistic control.' Lloyd Leipzig, former Vice-President of Advertising for United Artists and later Orion, says of Allen: 'His gut feelings about what should be done with his films are always right; they work for him.' Since *A Midsummer Night's Sex Comedy* (1982), Allen's movies have been produced by the Orion Pictures Corporation, which was created early in 1978 by five former executives of United Artists. Arthur Krim, Robert Benjamin, Eric Pleskow, William Bernstein, and Mike Medavoy, made up the entire top-level management of UA before they resigned because of 'individual and collective disagreements' with conglomerate owner Trans-america. Such was the reputation of these five men they were able to establish Orion with a reputed $100 million credit line. The new company made an arrangement with Warners to use the distribution structure of that company while still maintaining complete control over advertising, publicity, distribution, and booking for their movies. This unprecedented deal made it possible for Orion to enter the market immediately as the full equal of six established major studios. Allen has thus been able to continue his almost idyllic working arrangement:

> I have this deal with Orion. I keep my budgets low. I don't look for millions and millions. If a film loses, and a couple of them did, it's no more than $1m. That's chicken feed in this business. I don't make waves, so I'm left alone. It's a good deal for Orion. I don't cost much. My movies don't cost much. The company makes money. I get a living. Everybody is happy. If that wasn't the case, I guess they'd fire me. (*Hot Press*, May 6 1988)

Although Allen pays Orion if he goes over the budget during shooting, it is rare for his work to lose money. At $15 million, *Radio Days* was the most expensive Allen movie to date; in a risk-averse industry, Allen's approach is very attractive. When he decides to shoot a story in which he will not appear, he agrees with Orion to extend their deal by one picture and to make that picture a 'Woody Allen comedy'.

Many of Allen's contemporaries in the movie world have suffered after making box-office failures. Francis Ford Coppola, for example, threatened in 1988 that he would stop directing movies unless the producers ceased interfering with his work. Allen, in contrast, seems uniquely unaffected:

> I'm not for hire. I work at home. I write at home. I don't think big about budgets. I'm not into spaceships and million dollar special effects. I'm low down the totem pole of the spenders. I'm not even big in the spending league in television terms. They spend more on a thirty minute tv show than I do for a 100-minute movie. That's okay with me. (*Hot Press*, May 6 1988)

His efficiency is widely admired within the industry; as soon as one movie is finished, he starts on another – his self-sufficiency is astonishing:

> I have a long-term arrangement for making films, so it's not that I have to get an idea and sell somebody the idea, and go find an actor to play it, and spend two years making deals with people, and going to lunch and doing all that nonsense. As soon as I'm finished with the script, we're in pre-production the next-day – we're off! (BBC TV, 13 November 1987)

Allen is the consummate miniaturist in an age of expensive epic productions. His father once worked with intricate watch mechanisms and delicate jewellery, sensitive to the slightest touch, alert for the smallest of marks; Allen also prefers to work on a small-scale (his pictures rarely last much more than eighty minutes), and the movies he releases are evidence of a tremendous attention to detail. He explained,

> It's because I'm the writer as well as the director. That makes all the difference. How often on a film do you get endless discussions between director, producer and scriptwriter about the 'concept'? People often ask me: 'You write, you direct, you act – how can you do all that at the same time?' What can I say in reply? It's so much easier that way. Sometimes it's a physical strain, but it makes things so much simpler. (*Guardian Weekly*, 28 June 1987)

His control extends to the promotion of his work. For *Annie Hall*, he insisted upon subdued print ads and no television spots until the movie had already been running in theatres for several weeks, so that isolated scenes would not be allowed to distort the movie's theme. Safeguards are contractually spelled out, and the list continues to grow: for example, Allen's movies no longer play in South Africa according to a clause he added in 1986. After the French retitled *Sleeper* as *Woody and the Robots*, and *Annie Hall* was rechristened *The City Neurotic* by the West Germans for release in those countries, Allen had a clause inserted preventing foreign title changes. As Hollywood grows increasingly subservient to the demands of its sponsors, Allen's work looks entirely free from commercial interference.

'I consider myself eminently privileged,' said Allen. 'I work as an independent, answerable to no one. If an idea strikes me as the seed of an interesting film, I start to work on it without provoking too much curiosity, and if I go wrong in a scene, I can do it over again without too much drama' (Benayoun, 1986: 165). Over the years Allen has gathered together a group of actors and technicians who know his methods and tastes and can respond quickly and constructively to his instructions. Tony Roberts acted with Allen in the stage version of *Play It Again, Sam*, and has appeared in most of his movies; indeed, Allen used to rely on a very small ensemble to play both central characters (Diane Keaton, Mia Farrow) and secondary figures (Danny Aiello, Julie Kavner, Jessica Harper). Recently, he has felt adventurous enough to write for more varied characters, and has used several of his favourite English actors. He told Alexander Walker,

> I used to hesitate. A few years ago, I yearned to have Denholm Elliott play the husband in my film *Interiors*, but I went with E.G. Marshall. It didn't seem logical at the time that the character should be English. I didn't let that stand in my way when I cast Denholm in *September* – or Ian Holm [in *Another Woman*]. His 'Englishness' will never be noticed, he's so good. (Walker, 1988: 36)

Allen's meticulous preparation of the 'look' of his movies also involves a search for extras who have the facial expressions or accents or physique he feels he needs in the background: 'I have casting assistants from whom I request very precise types. They deploy themselves a bit everywhere, handing out "open call" cards. My staff are used to my needs because they've been working with me for years. I've had the same crew for something like ten years' (Benayoun, 1986, 164–5). He prefers not to look at the actor at auditions, examining instead their photograph and synopsis; this is partly out of shyness, but also because he is always seeking particular physiognomies for certain scenes. Allen's crew is composed of people he has employed for many years: Jane Martin, his assistant; Mel Bourne, his art director; Ralph Rosenblum and Susan Morse, editors; Dick Hymen, composer; Jimmy Sabat, sound mixer. The familiarity facilitates a disciplined, well-organized approach which does not necessarily encourage intimacy; Bob Ward, Key Grip on Allen's movies for more than a decade, has never exchanged a single word with him. Two cinematographers have played an especially influential role in Allen's development as a director: Gordon Willis and Carlo di Palma. Willis, who is based in New York, was responsible for some of the most beautiful photography in American cinema during the 1970s: of particular note is the Rembrandtesque lighting of *The Godfather* I and II; the surreal brightness of *All the President's Men*; and the rich textures of Allen's black-and-white *Manhattan*. Carlo di Palma first worked with Allen on *Hannah and Her Sisters*; his work is arguably more subtle than Willis', with greater sensitivity to the needs of the narrative. His work with Bertolucci and Antonioni (especially the latter's 1982 *Identificazione di una Donna*) is particularly memorable, and Allen has used his 'European' style to great effect in his most recent work. Whereas Willis helped Allen to achieve a nostalgic vision of New York in *Manhattan*, di Palma is more suited to Allen's optimistic stories, making the New York of *Hannah and Her Sisters* seem a warmer place, with soft colours and a less studied lighting.

Allen's ability to learn from his colleagues has made him a more ambitious director, willing to improvise during production. He told Benayoun:

> Danny Rose is an improvised film, the way I like them. It was shot in the streets, on well-planned locations, and we wanted a rough-looking appearance which gave us lighting freedom – I didn't have to wait for the sun. Here I could shoot on the inspiration of the moment, call up my friends and shoot quickly in familiar locations. (Benayoun, 1986: 165)

Rosenblum and Karen (1979: 265) remarked:

> Woody seemed to understand that as long as he had the ultimate authority, he didn't have to fear the opinions of others. He was always ready to try it your way, and if your way succeeded, so much the better. Above all, he wanted to learn from the people with whom he

worked, people with decades of experience in areas that were foreign to him – and he *has* learned, so that now, if need be, he could easily edit a picture on his own.

Allen makes a movie rather in the way he writes an essay: a succession of more or less complete-drafts, each time revising and adding new thoughts and scenes, improving on existing material, rearranging the order. He will film his script, then edit, then reshoot, then edit, and so on. *Stardust Memories*, for example, was first shot as a Fellini-esque comedy with rich colours and many outside locations; *Annie Hall* began as a 'murder mystery' parody; *September* was completed when Allen decided to burn the original negative and film an entirely different version. His method of shooting is now sufficiently flexible to accommodate, and sometimes encourage, improvisation; he allows his actors to change some of their lines if they feel uncomfortable, and he will occasionally write new lines during the evenings. He shoots much more footage than he can use, confident (unlike many other directors) that he will decide on the final cut. His direction, he claims, 'consists usually of "faster", "louder", and "more real" '. The description is typically understated. Allen's colleague, Mel Bourne, gives a more revealing account:

> Woody knows every inch what he wants. And he gets it, in spite of every opposition. Sometimes he makes changes which knock you sideways, but it's always clear in his mind what he does them for. The worst are those he is capable of making on the morning of shooting. He can come in, see a whole set ready to work in, then decide he doesn't want it. So out it goes ... Woody never wants to repeat anything. He'll be using new ideas, new thoughts and he'll not only work enormously hard to make them come alive, he'll expect us to do too. Woody doesn't care if you kill yourself, because he does the same with himself. (McNight, 1983: 189, 190–1)

A rare opportunity to observe Allen at work was given to the movie-writer Thierry de Navacelle during the filming of *Radio Days*, from 5 November 1985 to 9 May 1986. He observed:

> At the beginning, it is a shock to see this big director who has done fourteen movies, and more than a few good ones, hesitating, taking advice from actors, and saying out loud, 'I don't know how to do it'. And then, after seeing him doing it again and again, one begins to have an idea of what all this means. Woody gets all the elements together, the script in his hand, the set lighted, the actors ready, and

stands silently in the middle of everything, letting himself be taken by the atmosphere, by the sound of a voice, by a face, by an angle, by a line of the script. He knows what he wants, but at this point, he prefers to let the elements lead him and be ready to act when the inspiration strikes. And since each of the elements – the lines, the casting, the decor – has been intensely prepared, the magic, most of the time, works itself out. (Navacelle, 1987: 293)

'When I heard that Antonioni prepares a picture for six months,' Allen said in 1972, 'I couldn't figure out what the hell he is doing for six months.' It is because he can rewrite his screenplay so quickly, continuously, that allows him to be so flexible on the set. Possibly the knowledge that so many of his movies have been altered radically during the editing stage has encouraged Allen to regard the actual shooting in a less respectful light. Allen's models are European rather than American:

What I would aspire to in my fantasies at night are the films of Kurosawa and Bunuel and Bergman. Those are the great works of art in film, and nothing would please me more than if some time in my life, I could achieve a film of that consequence. (*Esquire*, April 1987)

He told me: 'I really do think that Bergman is, probably, the greatest film artist ever.' Contrary to the critics' image of him as a person obsessed with becoming 'another Bergman', Allen is quite open-minded about his own future movies: 'I don't want to do a series of films that always seem to make profound statements ... You want to do a certain number of films and try to do that, and I would like, in the course of my life, to do some broad comedies and a musical. You want to mix it up' (*Rolling Stone*, 9 April 1987). Allen has acquired most of his knowledge of direction from studying other movies and through trial and error on the set; on only five occasions has he worked under another director: *What's New Pussycat?* (Clive Donner), *Casino Royale* (Michael Ayringer), *Play It Again, Sam* (Herbert Ross), *The Front* (Martin Ritt), and, briefly, *King Lear* (Jean-Luc Godard). The final appearance was, it seems, particularly uncomfortable for Allen; he told Alexander Walker,

Godard was very evasive about the project. He kept telling me it was about a Lear jet that crash-lands on the coast. When I got to the shoot, there's no script and Godard is wearing a bathrobe and pyjamas and smoking a big cigar. He reminded me of Groucho Marx playing Rufus T. Firefly, the great genius no one dares contradict. I did a lot of the things he asked me to do that couldn't look anything but foolish on the screen. But ... then, he's Godard. (*London Evening Standard*, 11 August 1988: 25)

Allen's traditional reverence for plot and planning must have been rather shaken by the experience with Godard; perhaps there is also an element of repression here, with Allen's artistic ambitions coming up against his own insecurity: 'What if I fail and lose the audience I have?' The freedom Allen has rests, to a large extent, on his enduring popularity with a fairly specific section of the movie-going public; he is admired by a discriminating audience, middle-class and college educated, who live and work mainly in the big cities. When I asked him to describe his *own* conception of his audience, he replied: 'I think of it as a pretty small audience which varies from film to film.' Allen has never truly penetrated the mass market (*Annie Hall*, despite its Academy Awards, did rather modestly at the box-office compared to movies of a similar stature, and never achieved the commercial success of Mel Brooks' *Blazing Saddles*). Allen's audience is 'solid' – a high percentage of them keep returning to see each new Allen movie (Yacowar, 1979). The success of *Hannah and Her Sisters* suggested that Allen's *potential* audience is not as small as has commonly been claimed; Orion decided the movie merited a more ambitious promotion, and ensured that it opened in many more locations – 'We're selling it more as an entertainment rather than as the latest in the Woody Allen series' (*Variety*, 11 February 1986). The movie subsequently proved to be Allen's most popular work since *Annie Hall*, attracting many people who had seen few (or none) of his movies in between.

Instead of exploiting the success of *Hannah*, Allen seemed to step back, deliberately avoiding any project that resembled '*Hannah II*'; *Radio Days* was a modest, gentle, small-scale work, in sharp contrast to *Hannah*'s emphasis on character and plot. In fact, this endearingly 'little' movie was made up of a number of short stories which caused Allen to work with a huge cast and several elaborate sets. He evidently found the task far more exhausting than he had expected, and it discouraged him from attempting similarly complex projects. Allen commented during a BBC *Film 78* interview:

Writing is more fun than anything else, because nothing can go wrong that can hurt you, if you're just locked in at home ... You get a real good feeling when you think of an idea for a movie. You're home alone, and it's perfect. You see it in your mind's eye and everything gels. Then you write it, and it's not so hot because you had realistic problems. Then you film it, and it gets a little worse. By the time you've cut it and the film comes out, it's about 50 or 60 per cent of what you had conceived of. So it's always a big let down.

He has also been hindered in the past by problems such as a film technicians' strike in New York which forced him to change the setting of *Play It Again, Sam* from New York to San Francisco. Despite his efforts to adapt the story (using the city's hills as symbols of his character's changing fortunes), his familiar persona seemed rather lost in this alien place. It was the experience of making *Love and Death* in the Balkans, using contingents of the Red Army ('They were thrilled to be in a movie because their life was so boring ... just occupying Hungary') that frustrated him most. He encountered innumerable problems in Budapest – bureaucratic, logistical and climatic – and he returned to New York vowing to base his future movies in his native city, where he knows how to make the most of his surroundings. As was noted earlier, Allen's decision to centre nearly all his stories in New York also has a symbolic relevance, for he is both artistically and emotionally divorced from Hollywood. *Annie Hall* was Allen's first serious attempt to involve his city in his work, and it is strikingly anti-Hollywood in content and in style.

Annie Hall, in many ways, was a watershed for Woody Allen. It contained countless references to his early career, yet it also marked the emergence of a more sophisticated actor and director. Academy Awards are certainly not the most reliable gauges of artistic achievement, but, even so, Allen's three personal nominations (Best Screenplay, Best Actor and Best Director) had only one precedent: Orson Welles, for *Citizen Kane* (1941). For a comedian, the tribute was unique and unexpected. It was his most innovative and eclectic work to date, employing techniques such as split-screen, animation, instant replay and visual stream-of-consciousness devices. The camera is allowed to move more freely, and there is a deliberate three-colour scheme: the romantic New York scenes were shot on overcast days or at sundown; scenes from the past have a nostalgic, golden-yellow hue; and the California scenes were shot into the sun so that people almost seem to evaporate. It is as though Allen is trying to capture in images the variety of impressions, and subjectivity of interpretations, one experiences in the mind. When Alvy's thoughts wander or when his moods alter, so too do the images. Alvy Singer begins by staring at the camera, joking and, in time, confessing. He is 'sifting the pieces' of a remembered, ended love affair. Thus, from the beginning we know the basics of the story concerning Alvy and Annie; the images and scenes that follow are to be taken as fragments, scenes from a memory. The editing is remarkably neat throughout the movie, each scene seeming to be summoned up by its predecessor: Alvy's memory of his atrophied sex life with his ex-wife concludes with him sloping off for 'another in a series of cold showers', and then we cut to Alvy and Rob on their way to the squash court, with Rob saying, 'My serve is going to send you to the showers early.' The association is made as one does when remembering, between the showers of an unhappy marriage and the showers recalling the day he first met Annie Hall. The split-screen technique is well developed in the scene featuring Annie and Alvy with their respective analysts: we thus observe the two lovers engaged in the same activity yet separately; Annie's side of the screen is brightly lit and ordered, Alvy's is dark and shadowy, and Annie sits upright while Alvy is prostrate. Malraux's dictum about art being one's final defence against death is implicitly questioned during *Annie Hall*: art is seen to recall the unique but never genuinely to preserve it. We see that, despite Alvy's conflation of art and real life, the gap between fantasy and reality can still make itself felt: when asked by Annie's friend to 'score' some cocaine for him, Alvy jokes, 'sure, I'll be glad to. I'll just put it in a hollow heel that I have in my boot, you know'; after the flippant reference to the spy movie cliché, Alvy sneezes and blows two thousand dollars of cocaine over the motionless man. Annie's photographs of the happy scenes with Alvy and the fugitive lobsters seem more like epitaphs when they are separated, and, when Alvy tries to re-enact the scene with another person, there is nothing left; after Alvy and Annie break up, we see two actors rehearsing a scene in which the two lovers decide to stay together. Art here seems more like a desperate bid to deny a death that has already occurred. What catharsis there is in *Annie Hall* comes from the act of memory: Annie, when moving into Alvy's apartment, when sorting through his box of button badges, and when telling him about her first analysis, is on all three occasions unpacking miscellaneous objects as she simultaneously unpacks her concerns. When Alvy re-visits his childhood haunts, he laughs at the memory of his Uncle Joey and Aunt Tessie. At the end of the movie, the memories flow fast and freely, suggesting that they are the only things between Alvy and nihilism.

Great care was taken to make the movie's form match its content, and therefore as Alvy reshapes his memories so Allen reshapes his images, violating various principles of film rhetoric. The opening address to the camera denies the conventional gap between screen image and audience, as do the scenes with Marshall McLuhan appearing to humiliate the movie bore ('Boy, if only life were like this ...') and Alvy's quarrel with Annie over whether she said, 'The only question is will it change my wife' (Alvy turns to us for support: '*You* heard that because you were there so I'm not crazy'). Allen also subverts the realism of the narrative in order to reveal implicit feelings: in one scene a double-exposure enables Annie to rise from bed and start sketching while Alvy continues to make love to her body ('Now that's what I call "removed"!'). Alvy goes on to appear in Disney's *Snow White*, talking to the Wicked Queen about menstruation; by placing him in a cartoon, Allen makes Alvy seem childish and one-dimensional as he argues his case. Alvy is comfortable making life into art rather than bringing art into life: he sits with Annie on a park bench and describes passers-by as though he were casting a new movie – the lovers back from Fire Island, the Mafia linen supply man, and the winner of the Truman Capote Look-a-like Contest (who, in another audacious confusion of reality and fiction, is the real Capote as a victorious fake). Alvy uses movies as a means of avoiding problems in reality: he deflects a tension with Annie over how they treat each other into a quarrel over whether or not belatedly to enter a screening of Bergman's *Face to Face* (1975); when Annie is tempted to go with Tony Lacey's entourage, Alvy drags her off to see, yet again, Ophuls' *The Sorrow and the Pity*; finally, when Alvy sees Annie with her new lover, he takes solace from the fact that they are going to one of his favourite movies. In these movie moments, we sense the shimmer of a fear that has been hoarded, cared for, lovingly developed, polished with a fetishist's single-minded devotion. Alvy's movie moods have come to overshadow his capacity for spontaneity; even when preparing to make love, as he turns on his red lightbulb by the bed, he begins to think of preserving the moment: 'Now we can go about our business here and we can even develop photographs if we want to.' Nonetheless, at certain times the movies, and art in general, are seen as ambiguous – simultaneously preservation and loss, presence and absence. Watching *The Sorrow and the Pity*, the two lovers feel a strong sense of guilt and helplessness, but, as Alvy acknowledges, the movie is *supposed* to elicit such feelings. Even those photographs of Alvy, and that play of his, are not entirely without value; they manage, just, to reflect a faint memory of times past, of times when things were better. *Annie Hall* underscores Allen's view of the movies as a means of understanding the past and coming to terms with one's helplessness before time, loss, and death. 'Love fades', and movies fade; the evanescence of each new experience is poignantly captured in Allen's thematic and cinematic brevity.

It was perhaps inevitable that Allen's meditation on memory and the 'sifting' of the past presented him with the problem of an ending. In a sense, the ending occurs at the beginning, when Alvy tells us that he and Annie have parted. For such an anti-lineal narrative, which flits from one memory to the next, any formal closure is going to seem arbitrary and false. In fact, Allen could not decide on any ending; he and his co-writer, Marshall Brickman, wrote several conclusions but Allen continued to shoot additional material concerning how Alvy came to realize how much he missed Annie. Editor Ralph Rosenblum, who had salvaged Allen's first movie and had continued to work closely with him, persuaded him to omit the dramatic transitions and simply have Alvy say: 'I miss Annie – I made a terrible mistake.' Allen then suggested, 'What about memory – shouldn't we have them discuss old times?' Rosenblum asked his assistant, Susan Morse, to get him certain sections of film: a shot of Annie and Alvy driving uptown from the tennis courts, a shot of Alvy holding a lobster, a shot of the lovers on the beach, a shot of them in bed, shots of Annie arriving at Alvy's apartment, and many other discrete segments of scenes. Rosenblum recalls,

> Sandy quickly fetched me the reels, and I held them up to the light, showing her which frames I wanted – twenty feet of this, three feet of that, eight feet of this ... make this number one, this number two, and so on. She spliced them all together on a single reel, and I edited them down to a reprise of Keaton singing her nightclub number, 'Seems Like Old Times' (all the memory moments are silent). One of my favorite cuts in that montage was Woody and Diane on a pier. He points, and we cut to what they 'see', which turns out to be another memory cut of them kissing. That little transition helped augment the power of the reprise, although I put it together so intuitively I was

hardly aware of its existence until Woody and I screened the film some time later. (Rosenblum and Karen, 1979: 288)

Rosenblum, seeking some kind of neat conclusion, reminded Allen that the movie had begun with Alvy telling two jokes about love and life; it was decided that a complementary monologue should accompany the montage and close the movie. According to Rosenblum, Allen composed the lines in the back of a taxi cab on the way to work. Allen explained:

It was no big planned thing. I mean, we were sitting grousing all day, looking at footage, cutting, recutting, dealing with other problems. I remember sitting with Ralph in the cutting room at five o'clock preparing for a seven o'clock screening that night and saying, let's go down to the sound studio and I'll put a jump at the end of the picture and wing that joke about the eggs. At five-thirty that night we got into the recording booth, ran back uptown and stuck that joke in, and it stayed forever. (*ibid*; 287)

Marshall Brickman described the moment when he first saw the movie with its new conclusion: 'I'll never forget, suddenly there was an ending there – not only that, but an ending that was cinematic, that was moving, with that simple recapitulation of some of the previous scenes, with that music...'. Cocteau once described the aim of editing as the 'reorganization of chance'; *Annie Hall* is a fine example of such a procedure. It is an elegant cluster of fragments which seem to have found one another, by accident, at the last possible moment. Almost despite himself, Allen ended up with what he had hoped for: a moving invocation of times past.

Annie Hall ends on such a curious, melancholic note, it shocks one in the light of his previous comic conclusions. Allen recalls that his backers were initially disturbed by this; he felt he had stepped out of the 'safe' comic genre:

I think I was lucky in that I did comedy exclusively when I started, and I have this theory that the studios always think there's some mystery to that ... They think, 'Leave Mel Brooks alone; he knows what he's doing'. I got off on that foot with them and they've always left me alone. That's the way it's been on every film. I reshoot tons of material; I cast who I want; the films I work on are a complete mystery to the company that's paying for them. (*Esquire*, April 1987)

'In comedy it's very difficult to do *anything* filmically,' Allen argues, 'Everything has to be spare and quick and precise. The match has to be struck and the flare has to go up. None of the things that really good directors like. It's best in comedy to work directly on behaviour, not effects.' Movie comedy has never been easy for Allen; the jokes may come freely, but the problem is how best to employ them in the narrative. 'When you're editing,' says Allen, 'you have the anxiety of making the film come out. You cut one scene maybe twenty times, you see it over and over – it loses its punch ... The cutting-room reality wraps itself around you like a wet blanket' (Rosenblum and Karen, 1979: 266). 'Making a funny film,' he says, 'provides all the enjoyment of getting your leg caught in the blades of a threshing machine'. Like Chaplin, Jerry Lewis and Mel Brooks, Allen has always been highly conscious of the low cultural rating commonly accorded screen comedy, and he resents it. As early as 1970, Allen observed: 'the fun in directing is to get "fancy". But you have to present the comedian in as clear and simple a way as possible. In directing something serious, you can indulge yourself. It's not too much fun directing comedy.' It is also, one might add, not much fun for Allen to act in a comedy. The movie medium has always represented a major challenge to the versatility of comedians who began their careers on the stage in front of live audiences. They learnt to play 'off' an audience, using the laughter as a gauge for the success of their act. In movies, on a silent set, surrounded by unsmiling technicians, the comedian can easily become disoriented. The nature of the medium eludes some comedians; many, including Robin Williams, Bob Hope, Richard Pryor, and George Burns, do little more than perform stand-up routines which, although often very funny, are not cinematic. The barrier separating comic from audiences can thus be disruptive: without the audience's reactions, the comic may find that timing, intonation and expression lose that authenticity one needs to make one's material effective. Bill Cosby, for example, is a brilliant performer who thrives on the intimacy and immediacy afforded by a live audience; his movies have been great disappointments. Sid Caesar, hugely popular on television, was never at ease in movies. 'Comedy films are unlike other films,' said Allen, 'what's important in a comedy is the content of the shot, not the shot itself.' Alert to the disruptive effect of the wisecrack and the sight gag, he has slowly worked to integrate his humour: 'Whenever I don't use physical gags or slapstick, people cease to see visual structure in my films; but I have always been attentive to the visual side of them, even in my more talkative films.' In fact, Allen has gradually worked to hold his prodigious comic gifts in check, preferring to develop his sensitivity to the needs of narrative. *Sleeper* originally ran well over two hours, but the released version lasts only eighty-three minutes; most of the sequences that were cut (after viewings by test audiences) dealt with elaborate visual jokes which were often funny but which interrupted the essential flow of the narrative. These excised scenes are kept on what Allen's team call 'the black reels', occasionally returned to when Allen requires additional comic material for a new movie. With this spirit of self-denial, the trend is for leaner, 'tighter' narratives with few (if any) extraneous comic scenes. It is thus harder to quote from Allen's later movies; the one-liners have started to give way to a more subtle, extended form of humorous dialogue.

Allen's cinematic style does sometimes seem overbearing and manipulative, particularly in his dramatic work. *Interiors* has Allen intercutting shots of the sea in order to contrast with interiors, order, and artifice; the creaking symbolism is predictable and rather distracting. *September* cleaves to a theatrical discipline, with no exterior shots and a ritualistic use of candle-light; Allen's shooting style seems to ignore this, with an unusual reliance upon close-ups, and the result is an overly-mannered style which fails to exploit the full potential of the setting. However, in both movies there are a number of satisfying scenes. In particular, the wedding of Pearl and Arthur in *Interiors* is an excellent example of Allen's awareness of the camera's contribution to the narrative. At the beginning of the shot, the camera moves in to focus on Joey, the most alienated witness. As the couple exchange marriage vows, the camera moves back to incorporate side views of Renata, Mike, and Joey. When the ceremony nears its conclusion, the camera includes Frederick and Flyn, and as the newly-married couple embrace and kiss, the shot has a rear-view of the officiating magistrate and the family. This dilatory, informative shot suggests that the local, individual tensions within the family have been superseded, at least temporarily, by the celebrations. Such thoughtful fluency occurs increasingly frequently in Allen's work. *Hannah and Her Sisters* has a superbly sustained scene in which one seems to see the private anxieties of each sister gradually intertwine and infect them as a group. The camera encircles the three women in the restaurant as Holly petitions Hannah for financial backing and Lee (who is having an affair with Hannah's husband) quietly dissolves in her own remorse. The motion of the camera is broken when Lee can take no more and shouts at Holly, and the seamless unity of the scene breaks up into tiny visual fragments. Such subtle understatement is one feature of Allen's style; another is his readiness to surprise us with daring narrative techniques. Allen adapted a modernist literary device for the cinema when he invited us into his own life, intruding on the action with his own voice, commenting like a *kibbitzer* on the images he has devised. He gets up from the director's chair and talks right into the camera, sharing with the audience his thoughts and anxieties about the right way to get the movie moving again. In *Manhattan*, he begins with some voice-over ruminations as he struggles to find the perfect phrases for the city and his relationship to it. He abandons one approach, tries something 'more profound', turns that down in favour of a more elaborate metaphor, rejects that as 'too preachy', before finally finding an appropriate entry into the story itself. Allen thus delights in, at times, showing us the underside of the tapestry, the layers that make up the palimpsest: *Annie Hall* is an audacious clutter of techniques, *Hannah and Her Sisters* a playful series of scenes broken up by old-fashioned titles, and *Zelig* a deeply ironic litany of cinematic tricks and mannerisms. On occasions he can remind one of Billy Wilder's sly outsider, slipping within movie history and upsetting all its most treasured memories: the biopic, the movie star, the egotistical director, the legendary newsreels – all are satirised in Allen's work. Indeed, the effect of his own appearance in his movies is to make one imagine Chaplin directed by Wilder – the little comic, vulnerable and full of hope, but now depicted in often a mercilessly ironic, and sometimes embittered, light.

Manhattan is a memorable example of Allen's direction at its most intelligent and caustic. The theme of the struggle for personal integrity is complemented by the classical spirit of the movie, with its straightforward narrative, resolute black-and-white photography and Gershwin score. Indeed, Allen's choice of songs provides specific settings in which to interpret each scene: Tracy and Isaac relax in their apartment, amidst the sound of 'Our Love is Here to Stay'; they ride through Central Park as the soundtrack features 'He Loves and She Loves'; and Mary and Isaac experience a tense moment as we hear 'Let's Call The Whole Thing Off.' The most notable visual technique in the movie has a stationary camera being held on a physical space after the characters have vacated it, giving one a disturbing insight into the mortality that lurks beneath the surface. The central figures are forgiven little; Allen has rarely been so clear in his treatment of characters. Perhaps the most signficant fact about *Manhattan*'s construction is its elliptical treatment of Allen's own character: simply, less time is needed to register the meaning of Isaac's actions and personality. For example, when he returns home with news of his ex-wife's forthcoming book, he shuts the door: for just a few seconds, we see it has three locks and a security pole as defences against a hostile world. In earlier movies (such as *Play It Again, Sam*), this would be dwelled upon and underlined, with the Allen character pausing to discuss his insecurity ('That's a good airport terminal. I've thrown up there'); here, on the contrary, it is subtle, swift and stylishly fluid. New York itself is used in a thoroughly intelligible way: 'I really think,' said Allen, 'that we – that's me and cinematographer Gordon Willis – succeeded in showing the city. When you see it there on the screen it's really decadent.' It is also reconstructed, in the sense that Allen weaves together an impressionistic series of images of New York to produce a place redolent of his own past. Benjamin (1983, VI, 486) compared memory to the soil in which the fragments of ruined cities linger on, waiting not for the reconstruction of the lost whole but for their discovery as images 'that stand broken free from all former associations like delicacies in the sober chambers of our late insight'.

By the 1940s, inspired by the verisimilitude of war-time documentaries, movie-makers began to return to the streets they had left years before. The decline of the studios, the competition from television, and the development of lightweight equipment accelerated this quest for real worlds beyond the studio: movies such as *The Lost Weekend* (1945) and *House on 92nd Street* (1945) breathed an 'authentic' air of New York, and it is this tradition that Allen's later work draws upon. His cinematographers manage, in movies like *Manhattan*, *Broadway Danny Rose* and *Hannah and Her Sisters*, to capture impressions of the sheer corporeality of New York, capturing its massive constructions and shadowy suburbs. In contrast, Allen shoots in Los Angeles and makes the city appear as a stage set: paper-thin facades and palm trees, unnatural colours and blinding lights. Allen is the opposite of Hitchcock in his approach to the world around him; Hitchcock had a Catholic reverence for nature and the 'real', and would allow certain 'landmarks' to manipulate and dominate his narrative – the fight on Mount Rushmore in *North by Northwest* (1959), the murder at the United Nations, and the Riviera frolics of *To Catch a Thief* (1955).

In contrast, Allen often allows the locations to contribute to the narrative, adding another layer of meaning to the action and the characters. His selection of certain places in New York in which to base his stories are nearly always well chosen. In *Broadway Danny Rose*, we begin in the Carnegie Delicatessen with a group of theatrical agents and performers telling stories about Danny Rose; the setting is subtle, apposite and entirely believable, with the camera seeming to 'spy' on the group of raconteurs and the black-and-white images preparing us for a nostalgic story. *Manhattan* contains scenes set in Elaine's Cafe, the Russian Tea Room and the Hayden Planetarium, yet the places seem to mirror the moods of the characters, with idle chatter in Elaine's and romance with the stars. In *Hannah and Her Sisters*, the fateful meeting of Lee and Elliot occurs in the Pageant Book & Print Shop, and they start their affair in a room in the St. Regis Hotel; the bookshop, with its distinctive style and its popularity with intellectual New Yorkers, is a particularly propitious context for the two individuals seeking out new love, nervously citing Caravaggio and e.e. cummings. The movie also manages to include a gently ironic scene with the lover of New York sights, David the architect: 'You know, April, people pass by vital structures in this city all the time, and they never take the time to appreciate them.' April asks, 'What are your favourite buildings, David?' The reply is a cue for a self-consciously abrupt digression: 'You want to see some? Well, let's do it.' There follows a visual excursion through the City's landmark buildings: the Dakota, the Graybar building on Lexington Avenue, an ornate building on Seventh Avenue and Fifty-eighth Street, a red-stone church, the Chrysler Building, Abigail Adams' old stone house, and the Pomander Walk nestled off Broadway on the Upper West Side. The montage of sights is, in one sense, a reprise, for Allen's cameras have been to many of these places before – old movies are now part of those buildings, aspects of what we see in them. Allen is a unique lyricist of place; he has exploited the myths and meanings associated with his city and inflected them with his own stories and sensibility. The cinema starts with reality itself; it can shoot reality in many ways and from many angles, but it begins with a physical donnée – it is

spared the basic creative pain of evocation out of nothing. Dustin
Hoffman observed how Allen has understood this fact and seized
on it with enthusiasm:

> Woody Allen has told me that he has written in his contract that he
> can come back during postproduction to shoot maybe twenty, thirty
> percent of the film, and in that way do what a writer or sculptor does
> – you go back and you keep working on it till it's right. Most movies
> aren't that way. They always say, 'Don't worry about the sets; they'll
> be there'. And then they're not there. Studios are funny that way. They
> don't want you to go back again. Woody Allen told me, 'I never shoot
> sets. That's why I shoot Rockefeller Center, because I know it's going
> to be there'. (*American Film*, April 1983)

'The best film I ever did,' said Allen during 1987, 'was *Stardust
Memories*. It was my least popular film. That may automatically
mean it was my best film. It was the closest that I came to
achieving what I set out to achieve.' Technically, the movie has
moments that hark back to earlier works. Allen's constant shifts
between Sandy Bates' past and present, as well as the delicate
interplay between movie illusions and everyday reality, remind
one of *Annie Hall*. The movie's superb black-and-white cinematography recalls the subtle textures of *Manhattan*. However,
Stardust Memories moves beyond these examples in its exploration of movie history and its consequences. Isaac Davies
worried about 'how people are going to see us' in the future;
Sandy Bates is painfully aware that those people will see us,
largely, through images. He himself is being subjected to a
'retrospective', a weekend of his old movies, his past selves,
analysed by a group of eager fans and critics. His daydream
towards the end acknowledges the fact that, for these people, his
'immortal' image has already outlived his finite self. Death is one
long retrospective; it means little more than a 'season' of one's
old movies, filling the space one's body vacated. Malraux's art is
again cast as the last defence against death, but it has never
seemed so inadequate. At the beginning, Sandy Bates is trapped
in a train car filled with grotesque, inexplicably anguished people;
he looks out at another train on the opposite side of the tracks,
in which comely, laughing, glamorous, jewel-bedecked passengers
toast one another with champagne. The trains begin to move,
and Sandy flags a conductor to protest the injustice of his
condition; his ticket was, he claims, for the other train. When his
train finally reaches its destination, he steps out into a barren

junkyard, hovered over by seagulls, and peopled, to Sandy's surprise, by the glamorous passengers as well as the miserable ones. Not only is life awful, when it is over it is over for everyone; the good, the bad, the loved and the lonely, all end up dead together. Sandy Bates, the movie director who loses faith in the usefulness of movies, begins to turn his contempt in on himself. 'I didn't want this guy to be necessarily likeable,' said Allen, 'I wanted him to be surly and upset: not a saint or an angel, but a man with real problems who finds that art doesn't save you.' The 'whimsical' quality of the movies makes Sandy himself feel whimsical. In what is probably the most unsettling sequence in the movie, the director remembers the last time he saw Dorrie, his lover, in the sanitarium; the images seem to peel away, as though they are too painful to be gazed at, and the suffering of the person, for once, indicts the spectacle. Dorrie is seen in close-up; each time she utters a new phrase, the film cuts to a slightly different angle of her face: 'There's a doctor here that thinks I'm beautiful and interesting'/'Are you seeing anyone'/'You look thin'/'There's a doctor here that's crazy about me'/'Are you seeing any-'/'You-this-'/'People'/'Oh-'/'... be too close'/'There's no point to'/'... too much'/'... some fresh air'/'... feel better'. The unnatural abruptness of the sequence highlights the sense of violation - of emotions, of body, of language, of integrity. The camera finally, fleetingly, comes to rest on a shot of her face: she rubs the tears from her cheeks and says, 'How do I look?' The question is unanswerable; we are shamed into silence. 'He's pretentious,' exclaims Sandy's producer. 'His filming style is too fancy. His insights are shallow and morbid. I've seen it all before. They try to document their private suffering and fob it off as art.' The producer sees the ideal movie as a screen that shields us from harsh realities; Sandy sees it as a screen that reveals such realities. Allen's movies acknowledge both of these functions; that is the source of their ambivalance.

Cecilia, the movie-lover in *The Purple Rose of Cairo*, represents Allen's own fascination with the idea of movies – the pleasures they provide, the passions they project, the fears they unfurl. Cecilia (Mia Farrow) lives in the America of Allen's childhood, the America of the 1930s, when Hollywood was the collective all-American dream, just as the economic depression was its nightmare. Cecilia works as a waitress in a snack bar; she has a bull-headed, selfish husband (Danny Aiello), who spends his jobless days pitching pennies with his cronies and chasing women (he does not like movies, he is the kind of person who is blind to enchantment); Cecilia's sole pleasure is going to the Jewel theatre (the only movie house in her small New Jersey town) and watching, over and over, the movies that appear there. We see her first in the theatre, her face splashed by the lights from the screen, her eyes wide open and fixed on the Astaire movie that is playing, her head faintly moving to the rhythm of the music:

> Heaven, I'm in heaven
> And the cares that hung around me through the week
> Seem to vanish like a gambler's lucky streak
> When we're out together dancing cheek to cheek.

The song, the theme, the thought, frame the movie; it is its *leitmotif*, its principle of hope. Astaire's distinctive vocal, never sounding strong enough to cope with the music yet always succeeding despite itself, captures the fragility that seems so noticeable in Cecilia. When *The Purple Rose of Cairo* comes to the Jewel, Cecilia is captivated by the character Tom Baxter (Jeff Daniels); 'explorer, adventurer, poet', who is all set for 'a madcap, Manhattan weekend'. The more the rhythms of everyday life break down and deflate her (she is deceived by her husband, she loses her job), the more the consistent patterns and plot of the movie assuage her. She keeps returning to re-view the movie, memorizing its lines, absorbing its moods. One evening, as Cecilia is watching the movie for the umpteenth time, Tom Baxter's eyes stray from the other characters and he glimpses the figure in the audience. 'My God, you must really love this picture!' He steps down from the screen, takes the hand of Cecilia and they leave the theatre. After two thousand performances, he cries, he is free. To Cecilia, it seems like a dream, a dream made flesh. She makes an excuse to leave her husband so that she can go out in the evening and rejoin her hero; she is, literally, enchanted by his presence. Tom Baxter's escape from the screen, however, has other consequences both on and off the screen. On the screen, the action is brought to a halt; or rather, the plot is brought to a halt – the characters only now begin to *do* things, questioning, choosing, arguing, waiting for Baxter to return. As in Buñuel's *The Exterminating Angel* (1962), the characters in the movie are trapped, framed, and their familiar environment now feels like a prison. On the other side of the screen, the audience panic at this breakdown in conventions: a disoriented viewer exclaims, 'I just want what happened in the movie last week to happen again this week, otherwise what's life all about?' The producers of the movie have the problem of recapturing a person who does not really exist, and who is wandering around New Jersey at this very moment. In Los Angeles, perhaps the studio could have relied upon the police to capture the character quietly, but in New Jersey, 'anything can happen.' The projector cannot be shut down, because then all the remaining characters would disappear; one of them cries out, 'No! Don't turn the projector off! It gets black and we disappear ... You don't know what it's like to be annihilated.' The unique suspension of the formal division between fiction and reality could not have come at a worse time: the owner of the movie house is facing bankruptcy; the producers are on the brink of financial ruin; and the actor who played Tom Baxter, Gil Shepherd, is running the risk of ruining his career. The producer and the actor go to the town in order to restore the old order of things. Gil Shepherd happens upon Cecilia, and during their conversation he discovers that she knows where his character is hiding. Overwhelmed at finding herself in the presence of a real, flesh-and-blood Hollywood star, Cecilia agrees to arrange a meeting. However, actor and creation prove only too separable, and Tom rebels. Across America all the individual projections of 'Tom Baxter' begin to give signs of indiscipline; in some movie theatres 'he' nearly escapes into the auditorium (the legal ramifications of multiple Tom Baxters, like Zelig and his innumerable paternity suits, are frightening). Tom persuades Cecilia to spend an evening with him inside the movie, and they enjoy (this time on the same side of the screen) 'a madcap, Manhattan weekend'. Gil enters the movie theatre and demands a confrontation; he begs Cecilia to make a choice between a live actor and a fictional character. After a moment's deliberation, she chooses Gil. Tom returns into the movie, the plot moves on once more, and Cecilia goes home to pack her bags and start a new life in Hollywood with Gil. Yet Gil's love for her proves as evanescent as the movie images, and he returns to Hollywood without her. She is abandoned, stranded in her wretched small town with her violent husband ('I never just hit ya – I always warn ya foist!'). In the eviscerated reality of her sad, small town, all that is left to her is the refuge offered by the movie house. Tearful, helpless, she settles once more into her seat; the lights dim and shelter her sadness. The new Astaire/Rogers movie is showing; Fred Astaire, in black-and-white steps, tie and tails, is singing, 'Heaven, I'm in heaven...'. Cecilia, through her tears, is, for now, happy; for now she is in heaven.

The Purple Rose of Cairo is Allen's most satisfying expression of his anxiety over movies; his view of them (as escapism and enlightenment, deception and disclosure, crutch and catalyst) reflects his view of life. '*Something's missing*': the fantastic freedom of the movies diverts our gaze from the fact of unfreedom in the world outside, yet the enchantment in the movies may be our only hope in a disenchanted world. The extraordinary narrative echoes Allen's earlier experiments with form: 'God', in which the characters telephone the author for help with the plot, and 'The Kugelmass Episode', in which the reader 'loses himself' in a book. The movie also reminds one of Keaton's *Sherlock Jr.* (1924), with its oddly haunting story of the projectionist who dreams his way into the movie he is showing; Fellini's *The White Sheik* (1952), which explores an unexpected relationship between a famous actor and adoring fan; and Pirandello's *Six Characters in Search of an Author* (1921), in which the author is tracked by his creations. *The Purple Rose of Cairo*, nonetheless, has its own impressive kind of individuality. It is both a philosophical and moral story, a fable in fact, dealing with the problem of the relationship between illusion and reality, dreams and rationality. 'Something's missing' – even after one separates actor and image. Significantly, the director is absent in every sense: Allen himself does not appear in the movie, and in the scenes set in the studio office, we see producers, actors, but no director. Gil and Tom try, vainly, to settle the ownership of their existence; Gil argues that he performed as 'Tom', and therefore he created him. 'Didn't the writer do that?' says Tom. 'But I fleshed him out,' reasons Gil. Neither, one feels, is entirely right. Actor, image, writer and director – what is missing is our faith, the faith we bring to their collaboration, the trust we place in their being. Tom's returning of Cecilia's gaze seems to be an unexpected recognition of this fact. Screen escapism has rarely been so delicate, so enchanting. The movie within the movie acts as a close-up on the pleasure-centre of motion pictures: 'We'll go to Casablanca, Tangier, Monaco or Egypt ...', says one of the characters, and, of course, they can. To enter wholly into the events and to enjoy complete identification with the characters requires the kind of imaginative activity that attends the state of dreaming. Astaire's arc-lit RKO heaven is a haven in a heartless world, a gentle place where

Cecilia is temporarily transported; more accurately, this is 'heaven' to her, the only heaven her heart can hold onto. It is here where, in the darkness, lies the promise of illumination, a region of chance and risk within which alone the intimacy mythologized in the dancing of Astaire and Rogers is realisable. Cecilia will 'wake up' when this oneiric world no longer seems to satisfy her desire.

The movie also concerns itself with various kinds of hunger: emotional, sexual, physical. Cecilia hungers for something, something that is missing – food, money, love. Cecilia is the only character who gives without receiving: we see her serving food, but she never gets to eat it, she bestows affection on Gil and Tom, but gets little in return. Her husband, physically full and emotionally excessive, can only ask her, 'Any more meatloaf left?'; as she leaves him, all he can shout out is, 'I want my dinner!' Tom is 'fleshed-out', in effect, by Cecilia's adoration for him; he only ventures forth from the screen after seeing how she watches him. Gil feeds off her compliments, and takes her love and her hope. At the end, in the emptiness of the darkened theatre, Cecilia looks ravenous; she watches the movie with hungry eyes, her lean face made pale by the white lights from the screen. She is waiting, and is seduced by the illusion of plenitude. The movie shows us forms of seduction: our seduction by one another, by beautiful women and beautiful men and beautiful things; by alcohol, money, food, fame, America, art, and movies; seduction by our own hopes. *The Purple Rose of Cairo* asks us to consider our attachments to things less in the light of what things are than in the light of what mode of attachment we take toward them – for example, fetishistic, masochistic, voyeuristic, narcissistic, or, in general, partial. Like the philosopher in *Another Woman*, who eavesdrops on the drama in the next apartment, the movie-goer may allow a curiosity to turn into an obsession. Tom Baxter enchants his admirer, but in time he may well enslave her. In a nicely ironic inflexion of the fantasy/reality theme, genuine romance between Gil and Cecilia begins to dawn when they start, instinctively, to lapse into the dialogue of one of his old movies (dialogue which the fan knows as well as the actor himself).

Tom Baxter, freed from the constraints of the movie world, finds that his knowledge is not attuned to the imperatives of the real world. The limits of the reel world prove to be the limits of Tom's reality: he tries to pay the bill in a restaurant with stage money; he innocently questions a prostitute about her marriage prospects; when his lips touch Cecilia's, he pauses, waiting for the inevitable fade-out (his excitement upon learning of its non-existence in this world is unfounded, for he has no knowledge of sexual relations); when he plans a quick escape by stealing a car, he sits motionless, expecting the engine to start up by itself. The story has a seriousness which goes far beyond the surface drama of *Interiors* and *September* in the sheer breadth of its implications. The unfortunate characters left stranded on (or rather, *in*) the screen are forced to consider the existential and political ramifications of suddenly being presented with free will in the matter of plot, while also being faced with the immortal hell of never being able to finish the story. It is a move from Hobbesian order to Sartrian nausea, as though the film has broken, yet the images continue to show on the screen, washed up on some beach of indeterminacy. 'I'm a dramatic character,' shouts one of the frightened figures, 'I need forward motion!' We take it as 'natural' for movies to have a beginning, middle and end, a story, which has a certain duration and a comprehensible structure; when the movie in the Jewel peels off such conventions, leaving itself naked and open, unpredictable and unanswerable, the audience is astonished – 'It's a miracle!' The miracle is, in reality, that the plot (on other occasions) always does continue, and that the character we are drawn to never does catch our eye and step down to converse with us. Allen reaffirms the magic of movies by assaulting our most unthinking habits of mind; the process is no less than an act of re-enchantment. We see the beautiful power of this when the night-club *maître d'*, upon discovering that the laws of narrative have been suspended, takes the opportunity to realize his dream and bursts spontaneously into a frenzied, joyful tap-dance routine.

The movie also undermines the conventions of spectatorship – particularly the negative aspects of submitting, momentarily, to a fantasy world. Cecilia's needs have been ignored by society, and her precious movies, despite their appearance to the contrary, ignore them too. Physically one is always positioned so as to look *up* at movie images; Cecilia's face seems to have become fixed in this position, gazing up at people and things; she lives in a state of suspense engendered by an obsession with other people's stories. Her days are spent waiting – for her husband to assault her, for her employer to fire her, for Fred to dance with Ginger. Tom Baxter's action has shattered her own illusions of

impotence (neither her husband nor her movies used to acknowledge her sexuality and her independence), leaving her, at
the end, stronger than before. The ending is poignant but not
tragic; as she looks up once more and her face 'dissolves' into
the movie, the relationship will never be as submissive as it was
before. She has come to use enchantment; it will never use her
again. She has been to the source of the illusion and experienced
its own peculiar artificiality; the champagne is really ginger ale,
the elliptical narrative leaves one empty and poorer in memory,
and the glorious innocence of the characters proves to be the
product of ignorance. Like the future generation of hedonists in
Wells' *The Time Machine*, these people seem to live without
ever being alive. Tom Baxter has no knowledge of ambiguity or
contradiction, no awareness of mortality or love. He is beaten
up by Cecilia's husband, and he gets to his feet without any cuts
or bruises; he cannot be hurt, his 'character' is written as a hero.
Cecilia comes to realize that what attracts her to Tom in movies
is the very thing that proves so intolerable in real life: his lack of
responsibilities, his 'otherness', his lack of fears and anxieties.
On the screen his freedom is Cecilia's 'something's missing'; in
her own world his freedom is always missing something-it is
unreal, literally useless. 'People get old,' she tells him, 'and never
find perfect love'. Back in his fantasy world, Tom can find
perfect love, and Cecilia can look up and imagine it; it is the
projection of her needs that makes it seem real, and the fact of
his fantasy that is the source of our ambivalent response. A
movie world that comes to us fully formed is no world for us to
live in; we need to build our own utopia, dream our own dream.
We are at the mercy of what the medium catches of us, and what
it chooses, or refuses, to hold for us. Allen appreciates that
movies leave the world as it is, but he also knows that movies
are part of that world and affect the way we see it. The ambiguous
conclusion of *The Purple Rose of Cairo* turns on the knowledge
that there is nothing beyond the power of film to make us
accept; the movie world answers not to our needs but to our
hopes. The choice is not between fantasy and reality, for there is
(in reality) no choice; as Cecilia tries to explain to a baffled
Tom, 'You can't *learn* to be real – it's like learning to be a
midget.' As Allen has expressed it:

> Very simply put, the object of the movie was to show that we all have
> to choose between reality and fantasy, and we are, of course, forced to

choose reality, because the other way lies madness. And when we do choose reality, we get hurt, because reality hurts you. (BBC TV, 13 November 1987)

In such works as *The Purple Rose of Cairo* and *Zelig*, Allen dramatizes how human beings can become disabled by their dependence on the fantasies of society's cultural media; against this he posits doubt, anxiety, negation, failure, and finitude. His nightmare resembles the apocalyptic vision at the end of Thomas Pynchon's *Gravity's Rainbow*, where everyone has become so absorbed in plays, games and movies they are unaware of the tragedies in reality:

> The screen is a dim page spread before us, white and silent. The film has broken, or a projector bulb has burned out. It was difficult even for us, old fans who've always been at the movies (haven't we?) to tell which before the darkness swept in. The last image was too immediate for any eye to register. It may have been a human figure, dreaming of an early evening in each great capital luminous enough to tell him he will never die, coming outside to wish on the first stars. But it was not a star, it was a falling, bright angel of death. And in the darkening and awful expanse of screen something has kept on, a film we have not learned to see ... it is now a close-up of the face, a face we all know ... (Pynchon, 1975: 760)

Allen is fully aware of the sociological change the cinema has undergone from one sort of audience to another and of the impossibility of making movies that are totally modern and yet which do not encapsulate, as part of their relationship with an audience, the entire history of the movies. His public opposition to the 'colorization' of classic black-and-white movies reflects his fear that people are losing their historical perspective; by colouring these movies, the producers not only trample over the aesthetic value of the images, they also flatten the pictures, prising them from their place in history (looking like 'death warmed up'). Allen sees such trends as part of a more general movement away from a healthy, inquisitive attitude toward one's past. 'The man who loses his capacity for experience,' wrote Benjamin (1982: 186), 'feels as though he is dropped from the calendar. The big-city dweller knows this feeling on Sundays.' Against the timeless insularity of Hollywood, Allen (the city dweller) posits active, historic New York. He argues:

The trouble with this business is that people are still trying to predict trends. That's why you get *Police Academy Five* in the pipeline. Or eventually *Jaws Ten* maybe. That's not what this business should be about. The films I make, direct and star in try to avoid that. Sure, in taking all the key roles, I become a hyphenated animal, in which all the roles merge. But that's better than the other way. Films can't exist in a vacuum. They have to relate to the tempo of today. (*Hot Press*, May 1988)

Allen shares Pynchon's concern with the power of film to 'frame' reality, producing 'paracinematic' lives and 'movie children'. It is when he is faced with an uncomplicated view of movies as sheer entertainment, pure whimsy, that he rebels (as Alvy Singer rebels at Tony Lacey's home movie room). Indeed, Allen always seems eager to reassure himself of the moral worthiness of his work. Emerson, in his essay 'Self-Reliance', wrote: 'I shun father and mother and wife and brother when my genius calls me. I would write on the lintels of the door- post, *Whim*. I hope it is somewhat better than whim at last, but we cannot spend the day in explanation' (Emerson, 1985: 179). Writing on the lintels of the door is something one does on Passover, to avoid the angel of death; it is also on the lintels that writings of Deuteronomy are placed, in *mezuzahs*, to signify that Jews live within. Allen's movie work may seem whimsical, playful and light-hearted, but it is in fact more serious, and more searching, than that. Malraux's idea of art as a defence against death goes some way in explaining the importance of movies for Allen, but he also retains the anxiety of Emerson: 'I hope it is somewhat better than whim...'. The hope, for Allen, can never be realised to his own satisfaction.

> You can never seem to get the color the way you want it. When it comes time to take out the records you were working with and put in the real music, it's always a disappointment. When you're dead positive that this is the end, that it's finished, the distributors call up and say the first weekend's business is not what it should be. There's never a time when it's just a *fait accompli*, when the thing opens and everybody loves it, and audiences flock to see it – never. (Rosenblum and Karen, 1979: 266)

His work has an appeal, a usefulness, that not even he can entirely understand; the movies defy complete translation. These are moving visions, with themes and ideas and involute turnings we have not allowed ourselves to see completely, but which we sense and shelter in our memory of their presence. They are games that people play; they are games in the sense intended by Adorno when he noted that, 'The unreality of games gives notice that reality is not yet real. Unconsciously they rehearse the right life' (Adorno, 1978: 228). In Allen's city, the movie house is the home of hope, the refuge for remembrance, the place where one can experience renewal. Allen's characters turn away from thoughts of death in the movie theatre: Allan Felix in *Play It Again, Sam*, Alvy Singer in *Annie Hall*, Eudora Fletcher in *Zelig*, Cecilia in *The Purple Rose of Cairo*, Mickey Sachs in *Hannah and Her Sisters*, and little Joe in *Radio Days* - all find inspiration and enchantment in the movies. Leaving the theatre, a little dazed, wrapped up in themselves, feeling somewhat disjointed, they may view the world (and themselves) in a more benign manner. The movies are not an 'escape' for these people; rather, they are a catalyst for their compassion, exercising an effect upon their dealings with others and their understanding of themselves. Allen, in all of his work, is making the important observation that movies have become an important means of enjoying oneself, helping oneself, losing oneself, finding oneself, and knowing oneself. The past lives twice: once in itself, a second time in our reconstruction of it. The past is a multiple of our fantasies; reconstructed, it is not the past that was, but it is what remains of our stardust memories.

Few movie-makers have been so incessantly self-critical and anxious about what they do as Allen is. 'Maturity,' said Allen, 'has borne out my childhood. I'd always thought death was the sole driving force: I mean that our effort to avoid it is the only thing which gives impetus to our existence' (*Guardian*, 14 January 1979: 14). Movies, with their appearance of presence and absence, life and death, have an ambiguity that simultaneously attracts and repels Woody Allen. One of the most poignant expressions of this anxiety comes in the final image from *Stardust Memories*: an old Jewish man shakes his head and says, 'It's amazing. Rash. From this he makes a living?' As he continues to talk in Yiddish, the auditorium is emptied of people, leaving the grey vacant screen, the rows of chairs and the figure of Sandy Bates; he walks up the aisle, he pauses, turning back to gaze once more at the screen (as though expecting latent images to come into view), then he leaves, and all sound and all light fade away. We sense his disappointment, but also his indomitable hope. The movies are part of his life – it is no longer a question of whether or not he should embrace them. For good and bad, he lives in a movie world. As Schickel (1973) observes:

College may have made us appreciators of literary modernism, but the matinees of childhood maddened us with movies – and were the first on the scene ... His work has been shot full of ever more brilliant comment on the heritage that is, shall we say, the mother and father of us all.

6

Part of the Experience

*Philosophy is really homesickness, an urge to be at home everywhere.
Where, then, are we going? Always to our home.*

Novalis

I would trade that Oscar for one more second of life.

Stardust Memories

Mickey Sachs, a New York Jewish comic, is about to quit his
job. He has recently been under the impression that he has a
brain tumour, and now, despite the news that he is actually in
very good health, he is shocked by 'how meaningless everything
is'. True, he has been reprieved, he is not about to die pre-
maturely, but it is only a *temporary* reprieve: one day, at some
point, his life will come to a close. 'Doesn't it ruin everything for
you?' he asks a colleague. 'I gotta get some answers.' It is the
traumatic scene in *Hannah and Her Sisters* for Woody Allen's
character, the scene in which all those unspoken, unnoticed fears
and anxieties come out and confront him, shattering his sense of
orderliness and stability. It is the classic Woody Allen scene, the
scene in which dogma self-destructs, received opinion breaks
apart, and 'all that is solid melts into air'. It marks the end of
blind faith, it signals the beginning of the search for enlightenment. All of Allen's characters are driven by this urgent desire
for happiness and truth: the search for an authentic love; the
quest for a livable morality; the pursuit of genuine happiness.
From the *schlemiel* to the intellectual, the inspiration has always
been evident: life ought to be better.

Allen has remarked:

My films have certain set themes. For a start they deal with that greatest of all difficulties – love relationships. Everybody encounters that. People are either in love, about to fall in love, on the way out of love, looking for love, or a way to avoid it. God, there are a million variations. Then there are the communication problems. You know ... that thing called dependency. That is always linked to fear. Hand in hand. Dependency and fear. You can see them walking down the street. That's why life is painful. (*Hot Press*, 6 May 1988)

It should also be noted that few people have managed to make this painful life seem so incredibly funny. 'This world,' wrote Horace Walpole, 'is a comedy to those that think, a tragedy to those that feel'. Allen's work has come to find an approach that combines these two positions, producing a creative tension that reflects a world that is both comic *and* tragic. Allen is his own Don Quixote and his own Sancho Panza, a clown both damned and divine. This is the basis of his appeal as a comic, darkening his playful tricks and lightening his sober thoughts. This is also the basis for his lack of appeal for some people, who see little but another Chaplin struggling for Art. 'Why do all comedians turn out to be sentimental bores?' asks a disenchanted fan in *Stardust Memories*.

The city in Allen's movies is the arena for his activities, the place where his concerns are pursued; it is also an expression of those activities and concerns, reconstituted on the screen with his own images. *Manhattan* tells us that New York is 'his town', but much of the story contradicts that claim. Allen's character struggles for possession of the city against a number of human, and inhuman, opponents. It is not really clear what 'home' is in the modern world. Allen, of course, feels extremely ill at ease in the country, but then it could be argued that Allen (the rootless son of a rootless people) does not feel entirely at home anywhere – even in his native New York. Indeed, the sheer number of descriptions of New York as his 'home' suggests an anxiety about his roots and his role, and a hope that his repeated assertions of rootedness (like an incantation) might make it come true. At least in the city he has an audience, attuned to his essentially urban neuroses. One can be either public or private in cities, and, of course, one can be lonely – but it is hard to be *solitary*. The country really is a place for solitude, and in it sex, love, and death become part of immense and universal indifference. The country is not a place for gags, for that intense, anxious, intellectual wise-cracking which is one of Allen's greatest strengths. Nonetheless, his urban strengths remind one of his neurotic constrictions – the odour of Freudian paraffin is forever in the air. Urban life is, at some arguably Rousseauian level, exquisitely unnatural (artificial), and an art that is content with that constricted artifice is precisely that – constricted. Ingmar Bergman, as Allen would doubtless appreciate, is an informative contrast. *Fanny and Alexander* (1982), for example, is saturated with urban neuroses and modern wit, yet never constricted by it; for Bergman, the countryside can be blissful, baleful, indifferent, exquisite, and enchanting, rather indeed like life itself. Allen's vision of life is, at times, too redolent of the intense, cloistered inwardness of the night-club, jammed with acutely attuned urbanities using the vast and mannered resources of metropolitan culture, movies, plays, books, journals, philosophy, psycho-analysis, gossip, urban repression: the world as comic university. Brilliantly funny, but forever in need of nourishment.

Allen's thirst for ideas and insights forever places him on the edge of convention: he can never rest, draw to a halt, and come to a conclusion. He lives in fear of dogmatism, he strives for intellectual freedom. Writing about the philosophical disposition of the Americans, de Tocqueville noted 'a general distaste for accepting any man's word as proof of anything'. That distaste took shape as a traditional distrust of politics as collective activity, and of ideology as that activity's rationale. One of the ways in which this hostility toward political solutions manifested itself was in an ambivalence about the law. As de Tocqueville observed, Americans wanted 'to escape from imposed systems ... to seek by themselves and in themselves for the only reason for things' (de Tocqueville, 1969: 429). Comedy is one way of escaping from such constraints; Allen's comic characters are profoundly anti-authoritarian, ranging from Alvy Singer's almost unconscious rebellion in front of a police officer to Miles Monroe's refusal to tolerate *any* political or ideological solution: 'Don't you under-stand? In six months we'll be stealing *Erno's* nose. Political solutions don't work.' What faith these characters do have is soon undermined; Miles is staggered to learn that all his friends have been dead for two hundred years. 'But they all ate organic rice!' The problem for such characters is how to avoid despair. *Manhattan's* Isaac is on the verge of solipsism; if nothing works, why play along? What rescues him, and Allen's later screen incarnations, is a determination to keep looking for the true and the authentic, no matter how hopeless the search may seem. One of Allen's characters quotes the famous words of Tennessee Williams' Blanche DuBois: 'Whoever you are, I have always depended upon the kindness of strangers.' The Marx Brothers' anarchy was aimed at a cardboard world that offered little or no resistance to their assaults; ultimately, their iconoclasm is a product of extreme boredom - Harpo ignores conversations and cuts his neighbour's tie in two, Groucho will sometimes dwell overlong on wordplay, as though the story itself is not worth pursuing, and Chico's fast-talking style eschews any desire to communicate with his friends. Allen's world, on the contrary, is a recognizable one, concrete and three-dimensional, with the consequence that his humour is all the more outrageous and lethal. Furthermore, Allen uses his humour to try to change his world; the Marx Brothers use their humour to escape from their world.

Allen is forever trying to transcend dualism: he yearns to find some happy union of mind and body, comedy and tragedy, love and lust, fantasy and reality, the lover and the loved one. He senses the modern search for intimacy, and shows up its inadequacies. The cult of intimacy conceals a growing despair of finding it. The degradation of work and the impoverishment of communal life force people to turn to sexual excitement to satisfy all their emotional needs. Think of Allen's early characters: Fielding Mellish, begging his lover to let him join her in a leper colony; Miles Monroe, lost in a futuristic world with an Orgasmatron and an Orb for company; or Boris, whose search for erotic thrills leads him to be challenged to a duel. 'You go to a Bergman film,' Allen says, 'and you know you will be dealing with God's silence. Whenever you see a Scorsese film you know there's going to be a sociopath in it. With me it's this thing, the unfathomableness of desire. It's there over and over again. You can't help it, you need to deal with it to live.' It has to be said that in a great deal of Allen's work, including all of his early work, he does not so much 'deal' with this condition as passively observe its effect on him. One thinks of his characters' monologues, their on-camera self-analysis, and their exclamations of self-pity. There is also the sceptic in Allen's city, the person who cannot be satisfied with anything other than certainty: there is the student who demands that God's corpse be located in order to *prove* that He really *is* dead; there is the lover who insists on taking out an 'orgasmic insurance' policy. There is nothing 'relaxing' about the early Allen range of attitudes and dispositions towards the world, almost as if to be at ease and rest is simply to misunderstand the metaphysics of creation. Yet the spaciousness of great art has something to do with its power to make us relax, follow its contemplative flow. A life without the possibilities of such spacious relaxation is frenetically self-regarding, able to ridicule not just Michelangelo's *Pietà*, but even Treblinka. Allen begins to appreciate this during the mid-1970s, when he broadens his comic range and tries to accommodate a more speculative attitude toward his environment.

In his early work, Allen invited us to share in his bewilderment at the complexity of modern life; the world is not to be questioned, but rather to be coped with. The early movies of Allen's career are rich in such lighthearted acceptance of life's ironies: in *Take the Money and Run*, the prisoner craftily shapes a bar of soap to resemble a gun, colours it black with shoe polish, and succeeds in tricking the guards into leading him toward the prison gates; however, a storm breaks out, the rain comes down, and the guards turn round to find the prisoner pointing a fluffy ball of foam at them. In *Sleeper*, Miles Monroe wakes up in the future, only to find giant chickens chasing him and huge banana skins to slip on. In *Love and Death*, Boris, on the eve of his execution, discovers that God exists; the following day, he is shot ('I got screwed!'). By the time of *Annie Hall*, there is a new seriousness, an unwillingness to simply laugh away the problems of love and mortality. When one sees oneself as coming at the end of an oppressive tradition, parody becomes an important genre – a defensive and, potentially, a liberating one. Allen's early work shows him commenting upon past humour: Perelman in his *New Yorker* pieces, slapstick, Chaplin and Bob Hope in his movies. *Annie Hall* is at the interface between these early parodic works and the later, more original works. Alvy Singer is an ironic creation of Woody Allen, rather than merely an echo of Chaplin, Keaton or Hope. Alvy still tells jokes, but his face seems detached from the humour; in sharp contrast to the Hope-styled comedy of *Love and Death*, Allen here has a dead-pan expression. He still uses comedy, but he no longer settles with the comic. The concern with the lost times in *Annie Hall* reflects a recognition of the transience of life and the impotence of laughter in the face of mortality. Indeed, Allen here becomes obsessed with the need for a *sincere* form of comedy. The death's head displays complete expressionlessness – black eye-sockets – coupled with unbridled expression – grinning rows of teeth. Such an image haunts the shallow forms of humour: people laugh, but out of a kind of desperate nervousness, as though the hollow sounds would deafen them to their own fears. Allen began to seek a genuinely 'livable' humour - one that could embody his concern with the serious questions of life, death, and love. Thus, comedy as *style* started to supersede comedy as genre in Allen's movies. This is partly expressed in a way of seeing things which notices the comic in everyday life (rather than opposing that life with its fantastic witticisms). E.H. Gombrich once described a good joke as 'not an invention, but a discovery' (Gombrich, 1984); this is the shift in emphasis that occurs in Allen's later work. From using his humour to hide from reality, he now employs it to understand reality. One of his great predecessors at the *New Yorker*, James Thurber, expressed the reflective nature of this approach when he said, 'Humour is emotional chaos remembered in tranquility' (*New York Post*, 29 February 1960). In this sense, Allen's later use of humour involves its powers of rejuvenation: laughter as a catalyst for a renewed sense of wonder, momentarily abolishing the *ennui* of modern urban life. Allen knows the laceration of self-criticism, but now he also knows (and values) the balm of self-belief.

The early movies are noticeably *tentative* affairs, moving targets, unsure of their reception. Little is mediated, much is mixed up and muddled – a sight gag gives way to a smart one-liner, followed by a literary reference, and then a brief mime. The aesthetic schizophrenia has not completely disappeared. Movie-making is, for Allen, still an intensely ambivalent activity:

> I wish somebody would come in and tell me I can't make films anymore ... I don't have the discipline not to make them ... But it would sort of relieve the anxiety and the ambivalance I have about it if someone would come to me and say, 'That's it. It's over. You cannot make another film'. I'd suddenly heave a huge sigh of relief. (*Esquire*, April 1987)

He would also, of course, heave a huge sigh of regret: the movies are part of his past, and a process whereby he comes to review that past. There does seem to be something rather therapeutic in Allen's later movies: the man coming to terms with his mortality, the American responding to his society, the comedian working-through his influences.

For many of Allen's heroes, art fabricates an illusion of

meaning - a 'plot' in which everything fits – without which the burden of selfhood becomes unbearable. American movies have always been passionately devoted to story-telling, and Woody Allen has become one of the great modern story-tellers. The critic Walter Benjamin has spoken of the impulse to impart instruction as a defining characteristic of story-telling and as a condition of its vitality. Story-telling, he says, is oriented towards 'practical interests'; it seeks to be 'useful'; it 'has counsel' to give; the end it has in view is 'wisdom'. At the end of his night-club act, Allen often used to say: 'Um, what have we learned from all of this?' His movies are usually based on proverbs or aphorisms, such as *Annie Hall*'s story about 'needing the eggs'. Indeed, *Annie Hall* is perhaps the most notable example of Allen's story-telling technique: eclectic, imaginative, and intelligent, Alvy's use of his past is thoroughly imbued with this thirst for knowledge, this craving for understanding. Anything, literally anything, may be summoned up from memory in the cause of self-understanding. A chance remark by Annie moves Alvy to recall an old relationship, which leads him to remember the moment he first set eyes on Annie. The traumatic experience of his break-up with Annie makes him imagine himself dating the cartoon character he once saw when he was a child. Every event, every reference, every relationship, is sifted and analysed – a Jewish childhood, New York politics, former marriages, the Holocaust, certain books, certain movies, Marshall McLuhan, Ingmar Bergman, Walt Disney, and anti-semitic grandmothers. This kind of relatively unfettered eclecticism when dealing with the past is peculiarly American and an utterly different thing from the European author's sense of the past. The results and new juxtapositions can be brilliant, surprisingly original, and very un-European.

Throughout their history, the movies have served as a primary source of information about society and human behaviour for large masses of people. So significant a medium of communication should naturally reflect, to an extent, dominant ideas and interests, and the American movies have often done so in memorable ways. However, what is remarkable is the way that American movies, through much of their span, have altered or challenged many of the values and doctrines of powerful social and cultural forces in American society, providing alternative ways of understanding the world. Clearly, movies distort life, but it is often these very distortions that make them so significant: they testify to the anxieties, needs and interests of a particular historical period. As C.L.R. James (1950) has argued, the popularity of Hollywood's specious pattern of reconciliation is to some extent a reaction to the growing incompatibility of traditional American values in reality. In the movies, at least, the struggle for happiness finds temporary hope and inspiration. Capra's *It's a Wonderful Life* (not, it has to be said, one of Allen's favourite movies), for all its supposed lapses into mawkish sentimentality, is one of the most powerful examples of this redemptive impulse: a 'little man', George Bailey, has been driven out of business and deliberately humiliated by the most heartless of capitalists; he sits in a bar, desperate and dispirited, and mumbles to himself, 'Dear Father in Heaven, I'm not a praying man, but if you're up there and you can hear me, *show me the way*. I'm at the end of my rope. Show me the way, God.' At that moment, against all the conventions of Hollywood melodrama, George is knocked to the ground by a man he had earlier insulted. He is driven to the abyss. Looking at his life insurance policy, he thinks he is worth more dead than alive. When he wishes he had never been born, a magical guardian guides him back through his past – but a past devoid of his own existence. Life, for George Bailey, has become a movie – a *film noir* in fact – with him as a helpless spectator. This remarkable experience forces him (and us) to appreciate the beauty of participation. He sees his family, friends, his lover, all of their lives untouched by his, and he is forced to recognize just how much he needs them, how dearly he wants to be with them. He is back at the spot where he planned to kill himself, but now he wants to redeem himself: 'Get me back! Get me back! I don't care what happens to me. Only get me back to my wife and kids ... Please! I want to live again!' He repeats the affirmation over and over again, with extraordinary emotion: '*I want to live again! I want to live again! Please, God, let me live again!*' By allowing George to see what the world would have been like without him, the guardian angel gave him an adventure greater than he had ever imagined. Not surprisingly, because of George's kinship with Tom Sawyer, that adventure resembled Tom's trip to his own funeral, 'the proudest moment of his life'. The movie's lesson, in the angel's words, was that, 'You see, George, you really had a wonderful life.' Despite the extraordinary ending, the movie does not entirely allay the anxieties it has invoked. The evil businessman, Potter, escapes his anticipated come-uppance; the story's attempt at illustrating money's inferiority to friendship ends ironically in a sequence whose imagery implies that the extent of friendship can best be measured in terms of money; and the celebration of George's 'ordinarily wonderful' life inadvertently demonstrates that particular life's necessarily extraordinary quality (witness the wretchedness of life without him). Nonetheless, the movie's utopian longing is deeply moving; it seems to be saying, 'This *could* be so, if you are willing to believe it.' When one *does* believe it, one feels it *ought* to be so. George Bailey is forced to acknowledge that the American Dream is no longer a given, that it depends upon the will of its adherents. 'We can get through this thing all right,' he pleads with his customers. 'We've got to stick together, though; *we've got to have faith in each other.*' The self-doubt at one point makes him question all that he cares about: 'Why did we have to live here in the first place and stay around this measly, crummy old town? Who says this is such a happy family? Why do we have to have all these kids?' George experienced the movie's most pessimistic truth, that the value attached to even our dearest objects – even life itself – rests on the thinnest tissue of faith, even these cherished things can become nightmarish. That so many of us shed a tear at the merciful ending is perhaps a kind of recognition of how narrow the escape has been for that faith.

George Bailey's experience of the abyss, and his subsequent redemption, certainly makes him determined to *make* his life wonderful. It is only in Allen's more mature work that he allows his characters to seize such an opportunity. The early movies are too light to hold such ambition, and too humble to have such hope. The early Allen characters are excessively nervous, and merely glimpse at the deathly obstacles surrounding them. Death is the end of addiction to phenomenology, and maybe we all want to leave behind some memorial that we were, memorably (deathlessly) 'here'. However, Woody Allen, like a gifted student impatiently striving to become a 'great' artist, sometimes pushes too frenetically at the sources of his own creativity. In his attempt to understand himself and others, he plucks out the heart of their mystery. At such times he seems *manic*. A certain kind of achievement can come out of mania (Swift), but it is ultimately an art of acuity, wit, subversion and *Angst*, rather than affirmation and transcendence. One is left dissatisfied and a little demoralized: is *that* all there is? This question can be seen as the motivation for Allen's more mature work. The performer requires the alchemy of the story-teller who knows that we need art, lest we perish from the truth. Allen's later movies are rich little stories about the promise of *redemption*: redemption of a relationship (*Annie Hall*), of a city (*Manhattan*), of a career (*Stardust Memories*), of the self (*Zelig*), and, with *Hannah and Her Sisters*, the redemption of the idea of love itself. The hope is for a world in which one can be loved for one's own sake, and for a state of mind that allows one to appreciate that one really *is* being loved for one's own sake.

Allen's later work has sometimes been stylized by critics as overly 'nostalgic'. However, it is crucial to understand the *constructive* notion of nostalgia employed by Allen, which is radically different from the helpless longing for some bygone age commonly associated with mass-produced 'nostalgia' (a memory lane that leads one nowhere). Allen's nostalgia is set to *rehabilitate* the past for the present, rather than to seek refuge in the past from the present. Allen's sense of history is highly significant. The period in which we live is weighed down by a knowledge of earlier times: namely, the knowledge that otherwise rational human beings will facilitate the annihilation of entire populations if it suits their purpose, and that many good citizens, far from being appalled or angered or amazed when confronted with these acts, will accept them as an appropriate means of shortening a war, or instituting a radically new social system, or eradicating superfluous people. Seen through the prism of our contemporary knowledge of such evil, the past evokes nostalgia so fervid that the emotion has to be fiercely denied and denounced. Allen's poignant remark, 'if I had been born in Poland, or Berlin, I'd be a lampshade today,' makes clear his anxiety: the thought, 'will the survivors envy the dead?' haunts our time – not only because it describes a possible future but also because it articulates our own relation to the past, whenever we allow ourselves to look into the fully documented horrors that have already taken place in the twentieth century, so much more painful to live with, in the last analysis, than the horrors that may yet occur.

We now envision ourselves both as survivors and as potential victims. Allen's characters never fail to be shocked at the thought of the Holocaust, and they remain alert to the possibility of its recurrence. These characters struggle to retain a sense of history in a world that seems to exploit the past in increasingly shameless ways. Consider Alvy Singer's despair when he visits modern Hollywood, the studios and homes of his childhood idols now inhabited by doped-up pop stars and the producers of TV 'soap-operas'. Like children playing with a cherished memento, these people toy with the past with an arrogant carelessness. A society that has transformed nostalgia into a marketable commodity on the cultural exchange rapidly repudiates the notion that life in the past was in any meaningful way better than life today. Having trivialized the past by equating it with old-fashioned styles of consumption and outmoded attitudes, people now resent anyone who draws on the past in serious discussions of contemporary conditions or strives to employ the past as a standard by which to judge the present. Allen *does* employ the past in such a way. A knowledge, a memory, of better days informs his criticism of modern times. His work suggests that the modern world has its own form of suffering: that of having no words for the state of one's soul; of avoiding full wakefulness so as to shut out awareness of what is actually occurring. A major symptom (perhaps the problem itself) of what is occurring is the collapse of love, the closing-down of compassion. Allen's movies work against this trend, struggling to open up such concerns, and redeem what was, and is, worthwhile. As Eliot's 'Little Gidding' goes: 'We shall not cease from exploration/And the end of all our exploring/Will be to arrive where we started/And know the place for the first time.' It is a kind of excavation: *Annie Hall's* sifting, *Radio Days'* digging, and *Manhattan's* uncovering of the old city ruins. Allen shows how people once lived, and reflects on how they live now. He goes back to childhood, to beginnings, and discusses his development. This approach has been eloquently explained by Benjamin:

> Language shows clearly that memory is not an instrument for exploring the past but its theatre. It is the medium of past experience, as the ground is the medium in which dead cities lie interred. He who seeks to approach his own buried past must conduct himself like a man digging. This confers the tone and bearing of genuine reminiscences. He must not be afraid to return again and again to the same matter; to scatter it as one scatters earth, to turn it over as one turns over soil. For the matter itself is only a deposit, a stratum, which yields only to the most meticulous examination what constitutes the real treasure hidden within the earth: the images, severed from all earlier associations, that stand – like precious fragments or torsos in a collector's gallery – in the prosaic rooms of our later understanding. (Benjamin, 1979: 34)

Allen's collector's gallery is the cinema; his movies preserve these memories, and, in turn, reflect on their inexorable evanescence. Towards the end of *Radio Days*, Allen puts some wistful lines from the closing scene of Chekhov's *Three Sisters* into the mouth of a radio actor, who is watching the New Year arrive in Times Square; he wonders whether he and his colleagues will be 'remembered by later generations', and the fragility of his expression suggests a fear that even *that* immortaiity is of little comfort. 'I want to make sure that when I thin out I'm well thought of,' says *Manhattan's* Isaac; from this *memento mori* (he is standing next to a skeleton) Isaac draws the need for an assertive morality. Again, the recognition of death enriches the life.

Manhattan features a character who describes himself as a 'non-compromiser' who is 'living in the past'; he eventually realizes that living in the past is simply one other kind of compromise. He has betrayed himself. In all of Allen's later movies, one finds the fragility of trust expressed and, eventually, painfully accepted. *Manhattan* contains what is arguably *the* key phrase of the anxious Allen hero: '*I just don't want that thing about you that I like to change.*' New York, the movies, love affairs, society, all must change, but, if they have to change, why can they not be relied on to change for the better? *Annie Hall* showed Alvy Singer struggling against the nagging fear that 'love fades.' In the films that follow, it is suggested that it may not be love that fades, but rather the faith one has in love, and the problem becomes one of how to preserve that faith. In *Manhattan* we find Isaac preferring to follow remote, perhaps impossible, ideals rather than adhere to the corrupt human norms around him. He is on the rim of solipsism: riding with Tracy in a hansom cab, he says: 'On my prom night I went around this park five times, six times. If I'd been with a girl it would've been an incredible experience.' Isaac's feelings of betrayal when his former wife publishes a 'kiss-and-tell' book about their marriage serve to foreground his fear that trust is merely a convenient form of self-deception: when one falls out of love, it seems, truth crawls out from beneath the shell of the affair – silent criticisms are finally heard. As Isaac hears his ex-wife's attack on him, he winces with the pain of lost hope. Adorno captures this condition when he writes of divorce:

> It is as if the sphere of intimacy, the unwatchful trust of shared life, is transformed into a malignant poison as soon as the relationship in

which it flourished is broken off. Intimacy between people is for-bearance, tolerance, refuge for idiosyncracies. If dragged into the open, it reveals the moment of weakness in it, and in a divorce such outward exposure is inevitable. It seizes the inventory of trust. Things which were once signs of loving care, images of reconciliation, breaking loose as independent values, show their evil, cold, pernicious side. (Adorno, 1978: 31)

Tracy is the wonderful response to the Hobbesian melancholy of Isaac's Manhattan: she is more than an erotic answer to Isaac's fear of death ('How often can you make love in an evening?' 'A lot'. 'Yeah, I can tell. A lot. Thanks ... Well, a lot is my favourite number. Gee, really, *can you?*'); she is more than, in Isaac's words, 'God's answer to Job'; she is more than all of this, she is someone worthy of trust. More than just an answer, she is also a question; she is that 'foreign self', the loved one, whom Isaac has come to respect on her own terms, with all the anxiety which that involves. Isaac's race across Manhattan in pursuit of Tracy, who is about to leave for London (this is independence day), is his race away from the abyss; he once did not feel strong enough to believe in her love, but now, at the very last moment, he is prepared to take that risk. Tracy looks at this nervous, embar-rassed, apologetic man ('your slightest look easily will enclose me'), and says, 'Look, you have to have a little faith in people.' He looks at her, in the final close-up, with appreciation, admira-tion, bemusement, shame and pity, and with a little wonder: the young woman is wiser than the middle-aged man. She can trust. Isaac is moved, he is humbled. Maybe, it seems, there is still a chance of happiness for this embattled character.

At the end of Chaplin's *City Lights* (1931), the little man's love is finally recognized by the blind flower-girl whose sight has just been restored. However, Chaplin's tramp perceives the distance that remains between himself and the young woman; she longs for a rich, respectable suitor – not an outsider, an emigré, a tramp. An agonizingly poignant close-up of Chaplin's face ends the movie with an unanswered question: will the woman accept him for what he is and can the two of them possibly share a life together? At the end of *Manhattan*, it is *Isaac's* blindness that is cured: the final close-up shows him push back his glasses and gaze at the young woman in front of him, as though he is seeing her for the very first time. He has realized, possibly just too late, possibly just in time, that he has been loved for his own sake. The camera holds still on Isaac's face, as though encouraging him to see the constancy of the love Tracy has for him, but his expression evokes the lingering sense of doubt – the eyebrows rise up and arch, the eyes never quite settle on any one sight, but the mouth, thrillingly, is on the verge of a smile. This is not the end of anxiety, it is not the end of the differences between the two lovers, but it is a kind of promise to spend as long as it takes to work out what those differences are, and what they come to.

A problem for Allen's self-conscious, modern hero is the relationship between a partial vision of others and those others themselves. For example, he recognizes that he romanticizes Manhattan 'out of all proportion' and that he 'falls in love with trouble' and 'internalizes anger', but where does that leave him? Why do his actions and his needs seem as mystifying as ever? One of the unfortunate effects of the Freudian revolution, Allen implies, is that we have become so engrossed in the analysis of Oedipal structures, neurotic attachments and sexual desires, we have lost sight of love. Indeed, Allen's characters often seem to suffer under their analyst's intimidating worldview: 'You call your analyst *Donny*?' gasps Isaac. 'I call mine Dr. Chomsky ... you know ... or, uh, he hits me with the ruler.' One recalls the collapse of Alvy's marriage in *Annie Hall*: 'Why do you always reduce my animal urges to psychoanalytic categories?' Allen himself is at times drawn into the reductionist game – separating the comic from the tragic, the pleasurable from the practical – but he is usually alert to its dangers. Tracy's face, one could say, stares back at the analyst, daring him to 'explain' her.

The sophisticated appreciation of the fragility of trust one finds in *Manhattan*, and the ensemble writing Allen did so well in *The Purple Rose of Cairo*, are continued and developed further in *Hannah and Her Sisters*. *Hannah* is the first of Allen's movies with him as an actor that is not entirely dominated by his presence and character. The stylistic homage is once more to Bergman, but this time to the warmth of *Fanny and Alexander*, rather than to the earlier melancholy; like *Fanny*, it begins and ends at family celebrations, albeit traversing two years rather than one, and deals with emotional ructions in the various members of a thespian family. Interestingly, Allen originally intended *Hannah* to cover one single year, like Bergman's movie, but lengthened it for reasons of pacing and character development, allowing the movie to determine its own form, where once he would have been slave to his influences.

Knowing the symbolic aspect of Allen's movies, it is significant (and rather ironic) that the character played by Max von Sydow, present in so many Bergman psychodramas (including *Shame, Hour of the Wolf*, and *The Passion of Anna*), is easily the most intelligent and closed-off person in the movie, and ends up unloved, unnoticed, and alone: the iconic touchstone discarded. Indeed, the opening caption, 'God, she's beautiful', inaugurates an unprecedented (for Allen) sense of personal wonder. *Hannah* is a remarkable example of sophisticated screen comedy, and in terms of Allen's own *oeuvre* it represents the flowering of the 'serious comedy' style that he had spent the previous decade developing. *Hannah* seems to bring together the various threads Allen had been spinning since the *Love and Death* period, and weaves them into a mature and densely-textured tapestry, which balances perfectly between the poles of tragedy and comedy. New York, art, personal integrity, intimations of mortality, the cunning of desire, intellectual uncertainty, ontological insecurity – all these themes are present, interwoven with a restrained comic feel that points up the seriousness of things as it offers balm to soothe that seriousness.

Allen's models for his narrative are Chekhov (for his musical texture and multiple points of view) and Tolstoy's *Anna Karenina* (for its parallel plot lines: first, an adulterous affair, second, people's quest for meaning and happiness). The first of Allen's plots concerns Hannah (Mia Farrow), a celebrated stage actor (whose recent success was *A Doll's House*), taking time out to raise a family; her husband Elliot (Michael Caine), a bored financial adviser; and her sisters, both of whom feel dwarfed by their generous, gracious, accomplished sister. Holly (Dianne Wiest) is a failed actor with a crippling inferiority complex (and a cocaine addiction); Lee (Barbara Hershey) is an extremely attractive young idler who has allowed herself to become the lover/student of a misanthropic artist named Frederick (Max von Sydow). Elliot, sensing that his wife is so sweet and self-sufficient that even he has become superfluous, falls into a theatrical swoon over Lee, and the two embark upon a textbook liaison, complete with furtive messages, afternoons in hotel rooms, and considerable post-coital guilt. The second plot, which is woven through the first, has Allen as Hannah's former husband Mickey Sachs, a comedy writer and hypochondriac, so obsessed by his body breaking down that he will hurry to his physician over a spot on his shirt. 'I mean, *God*', he exclaims, 'how can

you just one day ... vanish?' For the duration, he raises a series
of complex metaphysical issues, all an extension of the question
posed by Alvy as a child in *Annie Hall* upon hearing the news
that the universe is gradually expanding and that the sun will
one day explode: '*What's the point?*' Even the prospect of a
family seems denied him: his relationship with Hannah collapsed
when it was found that he was infertile:

> *Mickey*: I'm so humiliated.
> *Hannah*: Could you have ruined yourself somehow?
> *Mickey*: How could I ruin myself?
> *Hannah*: I don't know. Excessive masturbation...?
> *Mickey*: Hey, you gonna start knocking my hobbies? Jesus!

He struggles to translate his passion and imagination into words
and practical actions, yet he stutters and he stalls. He feels
himself without roots, except for a vague sense of faith in his
native city; when he wanders down the street, worried about the
hospital tests he has been obliged to undergo, he says to himself,
'Okay ... take it easy ... Nothing's gonna happen to you. You're
in the middle of New York City. This is your town. You're
surrounded by people and traffic and restaurants...'. He clutches
at any philosophical insights that offer some promise of redemption – Socrates, Nietzsche, Freud – but nothing helps him come
to terms with 'the inevitable decay of the body'.

> Millions of books written on every conceivable subject by all these
> great minds, and, in the end, none of 'em knows anything more
> about the big questions of life than I do ... I read Socrates. You know,
> this guy used to kn-knock off little Greek boys. What the hell's he got
> to teach me? And, and Nietzsche, with his Theory of Eternal Recurrence.
> He said that the life we live, we're gonna live over and over again the
> exact same way for eternity. Great. That means I'll have to sit through
> the Ice Capades again. Tch, it's not worth it.

Forever at the back of his mind is the feeling that his sense of
tragedy is perceived by others as a kind of comedy: 'who the hell
are you kidding? You're gonna be a Krishna? You're gonna
shave your head and put on robes and dance around at airports?
You'll look like Jerry Lewis! Oh, God, I'm so depressed.' Mickey's
odyssey is comic, for to see this plainly Jewish character
conversing with a Catholic priest, taking communion, and discussing theological problems with Hare Krishna disciples, is to

see a man fighting his most established instincts – his irreverant Jewish wit and scepticism. Indeed, the scene with Mickey gazing at a 3-D image of Christ (whose eyes open and shut as one rocks from side to side) and piling his shopping on top of the New Testament, is reminiscent of the unshakable iconoclasm Allen once showed when interviewing Billy Graham on television:

> *Allen*: You could probably convert me because I'm a push-over ... And if you make it appealing enough and you promise me some wonderful afterlife with a white robe and wings ... I could go for it.
> *Graham*: I can't promise you the wings ... but I *can* promise you a wonderful, exciting life.
> *Allen*: *One* wing?

Mickey's existential queries, despite their often amusing form, give *Hannah* weight; they deepen its other half, which might otherwise seem merely a sex comedy. Although they never articulate it, the characters played by Caine, Farrow, Wiest and Hershey are no less terrified by the thought of their own lack of meaning, and each in turn is driven to the brink of despair. Yet *Hannah* is inflected by a comic tone that makes it one of the most liberating American movies since the Capra era. Allen had the movie lyrically staged and photographed, often in lengthy single takes, and each sub-plot has its own musical motif – songs such as 'You Made Me Love You' and 'Bewitched, Bothered and Bewildered'. Allen's technique accommodates the movie's swings in mood, from pathos to farce, despair to laughter, pessimism to optimism.

Allen has acknowledged that all three of the leading male roles – Mickey, Elliot and Frederick – embody different aspects of his own personality. Mickey, played by Allen himself, is nearest to the conventional screen 'Woody' character: a television comedy writer who quits his job, a 'little man' who wrestles with the most daunting metaphysical questions, a lover who cannot understand why the finest of intimacies sometimes give way to the greatest of distances. Elliot also has that sense of moral weakness and sexual appetite glimpsed in Allen's characters in *Manhattan* and in Martin Ritt's *The Front*. Frederick reminds one especially of the Allen character in *Stardust Memories*, a man making provocative but often quite plausible criticisms of contemporary *kitsch* culture, but doing so from a pathetically detached, impotent position. His universal principles float high above the particular problems of those near to him; 'Isn't it enough that I can love *you?*' he says, brushing aside Lee's complaints about his rudeness to outsiders. As she returns from an evening of love with Elliot, Frederick gazes carelessly at his sandwich and summarizes the night's television: 'You missed a very dull programme about Auschwitz.' The consequence of these three characterizations, Mickey, Elliot and Frederick, is that although Allen is on screen for an unusually modest duration, one feels that his presence persists throughout, imparting a sense of coherence and continuity.

Allen, irresistibly, continues to make some in-jokes about movies and actors, but now he can include them in a subtle and sophisticated way. For example, he has his old friend Tony Roberts appear as an ex-partner (now a successful figure in the corrupt California so memorably satirized in *Annie Hall*). Mickey, humiliated into having to admit that his former colleague now has *every* kind of creative superiority over him, asks Roberts if he will donate some sperm for Hannah: '*I* would be the father. You-you would just have to masturbate into a little cup.' 'I can handle that.' The dour, ascetic, acerbic Frederick is played by Max von Sydow, who has a certain notoriety for being Hollywood's 'Christ' in *The Greatest Story Ever Told* (1965). Bearing this fact in mind, Frederick's conclusions concerning modern culture and morality sound particularly ironic:

> the worst are the fundamentalist preachers ... third-rate con men, telling the poor suckers that watch them that they 'speak for Jesus' ... and 'to please send in money!' If Jesus came back, and saw what's going on in his name, he'd never stop throwing up.

In *Annie Hall*, Alvy Singer was searching for the perfect love, the love that continues to excite, the love that will never fade. The remarkable feature of *Hannah and Her Sisters* is Mickey's eventual recognition that, although loves fade, other loves are born. What our sense of 'perfection' threatens to do is to hold us captive in the present as the future arrives: Hannah's perfect wife, Lee's perfect beauty, Frederick's perfect morality, Mickey's perfect metaphysics – all suffocating ideals. The first sign of this realization occurs as Lee reads to herself from a poetry book; it is a turning point for her, and it is also a pivotal event for the narrative, leading us into the exploration of love. *Hannah*'s inclusion of an e.e. cummings poem complements the theme of vulnerability in the movie; cummings often used the lower-case 'i' to refer to his speaker, stressing the vulnerability of his anti-hero, wide-eyed with wonder before the world and readily assertive of his natural feelings, a figure corresponding to such characters as Pierrot, Petrouchka, Chaplin, and Allen. It is a mark of Allen's attention to detail that Elliot should choose what is arguably cummings' most beautiful poem, 'somewhere I have never travelled, gladly beyond', to express, voicelessly, his feelings for Lee:

> (i do not know what it is about you that closes
> and opens; only something in me understands
> the voice of your eyes is deeper than all roses)
> nobody, not even the rain, has such small hands

One of America's most gifted poets of love and death is thus memorably employed by Allen to illustrate his own thoughts on those two subjects. 'Did you ever get around to the poem on page a hundred and twelve,' asks Elliot. 'Yes,' replies Lee, 'it made me cry ... it was so beautiful ... so romantic.' As she holds up the book to show Elliot another favourite poem, he grabs her, kissing her passionately. The beauty of the thoughts gives way to the clumsiness of the desire; we see once again a love being ambushed by lust, the prosaic breaking up the poetic (in sex, as in comedy, timing is all).

Allen is still concerned with New Yorkers, but here he acknowledges what is wrong with them; he loves them, yet he can see their failings – and, in turn, his own. In *Hannah*, these failings are *alive*: we see their context, we witness the damage they do and the needs that drive them. Elliot at one point is heard telling his analyst: 'For all my education and so-called wisdom, I can't fathom my own heart.' Hannah's peaceful efficiency, encased by a poignantly precarious shell that seems set to shatter under the stress of Elliot's coldness, lies still in bed, in darkness, and whispers to herself: '...so pitch black tonight – I feel lost.' Mickey's quest for meaning seems to be self-defeating, yet even his suicidal tendencies cannot contend with his sense of responsibility:

> You know ... I was going to kill myself. The only thing that mighta stopped me, *might've*, is ... my parents would be devastated. I would, I woulda had to shoot them, also, first. And then, I have an aunt and uncle, I would have ... You know, it would have been a bloodbath.

The scene in which Mickey comes 'face to face with eternity' is titled 'The Abyss', and indeed the events cause him at last to find himself, his sense of his own uniqueness – as Wordsworth described such moments, 'Points have we all of us within our souls/Where all stand single.' For a period leading up to this moment, Mickey talks to no one except himself, as though negotiating with his own identity. We see him walking down a street, observing some joggers, reminiscing on past relationships, and staring out into space – while all the time his voice is heard, thinking out loud, his urge to speak overwhelming anything he might want to say. At the same time, the other characters begin to reveal how very vulnerable they really are: Hannah cannot bear to hear herself described as independent and 'too perfect'; Lee's guilt begins to break her spirit; Elliot's selfishness starts to shame him; and Hannah's parents lash out at each other's showbusiness vanities – 'she got drunker and drunker and finally she became Joan Collins'; 'All my life I've had to put up with insults from this non-person, this, this *haircut* that passes for a man.' This is, we must remember, a family composed mainly of *actors*, and actors (almost by definition) must find it exceptionally hard to embrace the belief that one is loved for one's own sake.

Allen allows his characters to glimpse the abyss and then, at the last moment, pulls them back, closing with a round of marriages and an enchantingly romantic flourish. His thematic point, in fact, is that comedy itself (along with love) can help us reconcile ourselves to a cruel, absurd universe. Life may be miserable but, as Alvy Singer also noted, it is all over far, far too quickly. Mickey Sach's search for meaning threatened to shatter what flimsy faith he still possessed. His apparently fruitless journey through the history of ideas has not really been such a failure. He has learned, on the brink of the abyss, the thought expressed by Adorno that 'The only philosophy which can be responsibly practised in the face of despair is the attempt to contemplate all things as they would present themselves from the standpoint of redemption' (Adorno, 1978: 247). As the demoralized Mickey slumps into a seat in a movie house, the sights and sounds start to work on his mood:

> the movie was a film that I'd seen many times in my life since I was a kid, and I always loved it. And, you know, I'm watching these people up on the screen, and I started getting hooked on the film ... And I

started to feel how can you even *think* of killing yourself? I mean, isn't it so stupid? I mean, look at all the people up there on the screen. You know, they're real funny, and, what if the worst *is* true? What if there's no God, and you only go around once and that's it? Well, you know, *don't you want to be part of the experience?* You know, what the hell, it ... it's not *all* a drag. And I'm thinking to myself, geez, I should stop ruining my life searching for answers I'm never gonna get, and just *enjoy* it while it lasts ... And ... after, who knows? I mean, maybe there *is* something. Nobody really knows. I know, I know 'maybe' is a very slim reed to hang your whole life on, but that's the best we have...

Mickey learns to see, once again, the promise of redemption; it is fragile, it may be broken, but it exists. There follows an assertion of a new commitment to life, in all its passionate messiness. As he had earlier remarked, reflecting on the collapse of his marriage to Hannah: 'Now instead of man and wife we're just good friends. Boy, love is really unpredictable.' From his new position, he is ready to accept this unpredictability. He denies neither the abyss that at any time may open up before our plans, nor the possibility, despite that open possibility, of living honourably, with good if resigned spirits, and with eternal hope. His capacity for love does not avoid this knowledge, but lives in full view of it. As George Bailey said: 'I want to live again!'

In this refreshed state of mind, Mickey falls in love with Holly - despite their previous, disasterous, date. 'Well, I hope you've changed,' he tells her, 'I hope so for your sake, because, uh, your personality left something to be desired ... namely a personality.' Indeed, from being a rootless, cocaine-snorting misfit, Holly has become a writer with a strong sense of tradition; indeed, her final audition found her singing 'I'm Old Fashioned' – 'As long as you agree/To stay old fashioned with me.' Mickey, in turn, has changed; he now has a willingness to empathize, listening enrapt as Holly reads him her screenplay. As all the characters congregate in Hannah's home for Thanksgiving, 'You Made Me Love You' plays on the soundtrack. Elliot gazes over at Lee, who has finally found a partner who loves her for herself, and he thinks to himself,

I acted like such a fool. I don't know what came over me. The complete conviction that I couldn't live without you ... What did I put us both through? And Hannah ... who, as you once said, I love much more than I realised.

Mickey arrives, moves over to Holly, puts his arm around her shoulders, and kisses her:

> It'd make a great story, I think. A guy marries one sister ... [*he kisses her*] ... doesn't work out [*kisses her again*] many years later...[*another kiss*] he winds up ... married to the other sister. It's, you know, it's a ... I don't know how you're gonna top that.

Holly, almost with a whisper, responds: 'Mickey ... I'm pregnant.' He looks at her, shocked, as though his hopes have, at last, come to fruition, and he embraces her. Love does, after all, preserve itself under betrayal; it allows, and forwards, its objects wish to find the edge of its own existence; it does not shrink from recognition that its object is headed for, or has survived, radical change, with its attendant destructions – which is the way love knows that a betrayal is ended, and is why it provides the context for a new innocence. There is always the promise of a wonderful life.

Hannah's architect laments the loss of so many fine sights, but the sense of hopefulness remains. As Mencken wrote: 'New York is not all bricks and steel. There are hearts there, too, and if they do not break, then they at least know how to leap' (quoted in Marqusee, 1988: 173). In *Hannah*, Allen has succeeded in entering other people's minds, and he ends by affirming a love which is characterized, among other things, by the ability to empathize. The wonder of friendship and the magic of love depend on the separateness of friends and lovers; it is this which makes their response to one another a gift, something they can treasure. It is only when one cannot accept the other person's separateness, give them space in which they can be themselves, that this separateness turns into something that separates. 'The heart,' Mickey remarks with undisguised pleasure, 'is a very, very, resilient little muscle'. As Larkin once wrote, 'What will survive us is love'; Allen, at last, appears in control of the demons in his soul. In the final, triumphant, exhilarating shot, he seems to be saying, 'I have learned to love.'

The ending of *Hannah and Her Sisters*, with its 'magical' pregnancy and its joyful atmosphere, is especially significant for those who have followed Allen's career, watching most, or all, of his movies. After the succession of disappointments his characters have suffered – the break-up of Alvy's affair, the uncertainty of

Isaac's relationship, the bitter failures of Danny Rose – this moment of affirmation, of celebration, we accept after many years spent in the company of these images. It is an occasion when countless memories of previous incarnations and old images seem to be invoked; the history of the star is glimpsed. One can think of similar moments for other performers: the sight of Laurel and Hardy in *Way Out West* (1937), one of their last great movies, dancing to the song 'At the Ball, That's All' and looking so poignant; Keaton and Chaplin in *Limelight* (1952), two great clowns united at last; Peter Sellers in *Being There* (1979), a final, fine performance by the great impersonator as a man who is content to be himself. For these moments, the story somehow ceases to matter, and we find ourselves loving them for their own sakes.

When Allen's characters look back on their past, they seem to be viewing their own private movies, finding similar moments of happiness. The search is for *'une promesse de bonheur'* in a society that does everything it can to discourage such promise. In *Stardust Memories*, for instance, Sandy Bates has settled into sarcasm in order to protect himself from the consequences of the nostalgia industry:

> *Dorrie*: That aftershave. It just made my whole childhood come back with a sudden Proustian rush.
> *Sandy*: Yeah? That's 'cause I'm wearing Proustian Rush by Chanel. It's reduced. I got a vat of it.

His joke carries a bitter tone; one is reminded of that other opponent of the commodification of culture, Frederick from *Hannah*, admonishing the pop star who has 'a lot of wall space' – 'I don't sell my work by the yard!' Yet at the same time as this bitterness we find in Allen an indomitable desire (indeed, a demand) for happiness. He knows it is not a hope he dare loosen his hold upon. As Emerson said, 'To fill the hour – that is happiness.' Sandy, imagining himself at the end of his life, examines those times when life seemed worth living, 'searching to try and find something to hang on to ... 'cause, uh, when you're dying, uh, life suddenly really does become very authentic ... And, I was reaching for something to give my life meaning, and a memory flashed through my mind.' The beautiful hour is uncovered; Sandy is in a sun-filled room, eating some ice-cream, and a record of Louis Armstrong singing 'Stardust' is playing in the background:

> It was one of those great spring days. It was Sunday, and you knew summer would be coming soon. I remember, that morning Dorrie and I had gone for a walk in the park. We came back to the apartment. We were just sort of sitting around. And ... I put on a record of Louis Armstrong, which is music that I grew up loving. It was very, very pretty, and ... I happened to glance over, and I saw Dorrie sitting there. And I remember thinking to myself ... how terrific she was, and how much I loved her. And, I don't know ... I guess it was the combination of everything ... the sound of that music, and the breeze and, and how beautiful Dorrie looked to me. And for one brief moment, everything just seemed to come together perfectly, and I felt happy. Almost indestructable, in a way ... It's funny that that simple little moment of contact moved me in a very, very profound way.

Perhaps he should have told Dorrie how much he loved her at that very moment, or perhaps to speak, to put that feeling into words at that precise moment, would have broken the beautiful spell; 'sorrow's crown of sorrows is remembering happier days!' Even this brief, precious moment of happiness is tinged with regret. Indeed, *Stardust Memories* moves one to see how pleasure and regret are so thoroughly entwined. Sandy's brief recollection of past happiness (the song 'Stardust' serving as *his* madeleine) leads him to find a more compassionate conclusion for his movie:

> We're on a train; and there are a million sad people on it. And I have no idea where it's heading. It could be anywhere. It could be the same junkyard ... But it's not as terrible as I originally thought it was, because, you know we like each other, and we have some laughs, and there's a lot of closeness.

This search for 'something to give my life meaning', something authentic and sincere, is also memorably expressed near the end of *Manhattan*. Isaac, having given up Tracy and been betrayed by Mary, lies down on his couch and speaks into a tape-recorder, trying to collect his thoughts together:

> Well, all right, why is life worth living? That's a very good question ... Um ... Well, there are certain things I guess that make it worthwhile ... Um, like what? Okay. Um, for me ... oh, I would say ... what, Groucho Marx, to name one thing ... uh, ummmm, and Willie Mays, and, uh, the second movement of the Jupiter Symphony, and ummm ...

Louis Armstrong's recording of 'Potatohead Blues' ... umm, Swedish movies, naturally ... *Sentimental Education* by Flaubert ... uh, Marlon Brando, Frank Sinatra...umm, those incredible apples and pears by Cézanne ... uh, the crabs at Sam Wo's ... tsch, uh [*sighs*] Tracy's face...

The list ends with the human face, the face of another, and the lonely recitation is left incomplete; the face is not there. He sighs, thinks for a moment, then sits up; he walks across the room to a cabinet, opens a drawer, and finds Tracy's final gift to him – a small harmonica. This memento embodies and revives the sense of harmony between Isaac and Tracy, the harmony Isaac had tried to shut away. In the smallest, least obvious of things, one finds the most intimate of memories. *Manhattan's* ending entertains our hopes with its sense of promise. Such movies encourage us to feel that to be human is to have, or to risk having, this capacity to wish; that to be human is to wish, and in particular to wish for a more complete identity than one has so far attained; and that such a wish may project a complete world *opposed* to the world one so far shares with others.

The painful choice Isaac has to make, between a life alone and a life with another, is, for Allen, the classic problem; it draws together his concerns with philosophy and love, sex and death, and hope and morality. The beginning of philosophy is sexual attraction is how Plato sees the matter in *The Symposium*. In this dialogue, Aristophanes (the comic poet) relates a story about the nature of love; he says that originally all human beings were spherical creatures but, after their misbehaviour, the gods cut them in two. Thereafter, each of the halves seeks to be made whole again; thus, each individual is a fragment. This expectation that there is another half that can complete us and make us whole once more is fulfilled in the experience of love. If sexuality is the dialogue's conclusion, this does not mean that its point was seduction; it can acknowledge that the only successful conclusion of such investigation is mutual satisfaction, and that what remains between the participants is not a thing left unspoken. Perhaps philosophy's acceptance of separateness ought to be acknowledged as its capacity to forgo further proof of love (*'you have to have a little faith in people'*). 'I gotta get some answers,' cries the Allen character – but how many answers will suffice to settle with life? In Plato's odd, somewhat intoxicated little gathering, the same question can be discerned. *The Symposium* concludes with the observation that 'Socrates was compelling them to admit that the man who knew how to write a comedy could also write a tragedy, and that a skilful tragic writer was capable of being also a comic writer' (Plato, 1951: 113). With a work like *Hannah and Her Sisters*, Woody Allen provides a similar argument. 'Every joke,' said Orwell, 'is a tiny revolution'. Allen's humour has, in a subtle way, changed the state of affairs.

'There's just something different about you. I don't know what it is, but it's great': love is permanently susceptible to the making of comparisons, the desire to alter, and the insensitivity to differences. We assimilate, either in the mind or in reality, someone whom we now love to someone whom we once loved: we forget what the person whom we now love is like, or we try to change them: 'Adult education is a wonderful thing. You meet a lot of interesting professors. You know, it's stimulating.' In refashioning present love upon past love, we forget, likely as not, what the person whom we once loved was like. 'Where ... where did the screw-up come?' Allen's writing admits his own contradictory, complex, vulnerable self; he invests himself in his work:

> I like to observe the little idiosyncrasies in people. I understand, I think, what makes people stand alone. I suppose in that way acting has been therapeutic to me. It sort of satisfied some deep protectiveness in my nature. A wish, perhaps, to insulate myself against the hurts I have suffered. Through my screen characters, I have grown a skin over my own skin. (*Hot Press*, May 1988)

It may also be through the creation of these characters that Allen has come to understand himself more deeply. Writing and acting are activities that involve a willingness to take risks; it is in taking such risks that, in spite of oneself, one reaches beyond the dictates of common sense and, however fleetingly, catches oneself unawares. By the time of *Hannah and Her Sisters*, Allen seems, at long last, ready to acknowledge his *own* character, 'There's just something different about you. I don't know what it is, but it's great.'

What remains for Woody Allen is the 'problem' of other people. Allen's heroes have come to realize that there is no 'correct' response to Tracy's comment in *Manhattan* about having a little faith in people; our faith always was, and is, so terribly, awfully fragile. Our knowledge of other people has layers. We can know others intimately and, by implication, sexually: the phrase 'carnal knowledge' acknowledges this. We can know them socially, as friends or acquaintances. We can know *about* them, either in the form of gossip, or, more diffusely, in the form of worldly wisdom. We can know about them 'objectively', academically, collecting information and constructing theories about them. Ideally, perhaps, these various facets of our knowledge should knit together; but they do not. On the contrary, they often generate confusion. It is not just our needs that are ambivalent; the knowledge of people to which these needs lead us is itself fraught with ambiguities, paradoxes and antinomies. Where people are concerned, what we know is rarely simple. Thus, the apparent stoicism at the end of *Annie Hall*, when Alvy comes to realize 'What great fun it is *just knowing her*', is not *entirely* convincing. 'Just knowing her' may be great fun, but for Allen's characters that is rarely straightforward and never enough. 'Something's missing' is a constant theme in the movies, and perhaps, because they *are* movies, there will always be something missing. Perhaps that is one of Allen's most subtle observations. For over three decades, the man behind those black-rimmed glasses has noted the anxieties, aspirations, guilt and neuroses of late twentieth-century Western life. He has assimilated all the postmodernist doubts and debates about love, about knowledge, about fiction and fact. Yet something else, something more, has happened. Allen's comic vision has recently acquired the kind of compassion that enables him, at last, to begin, nervously, to trust. Comedy has become the opposite of mockery; it allows Allen, and ourselves, to suspend moral or social judgement and to entertain imaginative possibilities that a more 'serious' stance toward a character or event would preclude. The logic of the comedy that absorbs scepticism requires that we discover outer and inner aptnesses with objects to succeed in the worst cases, and by means of precision and beauty of conduct in principle open to any normal human beings. It requires only the willingness to care: 'Well... *don't you want to be part of the experience...?*'

One of Allen's characters begs to know the answers to such questions as 'why is there so much human suffering?' and 'Is there a God?' and, 'Why does love fade?' He is told, 'These are the wrong questions.' Perhaps all the questions we ask of love, to measure, test, probe and preserve it, have the additional effect of cutting it short. Perhaps the reason we are unable to love is that we yearn to be loved, that is, we demand something from the other instead of delivering ourselves to the other, demand-free, asking for nothing but company. The thing that sustains Woody Allen's little New Yorker is the belief that there *must* be some trust inside us; in the lines he quotes from e.e. cummings – 'in your most frail gesture are things which enclose me/or which i cannot touch because they are too near.' Allen inspires us not *despite* his vulnerability but rather *because* of it. He is struggling, as we are surely struggling, to find the strength to found a life upon a love. As the character says in *Hannah and Her Sisters*: 'Maybe the poets are right. Maybe love is the only answer...'.

Bibliography

Adams, J. with H. Tobias (1966) *The Borscht Belt*. New York, Bobbs-Merrill.

Adler, B. and Feinman, J. (1975) *Woody Allen, Clown Prince of American Humour*. New York, Pinnacle Books.

Adorno, T.W. (1969) *Prisms*. London, Neville Spearman.

—— (1973) *Negative Dialectics*. London, Routledge & Kegan Paul.

—— (1977) 'Freizeit', *Gesammelte Schriften*. X, 2, Frankfurt, Suhrkamp.

—— (1978) *Minima Moralia*. London, New Left Books.

—— (1981–2) 'Transparencies on Film' *New German Critique*, 24–25. Fall/Winter.

—— (1984) *Aesthetic Theory*. London, Routledge & Kegan Paul.

Allen, W. (1975) *Getting Even*. London, W.H. Allen.

—— (1978) *Without Feathers*. London, Sphere Books.

—— (1981) *Side Effects*. London, New English Library.

Ardner, S. (ed.) (1978) *Defining Females*. London, Croom Helm.

Auletta, K. (1979) *The Streets were Paved with Gold*. New York, Random House.

Ayfre, A. (1964) *Conversion aux images?* Paris, Editions du Cerf.

Barthes, R. (1979) *A Lover's Discourse*. London, Jonathan Cape.

—— (1981) *Camera Lucida*. London, Fontana.

—— (1986) *The Rustle of Language*. Oxford, Basil Blackwell.

Bates, B. (1986) *The Way of the Actor*. London, Century.

Battaille, G. (1962) *Death and Sensuality*. New York, Walker.

Baudelaire, C. (1964) *The Painter of Modern Life and Other Essays*. London, Phaidon.

Baudrillard, J. (1985) 'The Masses: the Implosion of the Social in the Media' *New Literary History*, 16, 3, 577–89.

Becker, E. (1973) *The Denial of Death*. New York, Free Press.

Bellow, S. (1964) *Herzog*. New York, Viking.

—— (1979) Interview in George Plimpton (ed.) *Writers at Work*, 177–96. Harmondsworth, Penguin.

Benchley, R. (1922) *The Benchley Roundup*. New York, Harper & Row.

Bendazzi, G. (1976) *Woody Allen*. Florence, Nuova Italia.

Benjamin, W. (1950) *Berliner Kindheit um Neunzehnhundert*. Frankfurt-am-Main, Suhrkamp

—— (1979) *One Way Street*. London, New Left Books.

—— (1982) *Illuminations*. London, Fontana.

—— (1983) *Das Passagen-Werk*. 2 vols, Frankfurt, Suhrkamp.

—— (1985) 'Central Park', *New German Critique*, 34, 32–58.

Berman, M. (1982) *All That Is Solid Melts Into Air*. New York, Simon & Schuster.

Bester, A. (1969) 'Conversation with Woody Allen', *Holiday*. May 70–1, 83–4.

Birmingham, S. (1984) *'Our Crowd'; the Great Jewish Families of New York*. New York, Harper & Row.

Bloom, A. (1986) *Prodigal Sons: the New York Intellectuals and their World*. New York.

Boorstin, D. (1961) *The Image: A Guide to Pseudo-Events*. New York, Atheneum.

Brenner, L. (1986) *Jews in America Today*. London, Al Saqi Books.

Brickman, M. (1985) 'The Analytic Napkin' in M. Richler, ed. *The Best of Modern Humour*. Harmondsworth, Penguin.

Brode, D. (1986) *Woody Allen: His Films and Career*. London, Columbus Books.

Bruce, L. (1974) *Ladies and Gentlemen – Lenny Bruce!!* New York, Random House.

Burton, D. (1984) *I Dream of Woody*. New York, William Morrow.

Callow, Simon (1985) *Being an Actor*. Harmondsworth, Penguin.

Canby, V. (1982) 'Film: American Roles During the Holocaust' *New York Times*, 19 April.

Canetti, E. (1973) *Crowds and Power*. Harmondsworth, Penguin.

Catullus, G.V. (1977) *The Poems of Catullus* Tr. P. Whigham. Harmondsworth, Penguin.

Caughie, J. (ed.) (1981) *Theories of Authorship*. London, Routledge & Kegan Paul.

Cavell, S. (1979) *The World Viewed*. Enlarged edn, Cambridge, Mass., Harvard University Press.

—— (1981) *Pursuits of Happiness*. Cambridge, Mass., Harvard

University Press.

Cebe, G. (1981) *Woody Allen*. Paris, Veyrier.

Chandler, C. (1980) *Hello I Must be Going: Groucho and His Friends*. London, Sphere Books.

Cooke, A. (1986) 'The American in England: Emerson to S.J. Perelman' in *The Patient Takes the Floor*. London, The Bodley Head.

Cooper, L. (1922) *An Aristotelian Theory of Comedy*. New York, Harcourt.

Countryman, E. (1983) 'Westerns and United States History'. *History Today*. March, 18–23.

Cummings, E.E. (1970) *Viva*. New York, Liveright.

David, F. (1974) *Yearning for Yesterday, a Sociology of Nostalgia*. New York, Free Press.

Davies, C. (1982) 'Ethnic Jokes, Moral Values and Social Boundaries', *British Journal of Sociology*, 33, 383–403.

Davies, P. and Neve, B. (eds) (1981) *Cinema, Politics and Society in America*. Manchester, Manchester University Press.

Deleuze, G. and Guattari, F. (1977) *Anti-Oedipus; Capitalism and Schizophrenia*. New York, Viking.

Derrida, J. (1982) *Margins of Philosophy*. Brighton, Harvester.

Dickstein, M. (1977) *Gates of Eden: American Culture in the Sixties*. New York, Basic Books.

Didion, J. (1979) 'Letter from Manhattan', *New York Review of Books*. 17 August.

Douglas, M. (1974) 'Food as an Art Form', *Studio International*. September, 83–8.

Dunn, J. (1985) *Rethinking Modern Political Theory*. Cambridge, Cambridge Univerity Press.

Dureau, C. (1985) *Woody Allen*. Paris, PAC.

Eco, U. (1986) *Faith in Fakes*. London, Secker and Warburg.

Eliot, T.S. (1983) *Four Quartets*. London, Faber & Faber

Emerson, R.W. (1985) *Selected Essays*. Harmondsworth, Penguin.

Encyclopaedia Judaica. vol. 12.

Enzensberger, H-M. (1974) *The Consciousness Industry*. New York, Seabury.

Fekete, J. (1978) *The Critical Twilight*. London, Routledge & Kegan Paul.

Finkelstein, J. (1989) *Dining Out: A Sociology of Modern Manners*. Cambridge, Polity.

Foster, H. (ed.) (1985) *The Anti-Aesthetic*. London, Pluto.

Foucault, M. (1982) *The History of Sexuality.* vol. 1. Harmondsworth, Penguin.

Four Films of Woody Allen (1982) New York, Random House.

Freud, S. (1911) 'Formulations Regarding the Two Principles in Mental Functioning', in *Collected Papers* Tr. J. Riviere, vol. IV, 1924–50, New York.

—— (1960) *Jokes and their Relation to the Unconscious.* New York, Norton.

Fuchs, W.J. (1986) *Die vielen Gesichter des Woody Allen.* Köln, Taschen.

Gill, B. (1975) *Here at the New Yorker.* New York, Random House.

Gilliatt, P. (1974) 'Guilty With an Explanation', *New Yorker,* 4 February.

Gittelson, N. (1979) 'The Maturing of Woody Allen', *New York Times Magazine.* 22 April.

Gledhill, C. (ed.) (1982) *Star Signs.* London, BFI Education.

Gombrich, E.H. (1984) *Tributes.* Oxford, Oxford University Press.

Gornick, V. (1976) 'Face It, Woody Allen, You're Not a Schlep Anymore', *The Village Voice.* 5 January.

Gosling, J.C.B. and Taylor, C.C.W. (1982) *The Greeks on Pleasure.* Oxford, Oxford University Press.

Guthrie, L. (1978) *Woody Allen, A Biography.* London, Drake.

Harrington, J. (1973) *The Rhetoric of Film.* New York, Holt, Rinehart and Winston.

Hartle, A. (1986) *Death and the Disinterested Spectator.* Albany, SUNY.

Haskell, M. (1987) *From Reverence to Rape.* 2nd edn Chicago, University of Chicago Press.

Heller, J. (1984) *Catch-22.* London, Corgi.

Hekman, S.J. (1986) *Hermeneutics and the Sociology of Knowledge.* Cambridge, Polity.

Hentoft, N. (1982) 'The Silence of American Jews'. *Village Voice,* 8, 29 June.

Hertzberg, A. (1984) 'The Jewish Intelligentsia and Their Jewishness'. *Midstream,* 37, November.

Hirsch, F. (1981) *Love, Sex, Death, and the Meaning of Life, Woody Allen's Comedy.* New York, McGraw-Hill.

Hobbes, T. (1981) *Leviathan.* Harmondsworth, Penguin.

Howe, I. (1983) 'The Problem of Jewish Self-Definition', *Reconstructionist.* October.

Jacobs, D. (1982) *The Magic of Woody Allen.* London, Robson Books.

James, C.L.R., A. Grimshaw and K. Hart (1950) (eds) *The Struggle for Happiness: Essays on American Civilisation.* Unpublished ms.

James, H. (1907) *The American Scene.* London, Oxford University Press.

James, S. (1984) *The Content of Social Explanation.* Cambridge, Cambridge University Press.

Jarvie, I. (1987) *Philosophy of the Film: Epistemology, Ontology, Aesthetics.* London, Routledge & Kegan Paul.

Kael, P. (1987) *Taking it all In: Film Writings 1980–1983.* London, Arrow Books.

Kanin, G. (1981) *Together Again! The Stories of the Great Hollywood Teams.* New York, Doubleday.

Kellner, D. (1979) 'TV, Ideology and Emancipatory Popular Culture' *Socialist Review*, 45: 13–53.

—— (1984) 'Critical Theory, Mass Communication, and Popular Culture', *Telos*, 62, 196–206.

Kohut, H. (1971) *The Analysis of the Self.* New York, International Universities Press.

Kolowrat, E. (1963) 'A Loser on Top', *Senior Scholastic.* 22 November.

Kramer, D. (1951) *Ross and the New Yorker.* New York, Doubleday.

Kuhns, W. (1971) *The Post-Industrial Prophets.* New York, Weybright & Talley.

Lasch, C. (1979) *The Culture of Narcissism.* New York W.W. Norton.

—— (1984) *The Minimal Self.* New York, W.W. Norton.

Langer, L. (1975) *The Holocaust and the Literary Imagination.* New Haven, Yale University Press.

—— (1982) *Versions of Survival: The Holocaust and the Human Spirit.* Albany, State University of New York.

—— (1983) 'The Americanization of the Holocaust on Stage and Screen', in S.B. Cohen (ed.) *From Hester Street to Hollywood.* Bloomington, Indiana University Press.

Lax, E. (1975) *On Being Funny, Woody Allen and Comedy.* New York, Charterhouse.

Leavis, F.R. (1986) *Valuation in Criticism and Other Essays.* G. Singh ed., Cambridge, Cambridge University Press.

Lebrun, M. (1979) *Woody Allen.* Paris, PAC.

Lerman, L. (1972) 'Woody the Great', *Voyage*, 144–51, December.

Levitas, R. (1982) 'Dystopian Times? The Impact of the Death of Progress on Utopian Thinking', *Theory, Culture & Society*, 1, 53–64.

Litvinoff, E. (1987) *The Penguin Book of Jewish Short Stories.* Harmondsworth, Penguin.

Locke, J. (1924) *An Essay Concerning Human Understanding.* Oxford, Clarendon Press.

Lowenthal, L. (1968) *Literature, Popular Culture and Society.* Palo Alto, Pacific Books.

Lydon, M. (1982) 'Foucault and Feminism. A Romance of Many Dimensions'. *Humanities in Society,* 5, 3 and 4, Summer/Fall.

McCann, G. (1985) 'Play It Again, Woody', *Marxism Today.* November.

—— (1987) 'Radio Days', *Cambridge Film 87.*

—— (1988) *Marilyn Monroe.* Cambridge, Polity Press.

—— (1988) 'A Constellation of Selves', *Inprint,* March.

—— (1988) 'Woody Allen's September Song', *Blow-Up.*

McClelland, D. (1987) *StarSpeak: Hollywood on Everything.* London, Faber & Faber.

Macdonald, D. (1981) *On Movies.* New York, Da Capo.

MacIntyre, A. (1981) *After Virtue, A Study in Moral Theory.* London, Duckworth.

McLuhan, M. (1988) *Letters of Marshall McLuhan.* William Toye ed. Oxford, Oxford University Press.

McManners, J. (1985) *Death and the Enlightenment.* Oxford, Oxford University Press.

McNight, G. (1983) *Joking Aside.* London, Star Books.

Mamber, S. (1972-73) 'Woody Allen', *Cinema.* Winter.

Marcuse, H. (1964) *One-Dimensional Man.* Boston, Beacon.

—— (1970) *Five Lectures.* Boston, Beacon.

—— (1974) *Eros and Civilization.* Boston, Beacon.

Marqusee, M. (1988) *New York.* London, Conran Octopus.

Max, G. (1967) *The Groucho Letters.* New York, Simon & Schuster.

Mee, C.L. Jr. (1963) 'On Stage: Woody Allen', *Horizon.* May, 46–7.

Mellen, J. (1978) *Big Bad Wolves: Masculinity in the American Film.* London, Elm Tree Books.

Melville, H. (1988) *Moby Dick.* Oxford, Oxford University Press.

Monro, D.H. (1963) *Argument of Laughter.* Notre Dame, Ind. University of Notre Dame Press.

Morin, E (1960) *The Stars.* London, John Calder.

Moss, R.F. (1980) 'Woody Allen', *SR.* November.

Mulkay, M. (1988) *On Humour.* Cambridge, Polity.

Mundy, R. (1972-73) 'Woody Allen', *Cinema.* Winter.

Navacelle, T. (1987) *Woody Allen On Location*. London, Sidgwick & Jackson.

Orwell, G. (1970) *The Collected Essays, Journalism and Lectures of George Orwell*. Harmondsworth, Penguin.

Palmer, M. (1980) *Woody Allen: An Illustrated Biography*. London, Proteus.

Perelman, S.J. (1949) *Listen to the Mocking Bird*. New York, Simon & Schuster.

—— (1958) *The Most of S.J. Perelman*. New York, Simon and Schuster.

Petric, V. (ed.) (1981) *Films and Dreams, An Approach to Bergman*. New York, Redgrave.

Plato (1951) *The Symposium*. Harmondsworth, Penguin.

Pleck, J. (1981) *The Myth of Masculinity*. Cambridge, Mass., MIT Press.

Pynchon, T. (1975) *Gravity's Rainbow*. London, Picador.

Raban, J. (1988) *Soft City*. London, Collins Harvill.

Rich, Frank (1977) 'Woody Allen Wipes the Smile Off His Face', *Esquire*. May, 72–6; 148–9.

—— (1979) 'An Interview with Woody', *Time*, 68–9, 30 April.

Rieder, Jonathan (1985) *Canarsie*. Cambridge, Mass., Harvard University Press.

Riesman, D. (1976) *The Lonely Crowd*. Revised edn, New Haven, Yale University Press.

Roberts, T. (1988) 'Woody Allen: The Neurotic Philosopher', in Danny Peary (ed.) *Close-Ups*. London, Simon & Schuster.

Rosenblum, R. and Karen, R. (1979) *When The Shooting Stops ... The Cutting Begins*. New York, Da Capo Press.

Rosenfeld, I. (1944) 'Under Forty: A Symposium', *Contemporary Jewish Record*. February.

Rosten, L. C. (1941) *Hollywood: the Movie Colony, the Movie Makers*. New York, Harcourt Brace.

Rosten, L. (1978) *The Joys of Yiddish*. Harmondsworth, Penguin.

Roth, P. (1979) *The Ghost Writer*. Harmondsworth, Penguin.

—— (1983) *Zuckerman Unbound*. Harmondsworth, Penguin.

—— (1985) *The Professor of Desire*. Harmondsworth, Penguin.

—— (1986) *Portnoy's Complaint*. Harmondsworth, Penguin.

Rousseau, J-J. (1960) *Politics and the Arts: letter to M. d'Alembert on the Theatre*. Tr. Allan Bloom, Glencoe, Il, Free Press.

—— (1979) *The Reveries of the Solitary Walker*. Harmondsworth, Penguin.

Ruitenbeek, H.K. (1966) *Freud and America*. New York, Macmillan.

Saban, S. (1978) 'Through a Lens, Darkly', *Soho Weekly News*, 35–6, 3 August.

Sanders, R. and Gillon, E.V. (1979) *The Lower East Side; a Guide to its Jewish Past*. New York, Dover.

Sarris, A. (1978) 'Film Criticism in the Seventies', *Film Comment*, XIV, 1, January.

Schelling, T.C. (1984) *Choice and Consequence*. Cambridge, Mass., Harvard University Press.

Schickel, R. (1973) 'The Basic Woody Allen Joke', *New York Times Magazine*. 7 January.

Schofield, M., Burnyeat, M. and Barnes, J. (eds) (1980) *Doubt and Dogmatism*. Oxford, Oxford University Press.

Scruton, R. (1986) *Sexual Desire*. London, Weidenfeld & Nicolson.

Sennett, R. (1976) *The Fall of Public Man*. Cambridge, Cambridge University Press.

Simmel, G. (1903–1971) 'The Metropolis and Mental Life', in *On Individuality and Social Forms*. D. Levine ed. 324–39, Chicago, University of Chicago Press.

Singer, I.B. (1970) *A Friend of Kafka and Other Stories*. London, Jonathan Cape.

Skinner, Q. (1969) 'Meaning and Understanding in the history of ideas', *History and Theory*. 8, 3–53.

—— (1975–6) 'Hermeneutics and the Role of History', *New Literary History*, 7, 287–306.

Sklar, R. (1975) *Movie-Made America*. New York, Random House.

Sontag, S. (1983) *A Susan Sontag Reader*. Harmondsworth, Penguin.

Staiger, J. (1983) 'Seeing Stars', *The Velvet Light Trap*, 20, Summer.

Steiner, G. (1971) *In Bluebeard's Castle*. New Haven, Yale University Press.

—— (1981) 'The Archives of Eden', *Salgamundi*, 50–1, 57–89.

—— (1985a) *Language and Silence*. London, Faber & Faber.

—— ((1985b) *Real Presences*. Cambridge, Cambridge University Press.

—— (1988) 'The End of Bookishness?', *TLS*, 8–14, July, 754.

Stendhal (1975) *Love*. London, Merlin Press.

Stern, Z. (1980) *The Complete Guide to Ethnic New York*. New York, St. Martin's Press.

Sypher, W. (ed.) (1956) *Comedy*. New York, Doubleday Anchor.

Syrkin, M. (1982) 'What American Jews Did During the Holocaust', *Midstream*. October.

Tanner, T. (1987) *Scenes of Nature, Signs of Men*. Cambridge, Cambridge University Press.

Taylor, C. (1985) *Philosophy and the Human Sciences*, 2. Cambridge, Cambridge University Press.

Teitelbaum, D. (1980) 'Producing Woody: an Interview with Charles H. Joffe', *Cinema Papers*. Melbourne, April/May.

Thompson, J.O. (1978) 'Screen Acting and the Commutation Test', *Screen*. 19, 2, Summer.

Thoreau, H. (1983) *Walden*. Harmondsworth, Penguin.

Thurber, J. (1973) *Thurber Carnival*. New York, Harper & Row.

—— (1984) *The Middle Aged Man on the Flying Trapeze*. London, Methuen.

de Tocqueville, A. (1969) *Democracy in America*. New York, Anchor/Doubleday.

Trilling, L. (1972) *Sincerity and Authenticity*. Oxford, Oxford University Press.

—— (1980) *The Opposing Self*. Oxford, Oxford University Press.

—— (1981) *The Liberal Imagination*. Oxford, Oxford University Press.

Tyler, A. (1971) *Sex Psyche Etcetera in the Film*. Baltimore, Penguin.

Tynan, K. (1980) *Show People*. Weidenfeld and Nicolson.

—— (1967) *Tynan Right & Left*. London, Longmans.

Walker, A. (1988) 'Woody and the Max Factor', *London Evening Standard*, 11 August.

Warshow, R. (1964) *The Immediate Experience*. New York, Doubleday Anchor.

Wetzsteon, R. (1977) 'Woody Allen: Schlemiel as Sex Maniac', *ms*, November 14–15.

Wilson, J.D. (1935) *What Happens in Hamlet*. Cambridge, Cambridge University Press.

Wise, R.R. (1971) *The Schlemiel as Modern Hero*. Chicago, University of Chicago Press.

Wittgenstein, L. (1968) *Philosophical Investigations*. Oxford, Basil Blackwell.

Wollheim, R. (1986) *The Thread of Life*. Cambridge, Cambridge University Press.

Wood, M. (1975) *America at the Movies*. New York, Basic Books.

Yacowar, M. (1979) *Loser Takes All: The Comic Art of Woody Allen*. New York, Ungar.

Filmography

What's New, Pussycat? (1965). Director: Clive Donner. Producer: Charles K. Feldman. Screenplay: Woody Allen. Photography: Jean Badal. Music: Burt Bacharach. Editor: Fergus McDonnell. United Artists. 120 minutes.

What's Up, Tiger Lily? (1966). Script and dubbing: Woody Allen, Frank Buxton, Louise Lasser, Len Maxwell, Mickey Rose. Music: The Lovin' Spoonful. American International. 79 minutes.

Casino Royale (1967). Directors: John Huston, Kenneth Hughes, Val Guest, Robert Parrish, Joseph McGrath. Producer: Charles K. Feldman and Jerry Bresler. Screenplay: Wolf Mankowitz, John Law, Michael Sayers, suggested by the novel by Ian Fleming. Photography: Jack Hildyard. Editor: Bill Lenny. Columbia. 131 minutes.

Take the Money and Run (1969). Director: Woody Allen: Screenplay: Woody Allen and Mickey Rose. Photography: Lester Shoor. Editors: Paul Jordan and Ron Kalish. Music: Marvin Hamlisch. Produced by Charles H. Joffe for Cinerama Releasing Corporation. 85 minutes.

Bananas (1971). Director: Woody Allen. Screenplay: Woody Allen and Mickey Rose. Photography: Andrew M. Costikyan. Music: Marvin Hamlisch. Editor: Ron Kalish. United Artists. 82 minutes.

Play it Again, Sam (1972). Director: Herbert Ross. Screenplay:

Woody Allen. Photography: Owen Roizman. Music: Billy Goldenberg. Editor: Marion Rothman. Paramount. 84 minutes.

Everything You Always Wanted To Know About Sex* (*but were afraid to ask) (1972). Director: Woody Allen. Screenplay: Woody Allen. Photography: David M. Walsh. Editor: Eric Albertson. United Artists. 87 minutes.

Sleeper (1973). Director: Woody Allen. Screenplay: Woody Allen and Marshall Brickman. Photography: David M. Walsh. Music by Woody Allen with the Preservation Hall Jazz Band and the New Orleans Funeral Ragtime Orchestra. Editor: Ralph Rosenblum. United Artists. 88 minutes.

Love and Death (1975). Director: Woody Allen. Screenplay: Woody Allen. Photography: Ghislain Cloquet. Editors: Ralph Rosenblum, Ron Kalish. United Artists. 85 minutes.

The Front (1976). Director: Martin Ritt. Screenplay: Walter Bernstein. Columbia. 94 minutes.

Annie Hall (1977). Director: Woody Allen: Screenplay: Woody Allen, Marshall Brickman. Photography: Gordon Willis. Editor: Ralph Rosenblum. United Artists. 93 minutes.

Interiors (1978). Director: Woody Allen. Screenplay: Woody Allen. Photography: Gordon Willis. Editor: Ralph Rosenblum. United Artists. 93 minutes.

Manhattan (1979). Director: Woody Allen. Screenplay: Woody Allen, Marshall Brickman. Photography: Gordon Willis. Music: George Gershwin. Editor: Susan Morse. United Artists. 96 minutes.

Stardust Memories (1980). Director: Woody Allen. Screenplay: Woody Allen. Photography: Gordon Willis. Editor: Susan Morse. United Artists. 91 minutes.

A Midsummer-Night's Sex Comedy (1982). Director: Woody Allen. Screenplay: Woody Allen. Photography: Gordon Willis. Editor: Susan Morse. Orion Pictures. 87 minutes.

Zelig (1983). Director: Woody Allen. Screenplay: Woody Allen. Photography: Gordon Willis. Editor: Susan Morse. Orion Pictures. 80 minutes.

Broadway Danny Rose (1984). Director: Woody Allen. Screenplay: Woody Allen. Photography: Gordon Willis. Editor: Susan Morse. Orion Pictures. 85 minutes.

The Purple Rose of Cairo (1985). Director: Woody Allen. Screenplay: Woody Allen. Photography: Gordon Willis. Editor: Susan Morse. Orion Pictures. 81 minutes.

Hannah and Her Sisters (1986). Director: Woody Allen. Screenplay: Woody Allen. Photography: Carlo Di Palma. Editor: Susan Morse. Orion Pictures. 107 minutes.

Radio Days (1986). Director: Woody Allen. Screenplay: Woody Allen. Photography: Carlo Di Palma. Editor: Susan Morse. Orion Pictures. 89 minutes.

September (1987). Director: Woody Allen. Screenplay: Woody Allen. Photography: Carlo Di Palma. Editor: Susan Morse. Orion Pictures. 83 minutes.

Another Woman (1988). Director: Woody Allen. Screenplay: Woody Allen. Photography: Sven Nykvist. Editor: Susan Morse. Orion Pictures. 81 minutes.

New York Stories (1989). Directors: Martin Scorsese, Francis Coppola, Woody Allen. Screenplays: Richard Price, Francis and Sofia Coppola, Woody Allen. Photography: Sven Nykvist, Nestor Almengros, Vittorio Storaro. Editors: Thelma Schoonmaker, Barry Malkin, Susan Morse. Touchstone Pictures. 117 minutes.

Crimes and Misdemeanors (1989). Director: Woody Allen. Screenplay: Woody Allen. Photography: Sven Nykvist. Editor: Susan Morse. Orion Pictures. 104 minutes.

Index